THE BITTERNESS OF JOB

The Bitterness of Job

A PHILOSOPHICAL READING

John T. Wilcox

ANN ARBOR

THE UNIVERSITY OF MICHIGAN PRESS

For Benjamin, Nathaniel, and Adam

First paperback edition 1994
Copyright © by the University of Michigan 1989
All rights reserved
Published in the United States of America by
The University of Michigan Press
Manufactured in the United States of America

1997   1996   1995   1994   4   3   2   1

LIBRARY OF CONGRESS CATALOGING-IN-PUBLICATION DATA

Wilcox, John T.
    The bitterness of Job : a philosophical reading / John T. Wilcox.
        p.   cm.
    Bibliography: p.
    Includes index.
    ISBN 0-472-10129-3 (alk. paper).   ISBN 0-472-08247-7 (pbk. : alk.
paper)
    1. Bible. O.T. Job—Criticism, interpretation, etc.
    2. Suffering—Biblical teaching.   3. Good and evil—Biblical
teaching.   4. Theodicy—Biblical teaching.   I. Title.
    BS1415.2.W53   1989
    223'.106—dc20   89-35811
                                                              CIP

I trust what doesn't regard and kills,

graceful design of the sidewinder
in dry white dust, path to a pool
in high rock, flesh and bones
and dying stench of deer, decay

and the fossil glyph speaking
creatures in the Pleistocene sea:

death imprinting life imprinting death.
I am possessed.

Death valley under exploding stars.
Hallelujah.

Salty Badwater's land dive
below sea level.

Mount Whitney's ice-granite
jabbing at blue void,

nadir and zenith, beyonds
gasping for blood in the valley
of bat and dust devil.

Desert, you are prayer's natural
occasion, purest water from the rock
and most naked temptation to
own and not be owned.

Give it up.

—From Patricia Wilcox, "Death Valley Suite"

Preface and Acknowledgment

The Book of Job is a masterwork of the human spirit—or, many believe, of God's Spirit. It deals with some of the grandest and most difficult issues arising out of its religious tradition; and these issues speak to perennial, deep human concerns. It employs a language of intelligence, learning, and psychological power. In consequence, it has been eulogized in the most sweeping terms, and its conceits, its prose, and its poetry have inspired imitators and adaptors in every age.

But Job is also one of the most perplexing books ever written. In its smallest details, and in its largest issues, it is full of mysteries. In the form in which it exists today, no one knows the meaning of many of its words and phrases; clearly, many lines have been altered or corrupted; sections seem transposed out of their original locations; passages may have been lost; additions seem to have been introduced. We do not know but roughly when it was composed, or how many authors, editors, and revisers labored over it. Centuries of readers have disagreed about what its message or import is—and often about what problems it addresses!

In the light of its greatness and in the dark of its riddles, one might think the counsel of wisdom to a reader would be silence. Near the end of his ordeal, confronted with the grandeur and mystery of the Creation, and with his own smallness, Job lays his hand on his mouth and refuses to speak further (40:4–5); he confesses that he had "uttered what I did not understand, things too wonderful for me, which I did not know" (42:3).[1] Any commentator who has chattered about the Book of Job might feel an analogous repentence. The book, like the Creation depicted in it, is awesome and baffling; one is tempted to join the silent and chastened Job. Nevertheless—or even because of all this—commentator after commentator succumbs to the opposite temptation, and fancies himself equal to the task of saying something sensible about this Mount Everest[2] of a book. As Nietzsche said, the difficulty of a task is not the least of its lures; and one observer has said that, as every actor, in the back of his mind, hopes someday to play Hamlet, so every biblical scholar hopes someday to write a book on the Book of Job.[3] I did not know that, when I began the present study; perhaps if I had known it, I would not have begun. And I did not *plan* to write on Job. Instead, Job and his problems simply fell into my path, a few years ago, when I was on my way to another destination. To be a good citizen, I had to read Job again and a little of the Job scholarship, and to give an introductory lecture; but then I was hooked. Then when friends asked, "Why are you studying Job?," I wanted to reply, "Why isn't everyone else? How can they resist it?"

I am not a biblical scholar, nor was I ever one, except as an amateur; I have been a philosophical scholar, and a secular one, most of my adult life. But is it so odd to have a *philosophical* study of the Book of Job? Until recently, most Western philosophers wrote on Job; in the last century philosophers have increasingly left the work to the specialists in the Near Eastern languages (and to creative writers and literary critics). Those specialists have made tremendous progress, and when I speak in this book of "the scholars," I am referring to them—with much respect. They have made great advances in our understanding of the bits and pieces of Job—the words, phrases, allusions, details. Many of them, however, seem innocent of the larger philosophical options available—or even, at times, of the theological options. So I believe it is time for other studies to focus on those larger issues, and that is what I attempt here.

Moreover, in retrospect, I understand to some extent how I was one who was lured into this study. There are influences in my background that prepared me for this encounter. I have seen my share of injustice in life, perhaps more than some, certainly less than others. But if the Book of Job is right, all of us have seen enough to have a personal sense of the issues here, if we are honest; so I would not stress my personal involvement. What I mainly mean is that my scholarly and philosophical background have been helpful. As an undergraduate I was fortunate to be introduced to Job by men of learning and humanity;[4] the impression of profundity has remained. Then for years I was associated with Charles Hartshorne, the grand old man of process philosophy; I was first his student and later his colleague. Few have as much to say about the Joban issues. Then I became a reader of Nietzsche, and I meditated on his reflections on the Moral World Order and on yes-saying. For thirty years I have thought about issues in the history of ethical theory in the West. And for the same length of time I have been married to a poet, and I have thought about how the poetic mind moves. John Rawls's account[5] of the moral attitudes gave me the clue to the notion of moral bitterness. These, I think, are my greatest large-scale intellectual debts.

I have read widely in the scholarship, but I have not attempted to read everything. On many issues, I have been content to be led by the arguments and the summaries of the scholarship that I found in the writings of Robert Gordis,[6] Samuel Terrien,[7] and Marvin H. Pope.[8] Their aid has been invaluable. I hope that this shortcut has not been inappropriate to the project at hand.[9] Of course I expect the scholar to discover some errors of detail here; but I believe the mistakes will be minor and unlikely to affect the substance of my conclusions.

Unless otherwise indicated, all biblical quotations are from the Revised Standard Version (RSV); sometimes I appeal to other versions, especially those of Gordis and Pope, and once or twice I attempt my own version. The RSV is widely known and widely available and is generally satisfactory for my purposes. In some passages there are important doubts about its accuracy on issues of concern to me, and at those points I mention the scholarly controversies. I do not try to resolve them. Only a world-class scholar in the relevant languages could attempt contributions to the textual controversies. I try throughout to build my case on what is genuinely known and clear about the Book of Job and to avoid interpretations based heavily on conjecture. I think, however, that my method, which relies upon the known and focuses on the larger issues, produces results that should be of some weight to the textual scholars in their debates over the details.

The Bible text from the Revised Standard Version of the Bible, copyright 1946, 1952, and 1971 by the Department of Christian Education of the National Council of Churches of Christ in the United States of America, is used by permission. The quotation from "Death Valley Suite" by Patricia Wilcox, copyright 1989, is used by permission of the author and of the *Denver Quarterly*. The selection from "A Masque of Reason" is taken from Robert Frost, *The Poetry of Robert Frost*, edited by Edward Connery Lathem, copyright Henry Holt and Company, Inc., and is reprinted by permission of the publisher. The selection from "What Are Years?" is reprinted with permission of Macmillan Publishing Company from *Collected Poems* by Marianne Moore, copyright 1941, and renewed 1969, by Marianne Moore; and with permission of Faber and Faber Ltd.

Many colleagues and friends have given this project encouragement, advice, and support of practical kinds. Patricia Wilcox's counsel throughout has been crucial. I have been helped greatly by Leon Goldstein, Saul Levin, and Samuel Morell; and significantly by Mario DiCesare, William Beardsley, Herbert Spiegelberg, John Flint, Norman Stillman, Edward Weisband, Martin Bidney, Francis Newman, Bernard Rosenthal, Turner Cassity, Jennifer Leonard, Nathaniel Wilcox, John Vernon, Donald Revell, Alice Kaminsky, Gerald Kadish, Dennis Schmidt, Lance Sussman, Thomas J. J. Altizer, Khalil Semaan, and Gary Rendsburg; by the anonymous readers for, and the staff at, the University of Michigan Press; and by the administration and staff of the State University of New York at Binghamton, which generously supported my research with a sabbatical leave and then with a Dean's Research Semester Fellowship. If there are debts of equal magnitude neglected here, I beg forgiveness; understanding oneself, and so knowing whom to thank, can be the hardest task of all.

Contents

Introduction:
The Structure and Origins
of the Book of Job

The Book of Job, however it may have been altered before it became canonical, still has an overall structure that is quite clear, and a few things are known about its origins. I will refer often to the parts of that structure and sometimes to those origins. A reader just beginning a study of Job can find in this introduction a schematic overview meant to serve as orientation; readers already familiar with the elements should not need these preliminary remarks, and may prefer to go directly to chapter 1.

Structure

Most of the Book of Job is poetic drama; it is a set of poems spoken by characters, as in a play. These poetic speeches begin in chapter 3 and conclude before the middle of 42, the last chapter in the book. The poetry is framed, as it were, by prose: there is a prose prologue in chapters 1 and 2, and most of chapter 42 forms a prose epilogue. In a sense, then, there are three parts to the book—prologue, speeches, and epilogue—but since the speeches make up about nine-tenths of the book, such an account is misleading: worse than saying that the Ten Commandments consist of the First and Tenth Commandments and some things in between.

The prose prologue tells a story of what Job had been like, the terrible sufferings he endured, and how he came to undergo them. This story, though it comprises only that short prologue, is the part of the book best known to people at large. The prose is beautifully polished[1] and the images are striking, so writers often quote from or refer to this story. Almost all literate Occidentals have heard of Job's uprightness and original happiness, and of how God allowed the

Satan[2] to test him by sending financial ruin, the deaths of his children, and miserable health.

The Satan had predicted that in such disasters Job would curse God, and Job's wife urges him to "Curse God, and die" (2:9), but he remains steadfast in his acceptance of God's will. Finally three friends, Eliphaz, Bildad, and Zophar arrive to comfort him. We do not hear again of the Satan.

After this prologue, the poetry, the heart of the book proper, begins. Within the poetic section itself, some further distinctions are needed. Most of the speeches, comprising the first and largest part of the poetry, are delivered by Job and his friends. Job laments, cursing the day of his birth (chap. 3). His first friend speaks, and Job replies; the second speaks, and Job replies; and then the third speaks, and Job responds. This set of six speeches, this whole "dialogue" between Job and the friends (chaps. 4–14), is called the first cycle of the speeches. Then follows a second cycle (chaps. 15–21) with exactly the same structure—speeches by the friends with responses by Job. Then follows what seems to be a partly degenerate, corrupted, or garbled third cycle, in which Zophar fails to speak, and Job appears to speak twice without interruption where we would expect Zophar to respond. Much of what Job says (most of chap. 27, and part of chap. 24)[3] in the third cycle seems to fit Zophar's views better than Job's.

In these chapters, Job and his friends "debate" the meaning of the evils they see about them, especially the evils that have befallen Job. Their poetic speeches are reminiscent of the psalms of praise and of lamentation, and often are as beautiful. In the prologue Job had accepted his fate without protest. But in most of his speeches, he complains of his suffering, his undeserved suffering, as he sees it; and he complains of the suffering generally of the upright and the innocent and of the prosperity and happiness of the wicked. His friends, who, in the prologue account, had come to condole and comfort, quickly lose their sympathy for him; they accuse him of sins that earn suffering, and they continuously articulate the view that God punishes the wicked and protects the innocent and the righteous. These alternating speeches, or psalms, usually said to comprise the central dialogues of the book, are not "dialogues" in anything like the full Platonic sense. There is no strong developmental order, especially not in the friends' speeches; and though some characters refer to what the others have said, no one ever concedes a point to anyone else, and no one ever offers a detailed analysis of anyone else's remarks.

If we say that the third cycle ends with chapter 27, then Job's opening lament and the subsequent dialogues occupy twenty-four of the forty-two chapters, two-thirds of the entire book. Then follows (chap. 28) a "hymn to wisdom," ostensibly still spoken by Job. Man's achievements in mining, smelting, and engineering are praised, but it is said that only God understands the way to wisdom—except that for man, "the fear of the Lord, that is wisdom" (28:28). Many scholars argue that this chapter does not fit well here, especially in Job's mouth.

Then Job brings his long speeches to an end. He reviews the elevated station he had had in the old days, and compares it with his present sufferings and ignominy (chaps. 29–30). He affirms his innocence, lists sins he is willing to be punished for, if he has committed them, asks to be "weighed in a just balance" (31:6), and signs his name, as in a legal suit (31:35).

At this point one might expect a legal trial, or God's hearing of Job's suit, to begin—and later God will respond, but not yet. We find next a new character we had not heard of before, a young man named Elihu, who "was angry at Job because he justified himself rather than God; he was angry also at Job's friends, because they had found no answer" (32:2–3). This Elihu then develops his own reply, in chapters 32–37, to Job's criticisms of God's governance of the world. If we include Elihu's speeches, then, we have thirty-five of the book's forty-two chapters devoted to the "debate" between the human characters in the drama—with Job usually attacking, and with Job's three friends and Elihu praising, God's governance. Elihu is not mentioned after his last speech.

Then the Lord speaks to Job "out of the whirlwind" (38:1, 40:6). The Lord speaks twice; these two speeches comprise almost three of the remaining four chapters of the book. In this "theophany," God challenges Job about his place in the cosmos; He asks Job what role he had in its founding, what power he has over it, and what understanding he has of its workings. Job confesses that he is "of small account" and lays his hand on his mouth, to speak no further (40:4–5). Then God speaks again. In His first speech, He has catalogued much of the

natural order, with no part of it described in great detail; His second
speech focuses on Behemoth and Leviathan, two great natural or
maybe mythical creatures of overwhelming might. Job says in response,

> . . . I have uttered what I did not understand,
>   things too wonderful for me, which I did not know.
> . . . therefore I despise myself,
>   and repent in dust and ashes.
>
>   (42:3, 6)

This concludes the poetic sections of the book.

The prose epilogue is only eleven verses in length. The theophany presented a challenge to Job, and, as we have seen, he responded with words of repentance. In the epilogue, God rebukes the
three friends, "for you have not spoken of me what is right, as my
servant Job has" (42:7, 8). The friends are told to sacrifice, and Job to
pray for them, and the Lord accepts Job's prayer.

Then "the Lord restored the fortunes of Job" (42:10), and the
remaining verses detail, with some picturesque color, Job's blessings
through the rest of his life. Job is comforted and aided by "his brothers and sisters and all who had known him before" (42:11), and his
possessions eventually become twice as great as before. He has new
sons and daughters, in the same number as before, and his three
daughters, especially beautiful, are given inheritances by their father.
The book concludes with the assurance that " . . . Job died, an old
man, and full of days" (42:17).

Unity

Seen from a distance, the Book of Job is remarkably well unified—
not, perhaps, as compared with a novel by Henry James, but certainly as compared with Psalms or Ecclesiastes. Indeed, it is more
unified than most books in the Bible. The preceding summary of its
structure should have made that clear. It is a story of one character,
Job, throughout; it has a prose beginning, a poetic middle, and a

prose ending; these largest elements bear clear relations to each other; and each of them is quite carefully structured internally.

Nevertheless, in minor details the book seems less than fully unified, as if it were not composed by one person, or as if whoever wrote its parts, perhaps at different times in his life, did not perfectly integrate them. Of course unity is a matter of degree, and whether one passage "fits" another depends upon the interpretations given to each and to the whole. And the importance of this in an *evaluation* of the book is controversial; unity as a literary virtue can be easily over-rated. At various points in my study I will examine some of the issues involved. But it may be well to indicate at the outset what some of the larger problems are.

There are differences between the prose "frame" of the book and its poetic substance. Job is resigned or "patient" in the prologue, but bitter and accusatory in most of his speeches. The story of the Satan and his testing of Job, which is the heart of the prologue, is not echoed in the poetry or even in the epilogue. The mystery and majesty of the Lord in the theophany seem foreign to the folktale humanness and staginess of the prologue. And so on. Some scholars see serious difficulties here, and some think that multiple authorship is required to explain the difficulties. It is widely believed that some sort of folktale about Job was known in the Middle East, and known in Hebrew, before our book was composed; and it may have been that the author or the major author of our book adapted that older tale but could not fully bend it to his purposes.

Then there is the problem of the Elihu section, which many scholars believe does not fit nicely into its setting. Elihu is not mentioned before or after his section; his language is somewhat different from the language in the other sections; when he is introduced, the prose suggests that the author had before him the speeches of Job and the friends, in a way that other sections of the book do not; some scholars find suspicious the explanation given (32:4) of Elihu's silence up to that point. Many readers do not see that this section adds much to the content of the book; they are ready for the theophany after Job's call for a trial, and they dislike this interruption and postponement of the climax. Of course, even if the insertion of the Elihu section, or its insertion without revisions to accommodate it, is a mistake, it may be one the original poet made, perhaps after he had

his earlier work before him. Surely a work like Job was not written in
a day. And the Elihu section may improve the work, even if it adds
problems in matters of detail. Smoothness of fit is not everything.

There may be puzzles about the theophany. One would think
that the theophany, God's appearance, would settle things—and in
terms of the drama, it does: Job repents and is silenced, and then the
epilogue immediately wraps up most of the loose ends. But many
readers have failed to see any relevance in what God says. How do
the God speeches really answer Job (or Job and his friends)? What's
the point? Again, all this must be dealt with below; indeed, this will
be a major preoccupation in the pages ahead. For now, I only indicate
another reason some readers have doubted the full unity of this work.

A lesser problem, I think, concerns the hymn to wisdom in chapter 28. It is a beautiful set piece, a powerful psalm; and—as I will
argue later—its point of view is certainly compatible with that in the
theophany. So we can easily believe that the great poet who wrote
one also wrote the other—though someone else could have, of
course. But what is Job doing, this early in the book, expressing the
point of view of the theophany? In most of his speeches, he attacks
the governance of the world; he should not, at that stage of the
drama, express a view close to that to which he needs to be led, and
to which he will be led later. Or so we might argue. So we might
conclude that something is wrong, and maybe that something has
been added to the book since it was originally composed—even if we
are glad that this great hymn has been preserved.

The anomalies in the third cycle of speeches suggest loss. The
cycles of speeches, generally, seem very carefully contrived, from
some formal points of view. Yet in the third cycle, as we have it
today, Zophar never speaks, and Job says things that might better fit
the mouth of one of the friends.

And in any event, the book has many lines and phrases and
words that seem garbled or misplaced, so almost certainly some
damage—not just change—has taken place since the book was first
composed. Much of the poetry and the prose is of the highest distinction; it is hard to believe that its author would have composed gib-
berish or deliberately written what are more easily explained as mistakes in copying.

And finally there are passages that bear the marks of deliberate editing, in which copyists seem to have purposely altered the meanings of lines, usually in the direction of what they would have taken to be orthodoxy and piety. So the text as we have it has *some* sort of history; it was not composed all at once exactly as we have it today. And in content it is not a full unity; there are minor details, at least, that do not fit well in their places. However great it is, it is less than it might have been, and perhaps less than it once was; and, given the evidence for additions, it is also, perhaps, more than it once was.

Authorship and Date

Let us assume, with almost all the scholars, that one person wrote at least most of the Book of Job—say the speeches of Job and his friends, and the response of God from the whirlwind. This person could have written the Elihu section, though many scholars doubt that he did. He almost certainly worked with an older, traditional folktale about the patriarch Job, though he may have composed our particular version of this tale, which forms the prologue and epilogue of our book. Assuming all this: who was this person? And when did he write the book?

Now Job himself and his three friends do not have normal Hebrew names, and they are associated with non-Hebrew places and peoples to the east of Palestine. The images and allusions in the book are broadly cosmopolitan, not narrowly restricted to those traditionally associated with the Jews. The book, a Hebrew book, is full of passages difficult to interpret. So some scholars suggest from time to time that the author of the book was not himself a Jew and did not write in Hebrew, and that our book is a Hebrew translation of a book composed in another language of the Near East. Most scholars, however, continue to reject this hypothesis; they hold that, despite its surface appeal, it does not really explain the facts very well. The overwhelming consensus is that the author was a Jew and wrote the book in Hebrew.

The cosmopolitan nature of the book, the evidences it gives of learning, and its lack of provincialism suggest, or even prove, that the author was, at least during much of his life, a person of education and travel, and therefore of wealth. Like Job during Job's prosperity, the author seems to have been a member of the upper class. I have not seen any speculation on the gender of our writer, but the scholars all speak as if it can be safely assumed that the author was male.

The dating of the book is extremely difficult. We know that the book was revered, translated, and paraphrased in the first century B.C.E.[5]; but how long had it been so important, and how long did it take for it to achieve such an important position? Many of the book's themes or issues seem virtually primordial; we know of works in other Near Eastern languages that deal with related themes,[4] and some of them can be dated as early as the beginning of the second millenium B.C.E. If our book refers to particular historical events, those references are too vague to give many scholars confidence that the import has been grasped.

There are some ways in which the Book of Job echoes other biblical works, or in which they echo Job, but these connections are only moderately helpful in dating the work. Some scholars, but not all, believe that Job was influenced by Jeremiah; if so, then it could not have been written before the sixth century B.C.E. Many scholars, but not all, believe that Job influenced second Isaiah (Isa. 40–55), and hence that it was composed no later than the fifth century. Those scholars who reject either of these considerations may argue for a century as early as the seventh or as late as the fourth, or even the third; so modern scholarly opinion is still divided over a range of four or five hundred years, with the years from 400 to 600 B.C.E. being probably the favorites. My tentativeness here should not lead the reader to think that all the scholars themselves are so tentative; some of them claim to be able to date the work accurately to a few decades—but none of their claims to precision have found widespread support among their peers. So it seems to me, as it seems to most of them, that the book cannot be very accurately dated—not now, at least, and perhaps never. It is a fairly late book in the Hebrew Bible; it deals with a folktale, and with issues, much older than itself; beyond that, not much is certain about its time of origin.[6]

Chapter 1

The "Orthodox Doctrine" of Evil

The Book of Job deals with many issues, but we need to focus first on the most obvious: the problem of evil in human life. The characters in the central dialogues debate the justice of God's reign. Though in the book as we have it, Job's stance is tension laden—though Job both praises God and curses Him—this tension escapes the notice of all the speakers. What is obvious to all is that they disagree; Job criticizes, while the others defend, God's governance of the world. Whatever the origin of the ambivalence in Job's speeches, an ambivalence we will explore later, for the characters themselves there are two sides in the conflict: the friends are defending and Job is attacking. Let us look first, then, at the issue as they all see it.

In a broad sense, the issue is whether human individuals get what they merit or deserve in life. The belief that they do has been widely found in many cultures, and it remains profoundly tenacious in our own. Indeed, one contemporary psychologist has labeled the belief "a fundamental delusion"—fundamental because it structures so much of people's perceptions of reality, a delusion because they believe it no matter how much evidence to the contrary is right in front of their eyes.[1] Spectators of suffering and of the grossest injustices tend to believe that the victims brought it on themselves. And the victims themselves suffer the further calamity of suspecting that

9

they are indeed to blame. Winners and losers, even in lotteries, suspect that the winners deserved to win and that the losers deserved to
lose. This view is always with us, and that is part of what gives the
Book of Job its perennial relevance.

In our book, this belief takes the special form of a belief in what
God does in the world; and it structures its notion of merit or desert in
accord with some widely held biblical ideas. Job and his comforters
have similar, perhaps identical, conceptions of what God should do,
of how God should govern the world. Roughly: God should punish
the wicked, should protect the weak, and should reward the righteous. Two of these expectations are analogous to the demands on
human rulers, or human beings who have power and influence. The
speakers in the dialogues believe that people with power should see
to it that the wicked are punished and the weak are protected; we
might say that they believe God to be under the same sorts of obligations, but that they disagree about whether God is discharging these
obligations.

The whole debate, in the dialogues, concerns God's dealings *with
people*. Most modern theorists of the problem of evil argue that when
God is conceived of as ruler over the whole cosmos, it is reasonable to
ask not only about people, but also about animals; some animals
suffer horribly, sometimes at our hands and sometimes as victims of
natural forces. Some theorists argue that this suffering, also, is an evil
that calls into question the goodness of God. The Joban dialogues
never address that issue. They sometimes mention animals, but they
never worry about animal suffering; they worry only about human
weal and woe. The innocent weak who ought to be protected, by men
and by God, are innocent people; and of course the righteous, who
should prosper, and the ungodly, who should be cut off, are people.
For the most part—almost totally—the debate is about the fate of
human *individuals*; Job does refer once to nations—God, he says,
"makes nations great, and he destroys them: he enlarges nations, and
he leads them away" (12:23)—but this reference is easy to miss. Over-
whelmingly the problem of divine justice is construed here in terms
of what fates await individuals.

Job's friends and Elihu are often said to defend "the orthodox" or
"the traditional" view. As I noted previously, we do not know exactly
when the book was written, much less what was really "orthodox" at

the time—if anything was.[2] Nevertheless, within the book itself there is warrant for the use of these terms.[3] Eliphaz says, "Both the grayhaired and the aged are among us, older than your father" (15:10). "For inquire, I pray you," says Bildad, "of an earlier generation, and heed the insight of their fathers . . ." (8:8). "Do you not know this from of old . . . ?" Zophar asks (20:4). And Elihu stresses his own youth (32:6–10), after it is reported that he "had waited to speak because they [the three friends] were older than he" (32:4).

This "traditional" view is often stated vaguely or metaphorically: "those who plow iniquity and sow trouble reap the same" (4:8). "But he [God] saves the fatherless . . . , the needy. . . . So the poor have hope . . ." (5:15–16). "Think now, who that was innocent ever perished? Or where were the upright cut off?" (4:7) Here we have the three elements of the traditional view: God protects the weak and punishes the wicked, just as a good human ruler does; God's justice is analogous to Job's own uprightness; and God also provides blessing to those who fear Him and serve Him. This seems to be what is meant when it is implied that God does not "pervert justice" or "pervert the right" (8:3); or, "far be it from God that he should do wickedness, and from the Almighty that he should do wrong" (34:10).

However, this traditional view is not exactly that the wicked should never prosper or that the innocent or upright should never suffer. God sometimes allows the wicked to prosper, but only briefly; soon, or eventually, they reap what they have sown. Bildad suggests that Job's children had sinned, and that that is why they died—God "has delivered them into the power of their transgression" (8:4). It is not suggested that the punishment came immediately after the sin. The papyrus, the reeds, can begin growth without water, but they soon wither (8:11–12); "Such are the paths of all who forget God" (8:13). The "tent of the wicked" stands, but only temporarily; it "will be no more" (8:22). Compensation to the wicked man "will be paid in full before his time . . ." (15:32):

> Do you not know . . .
> that the exulting of the wicked is short,
>   and the joy of the godless but for a moment?
> Though his height mount up to the heavens,
>   and his head reach to the clouds,

he will perish forever like his own dung;
  those who have seen him will say,
  "Where is he?" . . .
Though wickedness is sweet in his mouth, . . .
yet his food is turned in his stomach;
  it is the gall of asps within him.

(20:4, 5–7, 12, 14)

And when Job himself—through a copyist's error, or an editor's revision?—seems to agree with the friends, he also speaks of delayed retribution:

This is the portion of a wicked man . . .
If his children are multiplied, it is for the sword. . . .
Though he pile up silver like dust,
  and pile up clothing like clay;
he may pile it up, but the just will wear it,
  and the innocent will divide the silver.
The house which he builds is like a
  spider's web. . . .

(27:13, 14, 16–18)

The doctrine articulated by the friends may allow, in a similar way, for delayed reward for the upright. Bildad may suggest this (8:5–7, 21). He may have a notion about the righteous like his claim about the wicked—not that at every moment they get what they deserve, but that eventually they will receive their just deserts. Relevant here is the question of what kind of reward is promised to the upright; the answer may vary somewhat from passage to passage. At some points, it seems that the upright may expect to be blissful: "He will yet fill your mouth with laughter, and your lips with shouting" (8:21). In other places, it seems only promised that the upright will be protected from disaster:

In famine he will redeem you from death,
  and in war from the power of the sword.

(5:20)

. . . you will be secure, and will not fear.

(11:15)

. . . you will be protected and take your rest in safety.

(11:18)

In either case, probably, a good old age and many descendents are promised:

You shall know also that your descendents shall be many,
    and your offspring as the grass of the earth.
You shall come to your grave in ripe old age,
    as a shock of grain comes up to the threshing
    floor in its season.

(5:25–26)

However, neither of these refinements—that the reward may be delayed, or that the reward may be primarily long life and progeny— tells the full story of the background gloominess of the "orthodox doctrine" in these dialogues. The friends and Elihu discuss the reward of the upright much less than the punishment of the wicked. Moreover, the idea is often expressed, and as often implied, that no one is perfectly upright or righteous; and so that whatever evil may befall us we deserve it. There is something like a doctrine of universal sinfulness (of "original sin," in this sense[4]) hovering about the dialogues. The wicked are to be punished; but in one degree or another we all are wicked. The group contrasted with the wicked are sometimes called the upright, but often they are described as those who repent their sin, turn to righteousness, and call upon God to help. The wicked are described simply as the wicked, as evil-doers, etc., but the description of the contrast group is usually more complicated.

Eliphaz asks the suffering Job, "Is not your fear of God your confidence, and the integrity of your ways your hope?" (4:6) But if his speech is a genuine unity, what he means is clarified later. If we trust the rest of his speech, he does not mean that Job's "fear of God" and "integrity of ways" are so great that they alone can protect him. Early in this very first speech he presents a long, "uncanny" account of his belief that no one is totally "righteous" (or "just") or "pure" before God:

Now a word was brought to me stealthily,
    my ear received the whisper of it.

Amid thoughts from visions of the night,
   when deep sleep falls on men,
dread came upon me, and trembling,
   which made all my bones shake.
A spirit glided past my face;
   the hair of my flesh stood up.
It stood still,
   but I could not discern its appearance.
A form was before my eyes;
   there was silence, then I heard a voice:
"Can mortal man be righteous before God?
   can a man be pure before his Maker?
Even in his servants he puts no trust,
   and his angels he charges with error;
how much more those who dwell in houses of clay,
   whose foundation is in the dust,
   who are crushed before the moth."

                                                      (4:12–19)

This view would undermine any simple account of God's reward for those of "integrity." If Eliphaz's voice is right, no man is perfectly "pure" (4:17). And God punishes evil; this is why Eliphaz goes on to say (5:7) that "man is born to trouble as the sparks[5] fly upward" (or, with Gordis, "man gives birth to trouble, as surely as the sparks fly upward"). It is man's nature to bring trouble or sorrow upon himself. So even at the beginning Eliphaz does not accept a simple account of Job's "integrity"; Eliphaz believes that Job, like the rest of us, is impure—and that this is why he suffers. But God does not destroy us for our sins; He only chastens, and the chastening is actually beneficial:

Behold, happy is the man whom God reproves;
   therefore despise not the chastening of the Almighty.
For he wounds, but he binds up;
   he smites, but his hands heal.

                                                     (5:17–18)

This chastening view of suffering would seem to presuppose that we *need* to be chastened. Eliphaz praises the works of the Almighty, and says to Job, "As for me, I would seek God, and to God would I commit my cause" (5:8); then he details some of the ways in which God will protect a man. The picture is that all men sin, and thereby bring trouble, chastisement, on themselves; but God is mighty, so if the sinner "seeks God" and "commits his cause to God," He will protect him from calamities (5:19–24).

Part of this view is expressed again in Eliphaz's second speech. There too he says that no man is pure:

> What is man, that he can be clean?
>   Of he that is born of a woman, that he can be righteous?
> Behold, God puts no trust in his holy ones,
>   and the heavens are not clean in his sight;
> how much less one who is abominable and corrupt,
>   a man who drinks iniquity like water!
>
>   (15:14–16)

The last verse is meant personally—meaning that Job is abominable, etc.; but the logic of the whole passage is like that in 4:17–19, quoted previously: the heavenly beings are not pure, how much less pure is man! And in his third speech, after listing what he takes to be Job's sins, he asks Job for a conversion of sorts:

> Agree with God, and be at peace;
>   thereby good will come to you. . . .
> If you return to the Almighty and humble yourself,
>   if you remove unrighteousness far from your tents. . .
> Then you will delight yourself in the Almighty. . . .
> You will make your prayer to him,
>   and he will hear you . . .
>   you will be delivered through the cleanness of your hands.
>
>   (22:21, 23, 26, 27, 30)

The overall picture is the same: if a sinner repents, then becomes righteous, and prays to God for help, and trusts in God rather than in himself—or in any other power—then God will deliver the man. It is clear to me that the orthodox doctrine, in Eliphaz's mouth, does not say quite simply that the upright will be rewarded. It says that all are unclean and are punished. But it holds that a sinner may repent, mend his ways, pray to and trust God; and then he will be protected.

Most commentators have seen hints of this in Eliphaz, but I think they have underplayed it. And I think the same view is present in the other friends and in Elihu—perhaps not quite so clearly, but fairly clearly. Bildad's last speech expresses the kind of general pessimism about man that we saw twice in Eliphaz:

> Behold, even the moon is not bright
>   and the stars are not clean in his sight;
> how much less man, who is a maggot,
>   and the son of man, who is a worm!
>
> (25:5–6)

This view makes clear why Bildad stresses punishment more than reward, as he does: in his three speeches, only once does he offer any promise:

> If you will seek God
>   and make supplication to the Almighty,
> if you are pure and upright,
>   surely then he will rouse himself for you
>   and reward you with a rightful habitation.
> And though your beginning was small,
>   your latter days will be very great.
>
> (8:5–7)

This passage does not interpret itself. But I think the most plausible meaning, given Bildad's clearly negative focus, is that if you (Job) become pure and upright—which you are not, now—and if you repent and trust God, then He will protect you. This was Eliphaz's message.

Zophar speaks only twice. In his second speech he does not mention the righteous; he devotes himself entirely (20:4–29) to the fate of the wicked. In his first speech, he says that God goes easy on Job: "Know then that God exacts of you less than your guilt deserves" (11:6). Then he offers hope:

> If you set your heart aright,
>   you will stretch out your hands toward him.

If iniquity is in your hand, put it far away,
    and let not wickedness dwell in your tents.
Surely then you will lift up your face without
    blemish. . . .

(11:13–15)

And he goes on to express in varying ways the brightness and confidence Job can then expect. Now, given what he has just said about Job's guilt, he must not mean that if Job has no iniquity he can expect such a fine future—for Job, he has said, is terribly guilty! He must mean, as the others do, that though Job is guilty, he can reform himself, and petition God, and then God will help him. Now Zophar, unlike the other two friends, does not explicitly say all men are sinful, as Job is; but I believe that he means this. That hypothesis seems to me the simplest, given that the other two friends say this and that the three do not quarrel among themselves. Furthermore, his introduction to these verses needs consideration:

Can you find out the deep things of God?
    Can you find out the limit of the Almighty?
It is higher than heaven—what can you do?
    Deeper than Sheol—what can you know?
Its measure is longer than the earth,
    and broader than the sea.
If he passes through, and imprisons,
    and calls to judgment, who can hinder him?

(11:7–10)

Now maybe Zophar just means that *Job* cannot resist God's punishment, so *he* should repent, etc.; but the ignorance and impotence are really man's, not just Job's. So I suspect that Zophar means that the guilt is man's, too, and not just Job's. At least two of the friends—and probably all three—hold a doctrine of universal sinfulness. For them, the protection promised the "upright"—the "righteous," those who "fear God"—is not promised to the absolutely sinless, for there are none; it is promised to the repentant and reformed sinners who petition God for it and who trust God, and God alone, to provide it.

It is probable that this is Elihu's view as well. The two ways in which God "speaks" to man, in Elihu's account, are both negative—

both presuppose that man is at least tempted to be sinful. God speaks in dreams, "that he may turn man aside from his deed, and cut off pride from man" (33:17). God also speaks by sending suffering to chasten (33:19ff). Elihu portrays the transformed sinner as singing God's praises: "I sinned, and perverted what was right, and it was not requited to me" (33:27). Clearly Elihu focuses on the sinner who needs to change, and on the protections God can provide him, not on anyone who is totally without sin. So I am inclined to think that when Elihu speaks of a man who is "pleasing to God" (34:9, Pope) [or who takes "delight in God"], or who is "righteous" (36:7), and when he asks what Job would accomplish by being "righteous" (35:7), or having "righteousness" (35:8), he is not thinking of being absolutely without sin; I suspect he is thinking there, as at the beginning of his speech, of the righteous men Eliphaz and Bildad describe. This would square with his emphasis on the wicked and on God's punishment of them and warnings to them. But I do not claim that this interpretation is required by the text. The text requires us to interpret Eliphaz and Bildad this way, and it allows us, but does not force us, to interpret Zophar and Elihu this way.

So far, in explicating "the orthodox doctrine" in the dialogues, I have dealt with its account of God's dealings with the wicked and the "righteous." But there is a third aspect of God's agency in this doctrine: God protects the innocent weak—the poor, the needy, widows, the fatherless, the wounded, the dying. Yes, God is supposed to deal with men according to their deeds, and their hearts; but He is also supposed to protect those who cannot protect themselves. This is stressed several times, in the friends' defense of God and in Job's attacks (5:15–16; 24:3–12, 21). It is clear that God's supposed role here parallels the role of a good man, or a good human ruler; for Job and his friends often ask whether *Job* protects the weak, the fatherless, etc. (22:6–7, 9; 29:12–16; 31:16–23, 32), and Job accuses the friends of not helping *him*, as one of the weak (26:2).

As I say, this role seems a distinguishable third role that God (like the good man) is supposed to play. You might argue otherwise: you might argue that protecting the weak is keeping them from any suffering they don't deserve, and so that all three roles involve merit or desert, apportioning good and ill according to merit or desert. Even so it seems worthwhile to distinguish two kinds of "innocence";

infants have one kind, Job in the prologue, and reformed sinners, have another. Infants have done nothing; Job and reformed sinners have acted well. So if we speak of "merit" in both cases we mean it differently: Job merits much good; infants do not merit harm. If we say that newborns "deserve" protection, we do not mean it in the sense in which Job deserves prosperity. The Book of Job does not employ the language of rights, of course; but we might say that infants have a "natural" right to protection, whereas the righteous and the wicked earn their punishments and their right to reward. Even if we claim that all have sinned, we still have to distinguish between mature adults and infants. Mature sinners may repent and reform, call upon God and trust Him; but infants, even if we say that they sin, cannot do any of these. If God is to protect infants, He must protect them as infants, not as reformed sinners. Furthermore, in this book the analogy between God and the human ruler extends to the protection of the weak but not to the rewarding of the upright. In all the discussions of the upright and of the wicked their treatment of the weak is stressed; and Job claims to have restrained and punished the wicked. In these respects the upright are like God. But Job never suggests that he has rewarded the righteous, and the friends never say that he should have; that duty seems to belong to God alone.

There are some logical puzzles about the weak, however—the widows, the fatherless, the poor. Men and God are supposed to protect them. Job claims to have been their protector—that is part of his claim to be upright. Eliphaz claims (22:5–9) that Job has neglected them. Job claims that God neglects them; the friends deny this. But if the world were a thoroughly just place; if everyone got what he deserved; then wouldn't these unfortunates *deserve* to be widows, fatherless, and poor? Wouldn't they be not "unfortunates," but sinners, deservedly punished? And consequently wouldn't they deserve to suffer what such people usually suffer—exploitation by the powerful and unscrupulous? Yet clearly the ethics of Job and his friends includes the theme that men should protect such people; and clearly their theology includes the theme that God should protect such people. There is a strong tension here—perhaps a contradiction or incoherence. The ethics, with its norms for human conduct, clearly presupposes that people can be weak (widowed, fatherless, etc.) through no fault of their own; and that it is not true that whatever is (like widows being robbed) is right. The ethics clearly presupposes that the world is *not* a scene of perfect justice: it is our obligation to make it more just. And when God is given duties like those given men; when He is supposed to protect the innocent weak; then the theology also presupposes that the world is not perfectly just. The role of the good man, and the role of the good God, are specified in terms of their modes of dealing with such forms of injustice. But the "orthodox doctrine" claims that there is no injustice. Something has gone wrong. There is a terrible tension, perhaps inconsistency, implicit here. This point is not formulated explicitly in the book itself. But it is, in my judgment, very important; and it can be related to at least one point that is explicit, as we will see later.

There is another logical puzzle here; it might be seen as another way to present the same problem, but its ramifications are broader. God is supposed to protect the weak, and also to punish the wicked. But if He did—then what would be left for human rulers to do? If God protected the widows and punished robbers, why should men act to do the same? Wouldn't widows, and robbers, be already taken care of in the appropriate ways? (Throughout history, rosy "orthodoxies" have militated against compassion, social obligation, and reform.) Now you might reply that God deals with widows, and with robbers, at least partly through the agency of other people; but in that case it would at least appear that when such other people neglect these duties, then the innocent weak and the wicked will not be dealt with appropriately—by men, ex hypothesis, or by God, since God has delegated these duties to men. Many theorists of religion have conjectured that people postulate God's agency where it is clear that man's agency fails: so even though, e.g., some crimes go undetected by men, criminals are warned that God will detect and punish. This is a plausible suggestion; but if a religion claims that God will punish *all* crimes, regardless of what men do, that leaves unclear the role of human action against crime. And if God will protect all the weak, regardless of what men do, why should *we* bother? There may be answers to such questions—and sophisticated theologies have addressed them—but they are at least questions that naturally arise. And they have far-reaching practical implications. As we will see, the Book of Job is aware of the practical problems.

This discussion of the logical puzzles in the orthodox doctrine

leads very naturally into questions about how it was thought to be
"implemented"—by what mechanisms, so to speak, did God execute
His rewarding, protecting, and punishing? Again we do not have
explicit discussion of this; but there are hints and suggestions in
many places. I do not think we can press them into an elaborate
answer, but they provide at least a feel, a tone, a flavor, that intimates
what might have been thought.

We have already noticed the sowing-reaping metaphor: a man
reaps what he sows—*naturally*, we might say. This kind of metaphor
suggests a very intimate, intrinsic, natural connection between one's
deeds and one's destiny. We hear this tone in the plant-and-ground
metaphor as well:

> Can papyrus grow where there is no marsh?
>   Can reeds flourish where there is no water? . . .
> Such are the paths of all who forget God. . . .
>
> (8:11, 13)

In these figures we sense that action brings what it deserves in an
obvious and natural way, without any surprise, intricacy, or
obscurity; to say in these ways that "God" rewards and punishes
seems to say little more than that nature rewards and punishes, or
that actions have consequences.

In other passages it seems that God has to withhold or grant
what might otherwise be a natural outcome, or that He can augment
or diminish it. So Bildad suggests that when Job's children died, it
was because God "delivered them into the power of their
transgression"—as if death were a natural consequence of their sin,
but a consequence God can hold back. We might see an analogous
note in the prologue's account of Job's early prosperity. The Satan
says to God, "Thou hast blessed the work of his hands . . ." (1:10).
This traditional formula suggests that Job's prosperity is somehow his
own doing, a blessing from the work of his hands; it is not something
that someone who never worked would have achieved; but also that
it is God's doing—God blessed the work of Job's hands, though He
might not have. Of course, in this case, we seem to have *industry*
rewarded (because of righteousness), not merely the rewarding of
righteousness; or we have the rewarding of righteousness by way of

industry. In the other case, we seemed to have the direct consequences of transgression, not the consequences of transgression by
way of (say) sloth—or were the children also careless, to be feasting
and drinking, while a storm approached? In any event, in both cases,
it seems, we have God acting to support a "moral" connection He
might not have supported.

In some examples that are given, however, one sees no *natural*
connection at all; all we see, or hear alleged, is the moral fittingness,
the justice, of the outcome. Job's oxen and asses were stolen by the
Sabeans, and the Chaldeans stole his camels; the friends seem to
think that these kinds of losses were due to Job's exacting pledges
from his brother, and neglecting the weary and the hungry (22:6–7).
But it is hard to see any natural connection at all, unless we assume
that his brother had friends among the Sabeans, or the weary and
hungry were related to the Chaldeans! The more likely explanation
would be that God arranges things in ways we do not fathom, so that
sins are punished; that God moves in mysterious, not natural, ways.
And surely God's bringing or allowing wind (1:19), fire from heaven
(1:16), and disease (2:7; 18:13) to afflict people cannot always be understood naturalistically.

Indeed, some of the results of sin and of righteousness seem
downright unnatural, violate what our sense of nature would lead
us to expect—they border on the miraculous. If Job clings to God,
Eliphaz says,

> In famine he will redeem you from death,
>   and in war from the power of the sword. . . .
> At destruction and famine you shall laugh,
>   and shall not fear the beasts of the earth.
>
>   (5:20, 22)

We would expect stockpiles of grain, not righteousness, to protect us
in famine; and military prowess in war. We would expect beasts to
have their own laws, and not to even recognize our fidelity to God.
But somehow, the orthodox doctrine alleges, these natural expectations are overthrown.[6]

One thing is clear: if old age with many descendents is the chief
reward, or the crucial reward, then the orthodox doctrine must deal

with *all* sources of premature death or great incapacity; and among
these are the actions of other men, meteorological phenomena, the
ways of animals, and multitudes of illnesses. It is most implausible to
regard these as always connected with righteousness in any natural
way, at least as we understand nature today. The man who drowns
swimming below Niagara Falls and the robber who dies of bone
cancer may both, in different ways, deserve their fates; each may reap
what he sows, metaphorically; but the metaphorical connection is
different in the two cases. The relationship can be understood naturalistically in only one case. We might say that the man who drowns
reaps what he sows, but that the robber only reaps what he deserves
to reap. If all good and ill that befall us are "reaping what we have
sown," the metaphor is attenuated in many cases; God's action to
bring about such "harvests" must be quite elaborate, and the mechanisms must be quite obscure to the human observer.

I have spoken of logical puzzles in the orthodox doctrine. But
what rationale is given, in the book, for this doctrine? Why do the
friends, and Elihu, believe it in the first place? Answers are not easy,
because the comforters are more given to expounding their view than
to arguing for it; but I think that there are six, or possibly seven, kinds
of considerations influencing them.

First, as we have seen, the orthodox doctrine *is* orthodox and
traditional—it has been taught by the fathers of an earlier generation
(8:8). To reject it is hard, and perhaps unreasonable, because to do so
goes against the wisdom of the ages. Second, the experience of the
friends themselves, they say (4:7–8, 15:17—though 8:9 might count
against this) bears out the truth of the doctrines. They say that they
are old (15:10), and that they have found it to be true. And, third,
Eliphaz perhaps appeals to the authority of inspiration, when he
reports (4:12–21) his dream vision of man's radical fallenness.

There may also be some "theoretical" considerations that weigh
on these relatively untheoretical comforters. It should be noted that
Job begins the discussion, not they; he begins it with a lament, in
which he curses the day of his birth. He does not raise there any
questions of divine justice. He tells of his own sorrows; but implicitly
he tells of the sorrows of many people. He wishes that from birth he
had been in the place of death, and what he says of that place suggests that many are better off there:

There the wicked cease from troubling,
　　and there the weary are at rest.
There the prisoners are at ease together:
　　they hear not the voice of the taskmaster.
The small and the great are there,
　　and the slave is free from his master.

$$(3:17-19)$$

Eliphaz responds immediately with the orthodox accounts (4:8–11, 5:2–7) of what happens to those who "plow iniquity" (4:8), and he presents his opening account of universal sinfulness (4:12–21). If there is any logic in the structure of the book here, then a reason for the orthodox doctrine is that it is a response to the riddle of human suffering. Why is it that so many suffer? Because they are sinful. Why is it that all of us suffer? Because we are all sinful. The fact of suffering, and the fact of universal suffering—if it is a fact, if we are "born to trouble as the sparks fly upward" (5:7)—call for explanation. The orthodox doctrine is a theory that explains (and justifies) human suffering, and this seems to provide much of its appeal for its defenders.

It is sometimes alleged that the Book of Job also deals with questions of the rationale for righteousness. As I have noted, many theorists speculate that the function of much theology is as a buttress for law and morals, that people conceive of God, or the gods, as providing sanctions for righteousness. Why should we be upright in those situations where we can escape the notice of others? A common answer is that we cannot escape the notice of God, and that He will reward and punish, whether people do or not. So religion functions as a support for propriety, by maintaining that propriety pays. Clearly the orthodox doctrine in this book could function in this way, for it makes the required connections between righteousness and prosperity. So maybe this is one more reason the friends defend the doctrine. But, interestingly, this is not stressed in the dialogues. Job himself *never* speaks to this issue; and it is not clear that the friends speak to it, either. There are a few of their speeches, to be discussed in detail in chapter 5, that might refer to this issue, but it is not clear that they do, and they focus on other issues. Nevertheless, this issue might be related to what is discussed; and in the prologue the Satan had seemed ironic about rewarding righteousness: "Does Job serve God for nought? . . . But put forth thy hand now, and touch all that he has, and he will curse thee to thy face" (1:9, 11; see also 2:4–5). So maybe the question of the rationale for righteousness, or for serving God, *is* important to this book, and maybe it is even true that another appeal of the orthodox doctrine is that it gives an answer to that question. These issues will require careful exploration later.

Another consideration, though probably not a stimulus, lies in the friends' perception of the weakness of human beings and of the power of God. Eliphaz sounds this theme in his first speech:

> Call now; is there any one who will answer you?
>   To which of the holy ones will you turn? . . .
> As for me, I would seek God,
>   and to God would I commit my cause;
> who does great things and unsearchable. . . .
>
> (5:1, 8–9)

If God is powerful, and men (and even "holy ones"?) are weak, the part of prudence is to appeal to God, and to do what He wishes; and God will be *able* to punish, protect, and reward, as the orthodox doctrine says He does. Of course, this line of thought presupposes orthodoxy, rather than giving us an independent reason for believing it; but it does at least show how the doctrine *could* be true. So surely it gives the doctrine's defenders more confidence that they are right.

And there is one more consideration that Elihu raises. I mention it hesitantly, since it appears only in his mouth, and since it seems so weak as an argument; still, it does seem to weigh with him at least. He asks Job:

> Shall one who hates justice govern?
>   Will you condemn him who is righteous and mighty,
> who says to a king, "Worthless one,"
>   and to nobles, "Wicked man";
> who shows no partiality to princes,
>   nor regards the rich man more than the poor,
>   for they are all the work of his hands?
> In a moment they die;
>   at midnight the people are shaken and pass away,
>   and the mighty are taken away by no human hand.
>
> (34:17–20)

Now this is complex, but the basic problem here is that—like much else in the book—this passage seems to confuse justice with power. A modern reader, at least, is apt to respond to the first question—"Shall one who hates justice govern?"—with a division of the issues. *Should* one who hates justice govern? No—one who loves justice should govern. But *does* one who hates justice govern? Perhaps—that is precisely what Job charges, that is what the issue is. So to assume that the answer is no is to beg the question. The fact that God is powerful does not entail that He is just. Many powerful human rulers are unjust. *Should* that be? No. But *are* they? Yes. So this argument of the young Elihu is extremely weak. In the book as we have it, Elihu speaks last, before the theophany, so Job has no chance to reply to him. But this argument hardly merits a reply.

Chapter 2

Job's Response to Orthodoxy

When Job speaks in the dialogues, he addresses five of the six or seven concerns that, as we have seen, underlie his friends' defense of orthodoxy. He does not speak to the very last concern, the weak argument advanced only by Elihu. But in the book as we have it he does not speak in reply to Elihu at all, and the idea there is so flimsy that he could hardly have anticipated it.

Nor does Job address the issue of the rationale for righteousness: "Why should I be righteous, unless it pays?" I have admitted the bare possibility that the comforters raise this issue, though they clearly do not stress it; Job himself does not even mention it, which gives us an additional reason for doubting that the friends do, for doubting the interpretation of their speeches that holds that they do. At the very least, this is not *Job's* worry: *he* is not wondering why he should be upright. True, the orthodox doctrine would give him a reason; but he is not looking for a reason. So he does not mention this concern. (I will return to this issue later.)

Job takes cognizance of the other supports of orthodoxy but is unmoved by them. He knows that what the friends say is traditional and widely accepted. Job says to them, "No doubt you are the people" (12:2)—or "the people that count" (Gordis), or "gentry" (Pope). He says of Eliphaz's counsel, "I have heard many such things" (16:2). And when once he responds to Bildad with the surprising line,

"Truly I know that it is so" (9:2), seeming to agree with the friends, if he is not sarcastic, he may just mean that he has heard their view before, that he knows that theirs *is* the orthodox or traditional view. But he is challenging this orthodoxy. He is bitter because he expected this tradition to be right, and he is finding it wrong.

Job conveys a conviction that it is not necessary to accept what his friends and "the people" have believed—that he has the ability to determine the truth on his own. He does say that "Wisdom is with the aged, and understanding in length of days" (12:12)—but he cannot mean that the friends, in virtue of *their* age, are right; for in the same chapter he says, "But I have understanding as well as you; I am not inferior to you" (12:3)—and "What you know, I also know; I am not inferior to you" (13:2). Just before the "length of days" passage he asks, "Does not the ear try words as the palate tastes food?" (12:11) I think that what he means is that, as we have an ability to discriminate among foods, so we can discriminate among words, determining which are true and which are false. We do not need, in either case, to accept whatever is given, to rely upon tradition or upon what our friends say. Of course most modern, and even ancient, thinkers would quibble with Job's analogy here: the palate determines how foods taste, or seem in the mouth—whereas how words sound, or seem in the ear, so to speak, is not a sure indicator of their truth; fair words can be false; and what seems fair to me may seem foul to you. Plato thought the determiner of truth was more like a dietition than a cook. But the main point of Job's analogy is probably not affected; his point is that we have the ability to test words for their truth, and so to find that the friends' words are empty, are "proverbs of ashes" (13:12). (*How* we do such testing is not explained, although, as I will show below, there are hints of a broad kind of empiricism.) As Job rejects the friends' appeal to tradition, so he rejects their other appeals. We have seen above that it is Job, not one of the friends, who first introduces the theme of man's misery; but Job cannot accept the friends' explanation of it. And Job insists just as much as the friends upon God's might and man's frailty; but he denies that God is using His power as the tradition claims. As for terrifying visions and dreams in the night, Job acknowledges that they occur; but he takes them as further evils needing justification (7:13–15), not as evidence that life is already just. To Eliphaz, they bring messages of universal import (4:12–21); to Elihu, they bring personal messages for individual warning (33:14–18); but Job takes them, at least in his case, as more evils, sent to torture further the innocent. Implicitly he denies that the alleged messages in them are true.

But Job's main quarrel with the grounding of orthodoxy seems to be, in a broad sense, empirical. Job reports what he himself has suffered and what he claims to know of the weal and woe of others, and he claims that the facts are not what the tradition holds them to be. The world, he says, is not like that. And he probably means that the truth about this is no secret, that men of experience know it:

> Have you not asked those who travel the roads,
>   and do you not accept their testimony
> that the wicked man is spared in the day of calamity,
>   that he is rescued in the day of wrath?
>
> (21:29–30)

He may even mean that the truth is so obvious that the lower forms of life know it!—

> But ask the beasts, and they will teach you;
>   the birds of the air, and they will tell you;
> or the plants of the earth, and they will teach you;
>   and the fish of the sea will declare to you.
> Who among all these does not know
>   that the hand of the Lord has done this?
>
> (12:7–9)

Job denies all three parts of the orthodox view: he holds that the wicked prosper, the weak are not protected, and the righteous— construed simply, or in a more complex way—suffer the same or worse fates as others. Let us look at each of these in turn.

"The tents of robbers," Job says, "are at peace, and those who provoke God are secure" (12:6). Job waxes eloquent on this subject; he paints their lives in exaggeratedly rosy colors, echoing and satirizing the portraits of the lives of the righteous painted by the friends. The wicked "live, reach old age, and grow mighty in power" (21:7):

> Their children are established in their presence,
>   and their offspring before their eyes.

Their houses are safe from fear,
  and no rod of God is upon them.
Their bull breeds without fail;
  their cow calves, and does not cast her calf.
They send forth their little ones like a flock,
  and their children dance. . . .
They spend their days in prosperity,
  and in peace they go down to Sheol. . . .
When he [the wicked man] is borne to the grave,
  watch is kept over his tomb.

                                            (21:8–11, 13, 32)

We remember that the friends held that God punished the children of the wicked (5:4). Job does not question the justice of this kind of arrangement, as Jeremiah probably did, but he does deny that it really punishes the wicked, when the retribution comes after death:

You say, "God stores up their iniquity for their sons."
  Let him recompense it to themselves, that they may know it.
Let their own eyes see their destruction. . . .
For what do they care for their houses after them,
  when the number of their months is cut off?

                                            (21:19–21)

Since wickedness has its victims, and the victims are normally the weak, what orthodoxy says about God's protecting the weak is false, too. They suffer horribly:

Men . . . drive away the ass of the fatherless;
  they take the widow's ox for a pledge.
They thrust the poor off the road;
  the poor of the earth all hide themselves.
Behold, like wild asses in the desert
  they go forth to their toil,
seeking prey in the wilderness
  as food for their children. . . .
They lie all night naked, without clothing,
  and have no covering in the cold.

> They are wet with the rain of the mountains,
>   and cling to the rock for want of shelter.
> (There are those who snatch the fatherless
>   child from the breast,
>   and take in pledge the infant of the poor.)
> They go about naked, without clothing. . . .
> From out of the city the dying groan,
>   and the soul of the wounded cries for help;
>   yet God pays no attention to their prayer.
>
> (24:2–5, 7–10, 12)

As orthodoxy is wrong about the wicked and about the weak, it is also wrong about the "upright"—however we interpret this term. For Job himself is the counterexample, the living disproof. Job is suffering, as all can see; yet he insists that he has "not denied the words of the Holy One" (6:10), that he is "a just and blameless man" (12:4). He says, "there is no violence in my hands, and my prayer is pure" (16:17); "I am not guilty" (10:7):

> My foot has held fast to his steps;
>   I have kept his way and have not turned aside.
> I have not departed from the commandment of his lips;
>   I have treasured in my bosom the words of his mouth.
>
> (23:11–12)

Now these expressions at least suggest that Job believes he has done no wrong *at all*; and the extravagant way in which God praised "my servant Job" in the prologue inclines the reader to accept this self-appraisal as correct. Job is not simply Everyman; he is remarkably upright—even God takes special notice of him, in the prologue. At least two of the comforters, and perhaps all of them, believe that no man is completely "pure"; but Job, in this book, may be the exception. Nevertheless—despite his innocence—Job must appeal for mercy to his accuser (9:15).

However, it is possible that Job, in the book as we have it, actually accepts the view that no man is perfectly clean, and that he admits that he too has faults. He asks, "But how can a man be just before God?" (9:2) He echoes the pessimism of his friends:

Man that is born of a woman
   is of few days, and full of trouble. . . .
Who can bring a clean thing out of an unclean?
   There is not one.

(14:1, 4)

Of course, in neither of these passages is it certain that he really accepts universal sinfulness. In the chapter 9 passage, he stresses God's power; so he may be asking only whether a man can struggle successfully against God; as he says later in that chapter, "Though I am innocent, I cannot answer him . . ." (9:15). In chapter 14, a kind of converse passage, the stress is on man's weakness, not his impurity. In both cases the context suggests that the surface meaning is misleading in the passages I have quoted.

However, there are also some passages in which Job has seemed to some readers to confess minor faults of his own. "Why dost thou not pardon my transgression and take away my iniquity?" he asks (7:21), perhaps implying that he has a transgression to be pardoned; but the preceding verse was hypothetical, beginning with an *if*:

If I sin, what do I do to thee, thou watcher of men?
   Why hast thou made me thy mark?
   Why have I become a burden to thee?

(7:20)

So Job may not be admitting any guilt there either. The other passage some readers cite says,

For thou writest bitter things against me,
   and makest me inherit the iniquities of my youth.

(13:26)

So perhaps Job confesses some adolescent wrongdoing.

We seem to have a difficult problem of interpretation here. Job repeatedly and in varying language denies any sin, violence, wrongdoing, straying from God; he repeatedly complains that God treats him like a sinner, making him appeal for mercy, knowing that he is innocent. On the other hand, we have a few other passages that may suggest an admission of sin, perhaps of a minor sort, perhaps only in his early youth. So perhaps he is complaining not that God punishes one who is absolutely pure, but that God overdoes the punishment of one who is almost pure—that God treats minor faults like heinous crimes. Some commentators interpret Job this way. However, I can not find a single passage in which Job actually says this outright— that God punishes only the guilty but does not properly apportion punishment in accord with degree of guilt. This suggestion, that guilt and woe come in degrees, and that a just God should match the degrees—that the punishment should fit the crime in severity—while it is a natural suggestion, is not ever explicitly uttered by Job or by the friends. Job does ask, "Am I the sea, or a sea monster, that thou settest a guard over me?" (7:12) But there the contrast is between men and superhuman forces—for he immediately asks, "What is man, that thou dost make so much of him . . . ?" (7:17) Job never asks, "Am I a murderer, that thou settest a guard over me?"—contrasting murderers, say, with more ordinary sinners.

It may be relevant to this interpretation that Job repeatedly asks the friends, and then God, to tell him what wrongs he has done, or what the charges are (6:24; 10:2; 13:23–24; perhaps 23:3–7). Perhaps Job recognizes that he could have sinned in some way but is unaware of how. Perhaps, then, if the charges were made known, he could clear himself of graver wrongs, and confess and repent lesser sins. All this is possible, I think; again, however, none of this is explicit in any of Job's speeches. And I do not think it really fits the tenor of Job's calls for the charges. After one of them (6:24), he says to the friends, "Turn, I pray, let no wrong be done. Turn now, my vindication is at stake" (6:29). After another (10:2), he says to God, "thou knowest that I am not guilty" (10:7). Before another, (13:23–24), he says, "Behold, I have prepared my case; I know that I shall be vindicated" (13:18); and "This will be my salvation, that a godless man shall not come before him" (13:16). At the end of another call for a trial (23:3–7), he says, "an upright man could reason with him, and I should be acquitted for ever by my judge" (23:7). This is probably the meaning in the strange passage about the witness in heaven, too:

> Even now, behold, my witness is in heaven,
>   and he that vouches for me is on high.

> . . . [M]y eye pours out tears to God,
>   that he would maintain the right of a man with God,
>   like that of a man with his neighbor.
>
>   (16:19–21)

I think the plainest reading here is that if there were a trial, and a
heavenly witness testified for Job, there would be an acquittal. And
the famous and obscure "I know that my Redeemer lives" passage
probably indicates Job's innocence in just the same way:

> For I know that my Redeemer [or Avenger, Defender,
> Vindicator][1]
>   lives, . . .
>   and . . . I shall see God,
> whom I shall see on my side. . . .
>
>   (19:25–27)

In the context, it seems to me best to construe this "Redeemer" figure
as a Vindicator in a semilegal sense—a Defender of Job, perhaps God
Himself as Defender, against the charges impugning Job's integrity.
In both of these passages, then, I would read Job as expressing confidence in his innocence and confidence that somehow God (or some
aspect of God, or some heavenly being) knows of his innocence.

I think that half of this is probably the sense, too, of the earlier
"umpire" passage: "There is no umpire between us [Job and God],
who might lay his hand upon us both" (9:33). There Job sees himself
as unable to get a hearing: "For he [God] is not a man, as I am, that I
might answer him, that we should come to trial together" (9:32). Job's
presupposition, I would say, is that he is innocent, and that a trial
would prove him so. That is, I take the main point in all these passages to be the same: If there were an umpire, or a witness, or a
vindicator, Job would be found innocent. But in the umpire passage,
unlike the other ones, Job expresses no confidence that God knows or
cares about his innocence.

In Job's last speech (chap. 31), with its long list of sins for which
he would accept punishment, the most natural reading is that Job
believes himself innocent of all of them:

Oh, that I had one to hear me!
  (Here is my signature! let the Almighty answer me!)
  Oh, that I had the indictment written by my adversary!
Surely I would carry it on my shoulder;
  I would bind it on me as a crown;
  I would give an account of all my steps;
    like a prince I would approach him.

(31:35-37)

Willing to accept punishment for any real sins, Job believes that a just court would acquit him.

We have been discussing Job's rationale for rejecting the orthodoxy of the comforters. Job has denied that the wicked are punished or that the weak are protected. His evidence seems empirical: This is not how the world is; the traveler, and perhaps even the lower creatures, can see that this orthodoxy is false. As for the third claim of the comforters, that the upright are protected, this too is false, in Job's own case; Job is innocent but God persecutes him anyway. Job's friends, he says, "make my humiliation an argument against me" (19:5), but in this they wrong (19:3) him, for he is innocent:

Behold, I cry out. "Violence!" but I am not answered;
  I call aloud, but there is no justice.

(19:7)

Now we remember that in the version of orthodoxy developed by Eliphaz and Bildad—at least—there can be no man as pure as Job claims (or perhaps claims) to be. For them, Job should repent, reform, pray to God and trust God to help—and God would help. If Job did all that and then was not helped by God, their version of orthodoxy would be challenged. But they see Job as simply an unrepentant sinner, and hence they see his sufferings as no threat to their views at all. Job, on the other hand, cannot directly test what they say; for they require him to repent, and he knows of nothing needing repentance. So one might argue that, in the conflict between Job and the comforters over the fate of the righteous, the disputants never make contact: that their disagreement is really over the *possibility* of utmost purity, and not over *what happens* to the utterly pure. But this would be an odd conclusion. Job and the friends certainly see themselves as disagreeing over his case; and the friends never say, "Job, if you were as upright as you say, you would deserve your kind of fate"! (A totally upright man deserves to suffer?) So I think it fairly clear that their version of orthodoxy requires that the upright, whether in the reformed-sinner sense or in Job's extreme sense, be protected by God. For them, the pure, if there were any pure, would be rewarded; and even the impure, if they repent, etc., are protected. Job's case, if he really is pure, challenges the first part of this. So Job claims to know that all three orthodox themes are false—he claims that the wicked are not punished, the weak are not protected, and the upright are not rewarded. His support seems to be empirical: he has seen what happens in the world.

Much has been said—especially since Nietzsche—about the pessimism of Greek tragedy. *Oedipus* is a gloomy play; Oedipus believes that he is clever enough, and otherwise good enough, to avoid the kinds of crimes that bring destruction. He is mistaken; no man can avoid misery (or fated misery, at least). Other Greek plays present related views. The orthodoxy of Job's friends is similarly pessimistic, as we have seen. But in the dialogues Job goes even deeper into gloom: for he holds that destruction comes even to the righteous.

Finally, we should note that Job not only challenges the truth of what the friends say, he also challenges the kindness of the doctrine. We remember that, in this book as in much of high Hebraic thought, the content of the behavior required of man is largely practical compassion, the providing of protection for the ill, the widowed, the poor, the fatherless; what God requires of man is largely that he love and practice mercy. Over and over again this theme is introduced in the Book of Job. (It is also clear in this book that Job and his friends expect *God* to practice mercy, too—to be the help of the helpless.) But the friends' doctrine is not merciful or compassionate; when they hurl it at Job, *who is one of the helpless*, instead of helping him, they wound him further. Job makes a fairly large issue of this:

> He who withholds kindness from a friend
>   forsakes the fear of the Almighty.

My brethren are treacherous as a torrent-bed,
    as freshets that pass away. . . .
Such you have now become to me. . . .

(6:14–15, 21)

. . . [M]iserable comforters are you all.
Shall windy words have an end?
    Or what provokes you that you answer?
I also could speak as you do,
    if you were in my place;[2]
I could join words together against you,
    and shake my head at you.
I could strengthen you with my mouth,
    and the solace of my lips would assuage your pain.

(16:2–5)

How long will you torment me,
    and break me in pieces with words?
These ten times you have cast reproach upon me;
    are you not ashamed to wrong me?
. . . [Y]ou magnify yourselves against me,
    and make my humiliation an argument against me.

(19:2–3, 5)

Bear with me, and I will speak;
    and after I have spoken, mock on.

(21:3)

How you have helped him who has no power!
    How you have saved the arm that has no strength!

(26:2)

This theme—that the orthodox doctrine is used by the friends cruelly, whereas a man is supposed to help "him who has no power"—is fairly central in Job's complaints; he brings a practical, moral, religious charge against orthodoxy, at least as the friends employ it. The problem with their doctrine is not just its falsity, though it *is* false; its *utterance* is unrighteous, because cruel to the sufferer. From the number of times Job sounds this theme, we know that it is central; and given the background issue—that men and God should be helps to the helpless—its centrality becomes even more prominent. Theology and obligation focus on charity; but orthodoxy is itself uncharitable. There is a deep, deep problem here.

It may be the case that the author of our book was aware of the logical difficulty discussed above: that whereas theology and God's commandments stress helping the weak, orthodoxy suggests that the weak deserve to be weak, and so deserve to suffer the fate of the weak. Perhaps the author saw this paradox. At the very least, he saw the problem in uttering the doctrine: it makes the innocent weak suffer even more, though our obligation is to be comforters and protectors. He has Job say this repeatedly.

At the end of the book, after the theophany, Job's recognition of his ignorance calls for silence; but charity—a central duty—called for the silence (at least) of the orthodox friends. Interestingly, they *were* silent, for a whole week, in the prologue; but of course we can be aware of what our friends think as well as of what they say—and their thoughts can be about as cruel and as damaging as their words. If they think in their hearts that we deserve our misfortunes, that can hurt about as much as if they said so with their lips. So I doubt that mere silence can solve the problem here. This doctrine, even kept in the heart, violates a major obligation on a man of God. And we have seen anyway—at least if Job is right—that it is a false doctrine. Its falsity and its cruelty—where the opposite of cruelty is called for—demand its reform. This orthodoxy is not faithful to God, does not itself "fear God," not if God is the God of reality, and not if God asks His people to love mercy, kindness, charity, compassion.

Chapter 3

On Being "God's Servant"

As we have seen, the Book of Job deals with the problem of evil; the debate in the dialogues centers on the comforters' defense, and Job's critique, of the "orthodox doctrine" of evil. In the two preceding chapters we have explored that debate.

Nevertheless there is something misleading about approaching the Book of Job in this way. The book is, after all, a book *about Job*, a human character; it is a drama, not a debate—even if it includes a debate. "The problem of evil" is an intellectual or theoretical problem: the problem of reconciling the alleged goodness and power of God with the apparent amount and distribution of evil in the world. But the Book of Job is not just a treatise on that, or on any other intellectual problem: it presents a portrait, and tells a story, of an individual. It is, we might say, a psychological study—though one that involves the problem of evil.

Now this character Job is introduced in the prologue—by the narrator, and by Yahweh Himself—as a model among men: it is said that in some outstanding way he "fears God," is "blameless and upright," and "avoids evil" (1:1, 8; 2:3). Job seems what a man would ideally be: he is a kind of example God can point to with pride, the rarest of the rare, one of the few whom God calls His "servants" (1:8; 2:3). "There is none like him on the earth" (1:8; 2:3)—meaning at least that he is extraordinary; and perhaps even meaning that this is an idealized portrait, that no one is really as upright as this character, but that in him we imagine a more than human perfection.

But what *kind* of perfection is this? Or *how* is Job extraordinary? What does this book mean when it calls him "blameless and upright, one who fears God, and turns away from evil"? Some commentators treat this account with pedantic woodenness, as if it were Buddhist, so to speak; for they imagine that Job is being credited with the Noble Four-Fold Virtue, or the Four (Count 'em, Four) Virtues of (1) blamelessness, (2) uprightness, (3) fear of God, and (4) rejection of evil. There are passages in other Hebrew writings in which these terms have slightly differing meanings; but it seems to me totally wrongheaded to think the author of the prologue was making four distinct points each of the three times he wrote this account of Job's excellence. We know that "blameless and upright" was a formula, an idiom; we know that "feared God and turned away from evil" was also a formula or idiom. When the author puts them together he is merely being emphatic; we should look for four meanings here no more than in a modern writer who speaks of a "lighthearted, free and easy, devil-may-care" attitude. This is merely idiomatic rhetorical re-dundancy. Job is being described in a traditional formulaic manner. But if this is so, then what is the *content* of the description? What has Job done, or what is he like, to merit such a description? What has been compressed into this formula?

I think that the way to answer the question is to study the whole book, and to see what, within the book, entitles a man to this kind of high praise. But the prologue, where the praise occurs, seems to assume that we already know what warrants this distinction; for it tells us almost nothing concrete of what Job was like. We learn Job's name; his homeland ("Uz"—perhaps in Edom, at the southwest of Palestine, or perhaps in the Hauran, to the northeast, in or near Damascus); some details of his wealth (he was "the greatest of all the people of the east" [1:3]); the size of his family; and a little about how his children spent their feast days (1:1–4). Beyond these circumstan-tial facts, all we learn of Job the man is that he always offered burnt offerings for his sons, fearing that they might have "cursed God in their hearts" (1:5)! In the prologue, then, we are not told the content of Job's merit—why it was that he was singled out for such praise.

Accordingly, we must either leave the praise opaque, or we must assume that the book holds together as a work of art, and look at the rest of it to see there what makes a man "blameless and upright."[1] On this assumption, we are driven to the dialogues, where what men are like receives constant attention. There we can see what men are accused of, when they are said to deserve God's punishment; what Job is accused of, by the friends, when they deny that he is blameless and upright; what Job claims for himself when he defends himself; and what sins he vows willingness to be punished for, if he has committed them.[2] Though there are details elsewhere, the main sources are chapters 22, 24, 29, and 31. In them a clear picture emerges, which can be presented briefly. Most modern commentators divide ancient obligations into two groups—some ritual, and some moral; it is clear that ritual obligations are downplayed in the dialogues. There seems to be a reference to sun and moon worship (31:26–27); there may be another reference to idolatry (12:6); but there is no mention of the observance of the sabbath, of dietary laws, or of any other sort of ritual purity or cleanliness. (As I have noted, Job and his three friends, off to the east of Palestine, may not be Jews; but their debate does not reveal any distinctively non-Jewish traits, either; their ethnicity is not highlighted, as it would be if rituals were made central.) If we bring back into consideration the prose frame of the book, then we must remember that there are sacrifices in the prologue and that the friends are commanded to sacrifice (and Job to pray) in the epilogue. Nevertheless, even granting all this, ritual matters remain in the background of the book, while moral matters are in the foreground. (In this respect, the Book of Job resembles the great works of the eighth-century Hebrew prophets.) An upright man is honest; he is not a thief or murderer; he is not an adulterer, or a would-be adulterer; at least in Job's station, he provides for widows and orphans, for the poor, the blind, the lame, for strangers and travelers; he is not cruel or malicious, even toward his enemy; he does not allow cruelty on the part of his servants; he punishes the wicked and retrieves the prey of the wicked; he is not vain, and he does not put his trust in his wealth. This is the kind of man Job claims to be; we have no reason to doubt his claim; so this, I conclude, is primarily what the prologue asserts Job to be, when it praises him in its formulaic manner. We might say that when Job is described as "blameless . . . ," what is meant is that Job is remarkably moral, in the ways just explained. Job deals with his fellow men in exemplary moral fashion.

Now the action of the play is instigated by the Satan, who seems both to accept and to challenge God's praise of Job; he responds,

> . . . Does Job fear God for nought? Hast thou not put a hedge about him and his house and all that he has, on every side? Thou hast blessed the work of his hands, and his possessions have increased in the land. But put forth thy hand now, and touch all that he has, and he will curse thee to thy face. (1:9–11)

And then later: "But . . . touch his bone and his flesh, and he will curse thee to thy face" (2:5).

In a sense, as I say, the Satan seems to acquiesce in God's praise of Job: for asking "Does Job fear God for nought?" seems to grant that he does "fear God"; and if we are dealing here with formulaic redundancy, then to say that he "fears God" is to say all that God said— that he is "a blameless and upright man, who fears God and turns away from evil" (1:8; 2:3). So the Satan grants that Job has been exemplary. But he makes insinuations about him anyway: "Does Job fear God *for nought*?" The Satan suggests that it is possible to be like Job—that remarkable—and still not be all that one ought to be before God; that a man could be even more of God's "servant," even more "God-fearing," even more profoundly religious, we might say, than the upright Job.

And God does not reject this suggestion. He too seems to assume that what has been said so far in praise of Job is not all that might be said, and so the test is allowed. Some interpreters speak of a "wager" or "bet" between God and the Satan; in the book that we have, however, only the Satan expresses an opinion as to the outcome; God permits the test without predicting its result. So there really is no wager, and no stated disagreement between God and the Satan. Indeed, for our purposes the most important point is that they seem to agree: not that Job will fail—for God does not speak to that issue— but that the suggestion the Satan raises is a sensible one, that even a man like Job, "blameless," may not be all a man could be. Though no single word here should be translated as "test," the prologue does seem to describe a plan to test Job. God will "put forth His hand," "touch Job's bone and flesh" (or He will put Job and his possessions in the Satan's "power" [1:12; 2:6]); and presumably the outcome will tell whether the Satan's prediction was correct. A number of aspects of this "testing" need to be clarified. This chapter and the next two will address some of the issues.

In the first place, this whole Olympian (or perhaps Persian) court discussion between God and the Satan needs to be taken with more than a grain of salt, needs to be demythologized, in a very deep way, insofar as the problems the book addresses are concerned. Especially: If the prologue means, as the traditional folktale may have meant, that the explanation of Job's suffering is that he is being tested—that a discussion between God and the Satan explains why Job is suffering—then the poet of the book regarded the prologue as a pretense, as expressing a point of view that must be overcome. We must get ahead of our story here, slightly, to see why; the reason has to do with the structure and content of the book as a whole. Throughout the book many views are presented; surely the view of God Himself, in His speeches from the whirlwind, is normative. God's voice, in those speeches and in the epilogue, explicitly criticizes the words of Job and the words of the three friends. And what God says there implicitly criticizes the prologue, too—if we interpret it in this first way. Whatever the puzzles about the God speeches, we will see[3] that one thing is quite clear in them: God assures Job, lets us and Job see, that Job does not understand the world well enough to solve the problem of evil. God's message is a message of silence. Job sees, as in a blinding light, that when he spoke of such matters he had, as he says, "uttered what I did not understand, things too wonderful for me, which I did not know" (42:3). But if Job can not unriddle the problem of evil, neither can the friends. Moreover, neither can the man who composed the prologue. If the author of the prologue is really presenting an explanation of Job's suffering; if he is pretending to enter the divine counsel, to be privy to the divine deliberations; then he is as presumptuous as Job or his friends, and he too needs to repent in dust and ashes (42:6). Job does repent, but the challenge to Job is perfectly general; it does not depend for its force upon any peculiarity of that one Uzite named Job. No man understands the way of the evil in the world; and that includes the author of the prologue. The Book of Job may not display perfect unity; certainly there are literary layers in it; but if we read it as one work, then we must say that the theophany refutes the prologue—assuming that the prologue is presenting an explanation of Job's suffering.

However, it is not necessary to read it as explanatory. And, interpreted differently, the prologue is obviously right; Job *is* undergoing a trial. Sufferings—and not just on this scale—test a man, try him, tempt him; they torture his spirit and present him with divine, demonic, and pathetically human possibilities. It is never certain in advance how a man will respond to suffering. With his children killed, his property stolen, his health ruined, Job will be tried severely. Perhaps this is the way to read the Satan's predictions.

But if this is all that the Satan meant, then the case of Job involves trials that not even he foresaw (or trials that he satanically concealed). For Job is not only what we might call a "natural" man, who desires happiness and has difficulty bearing hardship; he is also a man with a moral sense, which in him turns into a sense of how the world ought to be, of how God is obligated to deal with the world. As we have seen, Job holds the expectations that his friends hold: he believes that the blameless and upright ought to be protected, and that the wicked ought to be punished. But this means, since Job himself is blameless and upright, that he is not merely suffering; he is suffering unjustly— "without cause," as God puts it in the prologue (2:3). Any man who loses his health is tried; but Job is a man who believes he ought not to have been afflicted, for he did not deserve to become ill, and consequently it is an injustice that he is sick. Job is tried not only by the loss of his health, but also by what he regards as the injustice of its loss. Job wishes he had never been born; when he does, he speaks as a natural man. But he also rails at the injustice in his case; when he does, he speaks as a man of moral principle, who has come to judge the course of his life—and God[4]—by moral standards.

And there is a third element in Job's trial that the Satan does not mention; and many of Job's readers today may not see it either, when they claim that Job is "egocentric." Job rails not only at the injustice of his own case; he rails at injustice in the world generally. Many philosophers believe that as a matter of logic one who complains of injustice in one case cannot consistently condone it in another, that a "principle" which would apply in only one case is no principle at all. Be that as it may, it is clear that Job's rage is not limited to his own case. In this sense, it is far from egocentric. Job complains not only on his own behalf, but on behalf of other men; he is outraged at injustice generally, at the undeserved suffering of all who are upright or weak and innocent, and at the unmerited prosperity of all the wicked.

It is fair to say, then, that the Book of Job does dramatize a trial— a triple trial—provided we take this as descriptive, and not explanatory, of Job's anguish. If we take the theophany as normative, then no man can explain the evil in the world; and so the prologue does not provide an explanation of Job's suffering. No one has the right to claim that Job suffers because of a divine plan to test him. But Job *is* tested, tempted, tried; in this sense the prologue speaks the plain truth. Job is tested by his afflictions, as the prologue suggests; he is more deeply tested by what he sees as the injustice of his afflictions; and he is tested finally by the injustice of all undeserved affliction and all unmerited prosperity.

In the prologue, as we have seen, God and the Satan seem to think that they can reasonably ask questions about a man as moral as the exemplary Job. But what more could be asked about a man already known to be "blameless and upright" in the Joban way? When the triple trial arrives, what parts of Job's life and psyche will be illuminated?

The narrowest reading would say that God wants moral conduct of the sort Job displays, but that He wants it not only in prosperity but also in adversity. Job's conduct toward his fellow men has been exemplary so far, but that means, always in fortunate circumstances (or not really "fortunate," since not a matter of luck; God sent these happy circumstances). Job's conduct has been blameless so long as God blessed the work of his hands and put a protective hedge around him. (And around other good men?) But would his conduct still be blameless in adversity (and injustice)? Would Job be a fair-weather friend to God, serving Him in good times, but deserting Him in bad? Cephalus, in Plato's *Republic*—of whom we also read that he made sacrifices—thought that it is easier to be just when you are rich than when you are poor;[5] your temptations are less. A distinction between behavior in prosperity and in distress certainly makes sense, and the Satan's remarks presuppose this distinction. So the Satan asks this question; but clearly he asks more than this. God and the Satan entertain a deeper question about Job. At the first level, they ask about

Job's behavior, his conduct, under fire; but they are also asking what lies behind the behavior. The Satan asks *why* Job serves God, what *for*—"Does Job fear God *for nought*?" The book virtually opens with a reference to the "heart"[6] —Job feared that his sons had "cursed God in their hearts" (1:5). And the test, or the question about Job, is clearly a test of *his* heart, from which his behavior arises. Adversity would reveal not just how Job would behave under stress, but also what has motivated him all along. God seems interested in that, and not in behavior only. Perhaps a man could be utterly upright in his conduct toward his fellows—and even in his conduct toward God, if that is different—and still not be God's servant in his heart. There might be more than one motive for upright behavior.

What these motives might be is only partially clarified in the prologue. Some readers have suggested that fear is a motive, and that God wants love instead; and they have fastened upon the word *fear* in the usual translation of the prologue—Job "feared God" (1:1) or "fears God" (1:8; 2:3); and "Does Job fear God for nought?" (1:9) In this interpretation, Job's conduct (in prosperity, anyway) is faultless, but it may derive from fear: perhaps Job obeys God only out of fear of His punishment for sinners. If that were so, Job would be ultimately interested in himself, not in his fellows whom he treats so well, and not in God whom he serves. But, this interpretation usually goes on to say, many Jewish (and, following them, Christian) writers taught that we should love our fellow men, and genuinely love God; so the test of Job is a test to see whether fear (i.e., self-interest) lies in his heart, or whether love is what motivates him. If we are self-interested, we might serve God, to escape His wrath (and to gain His blessing); in that case, we serve God "out of fear." If we love God, on the other hand, we serve Him for His own sake, not for what we stand to gain from His service. Some commentators who speak of "theocentric" and "egocentric" religion have this contrast in mind, and they think the test of Job is a test for theocentrism.

Now this interpretation is not obviously correct, even if we assume that a question of motivation is crucial in the testing of Job. For one thing, the term translated *fear* seems a broad term, sometimes translated *awe*, or *reverence*, or even *religion*. It may be that biblical religion had its original roots in fear, fear of disobedience, fear of

punishment; and perhaps that is why this term acquired such importance in Hebrew writings. Perhaps originally, or early, an upright
man was upright because he feared God—literally. But by the time of
many of the Hebrew books, the term seems to have denoted more
than mere fear. So we must be careful about assuming that its narrow
or early meaning is central here.

Furthermore, this narrow reading of *fear* makes nonsense of the
Satan's query, "Does Job fear God *for nought*?" The Satan does not
say, "Of course, Job *fears* God, but does he *love* Him?" Or, "Does Job
only fear God, or does he love Him?" God had said that Job feared
Him; the Satan grants the point, but asks whether Job's fear is "for
nought." He seems to grant the merit in "fearing God," but questions
the motives behind the fear. So it seems to me best to say—as I did
say—that "fears God" is short for "is blameless and upright, fears
God, and turns away from evil"; and that that means, in this book,
that Job deals rightly with his fellow men, as God commands. The
Satan grants that Job's conduct is admirable; he grants it when he
implies that Job does "fear God"; but he asks about the motivation—
does Job fear God *for nought*?

Still, even if the fear/love interpretation cannot be based simply
on the texts that speak of fear, the main point in this interpretation
may be correct. For the Satan does seem to ask about Job's motives—
for the ironic "for nought?" does suggest that rewards are what motivate Job. So take the rewards away, the Satan seems to say, and see
whether Job continues to fear/obey God. Perhaps there are higher
motives for obeying God, for doing His will. So then the test would
be a test of Job's motives, of the heart underlying his actions. A lower
motive is self-interest; a higher motive might be shown by serving
God "for nought," without reward. What that higher motive would
be, positively, is not made clear; but at least it would not be self-
interested. And to give this interpretation all possible concessions,
"love" *might* be the kind of disinterested motive God looks for.

We notice that as the prologue presents it, the issue in the testing seems an obvious issue; the Satan immediately asks about Job's
motives, and God immediately grants the Satan's request for a trial.
The transitions are quick; and this means, I suspect, that the author
counted on his readers to grasp the issue right off—to say, "Well, of

course this is a sensible question to ask. Of course someone who serves God for nought is better than someone who serves for reward. Of course self-interested motivation is lower."

I wish we knew why and how and when and to whom this point seemed so obvious. We know that a great deal of what passes for religion is self-interested. Socrates is usually thought to have held that all motivation is self-interested; many theoreticians have agreed with him. But here we have the whole action of the play generated by the opposite assumption, by the quite casual assumption that some people are better than that. Some are; the assumption is correct;[7] but much psychological theory that people have believed has denied it.

It is also worth notice, as hinted earlier, that this issue is connected with the issue of "orthodoxy" on the problem of evil. Orthodoxy—if it were true—would give a person a self-interested reason for "fearing God"; for the orthodox doctrine says that obedience always pays and disobedience never pays. It wouldn't follow, of course, that everyone who believed in the doctrine and obeyed God would necessarily be obeying *on account of* the reward and punishment; there still might be sterling souls who obeyed God out of disinterested motivation. Nevertheless, even for such persons it would be possible to give self-interested reasons for obeying. And to the extent that such reasons moved them, affected them, weighed with them, to that extent their motives would become self-interested. But orthodoxy is needed by the man of lower motivation; such a man either would not obey God, or else the orthodox doctrine would persuade him to obey. A man of more generous motivation might serve God without thought of reward, and so, perhaps, without belief in this orthodoxy. This argument is never presented in the dialogues; and yet the prologue, with breathtaking casualness, simply assumes that people could be beyond caring about the rewards that orthodoxy promises!

To return to our main concern: at one level, we see, the test of Job is a test of his conduct in suffering; at another level, it is a test of the motivation behind his conduct. The Satan pretty clearly suggests that both levels are involved in the test. However, if we look ahead in the book, we receive hints that the test is even deeper, or broader, than that. The dialogues, as we have seen, focus on *moral conduct*; I am interpreting Job's initial excellence in terms of such conduct, and

interpreting the test as revealing such conduct and the motives behind it. But this may give us an unduly narrow focus. For clearly, at
both levels we interpret religion (or faith, or "fear of God") in *moral*
terms: and perhaps religion is broader than moral action and its motivation. Of course, religion is often interpreted morally; Abou Ben
Adhem loved his fellow men, and so "Ben Adhem's name led all the
rest."[8] But perhaps that is a mistake, or perhaps that is not the view of
the Book of Job. Perhaps a right relation to God, in this book, transcends morality altogether. Perhaps Job could be moral, and moral
from disinterested motives, and still not be all that God calls him to
be. Eventually I will argue that this is part of the message of the
theophany.

For biblical religion, morality is crucial; in the prophets, especially, we see this theme clearly articulated. Amos has God thunder:

> I hate, I despise your feasts,
>   and I take no delight in your solemn assemblies. . . .
> But let justice roll down like waters,
>   and righteousness like an everflowing stream.
>
> (Amos 5:21, 24)

The New Testament (N.T.) presents Jesus as adopting a similar
stance, on his own authority and on the authority of the scriptures.
Jesus said, "Go and learn what this means, 'I desire mercy, and not
sacrifice'" (Matt. 9:13, quoting Hos. 6:6). The New Testament presents this emphasis as central in Jesus' struggle against the Pharisees;
and Paul presents it as central in the struggle to open the church to
the gentiles. Clearly much of the Old Testament (O.T.) and much of
the New emphasizes moral behavior at the expense of ritual. And the
dialogues in the Book of Job do the same. But it may be that the moral
is too limited, too narrow, to encompass all that a right relation to
God involves. We will see, when we reach the theophany, that this *is*
the view there. At that point we will see how the testing of "God's
servant" Job leads him eventually beyond the realm of the moral
altogether.

It is at least arguable that being religious, "fearing God," is more
than behaving, and being disposed to behave, well toward one's
fellows—and more than any kind of behaving. Perhaps a religious

orientation is a whole way of life, not just a way of acting—for living is more than acting. To live is to act; but it is also to undergo, to experience, to suffer, to be a patient in relation to the world's agency; and—involving both—it is to be an observer, a witness, a spectator, a knower of the scene about oneself. My life is, in part, a matter of whether I rob my neighbor, help him in time of need, and the like— of things I *do*; but it is also a matter of becoming sick, of growing old, of being injured, and eventually of dying—not things I *do*, in any action or behavior sense, but things I undergo; and it is also a matter of seeing or knowing or believing what is going on in and about me. A part of my life is my knowledge of genocidal atrocities committed against my fellow men, even though I did not take part in those atrocities—indeed, even though some of them took place before I was born. If religion is a way of dealing with the whole of life, then there are ways of suffering and of apprehending, there are ways of re- sponding to life—not just ways of behaving—that can be religious or irreligious. One way of understanding the testing of Job is to see it in these terms. Job has been exemplary as agent; how is he as patient? When he acts or behaves (in relation to his fellows), he does well; but how is he when he undergoes, when he suffers (or suffers what he does not deserve)? And even: how is he when he witnesses others' unjust suffering, and the prosperity of the wicked? How does he deal with those sides of life? One might say that these questions still address Job's "heart"; but at our second level, Job is tested to see what kind of heart gives rise to his moral conduct; at this third level, he is tested more broadly—to discover his heart, his posture, his spirit, in relation to the sides of life that do not call for moral action in re- sponse. How is he there? In the dialogues we are presented with an answer; it is an answer that the theophany reduces to dust and ashes.

Chapter 4

Cursing God

"The patience of Job" is an ambiguous expression; Job is a patient, in the traditional sense that opposes *patient* to *agent*. He is a sufferer in our book; and in the prologue he endures his suffering with patience, or even with resignation. In common speech the expression usually refers to his resignation, his ability to wait or to endure without rancor. So we speak of situations that "would try the patience of Job"; it may be that this patience was known in folklore even before our book was written. But patience, in that sense, is not a trait of the character portrayed in the central dialogues. I will argue that *bitterness* is what marks that Job, or rather "moral bitterness" (to be explained later); that Job curses God, out of that bitterness; and hence that the Satan was right when he predicted that Job would curse God to His face, once the protective "hedge" (1:10) had been removed.

As we have seen, the Book of Job deals with the problem of evil but is also a portrait of, and a story of, an individual. That individual undergoes agonies of body and of mind, and the prologue, speaking mythologically, presents those agonies as a test. Using clues from the whole of the book, we have had a preliminary look at what more God might want from a servant as upright as Job; we have considered three ways in which Job's exemplary righteousness might be transcended. Now let us see what actually happens when Job is tested, how Job actually responds to his ordeal.

Job's righteousness lay in his conduct toward his fellows, in his morality; so in part we wondered whether the suffering Job would become immoral. One might think that the trial would tempt Job to become the opposite of all that he was before, to become no longer morally "blameless and upright." This expectation is strengthened by the way *we* often use the term *temptation* in daily life and in literature: we are tempted to gain unjust advantages for ourselves or to treat others unethically. David was tempted when he saw Bathsheba, and he committed murder (2 Sam. 11:1–24). Nostromo was tempted, and he stole the silver;[1] Michael Kohlhaas was tried, and he became a murderer and a destroyer.[2] In each of the latter two cases, incidentally, as in Job's, injustice provided the context—and in those cases it produced more injustice. But if Job is seriously tempted to immoral behavior, to mistreating his fellow man—to upsetting boundary stones, to neglecting the widows and orphans, to abusing the stranger—we never hear of it. If that be the test, Job passes it with such flying colors that we never hear he has even considered it. In the entire book he never once suggests that he is thinking of becoming an evil-doer, of abandoning his moral uprightness. He never says, "Since the wicked are prospering, and the upright are suffering, I had better become wicked myself. I am a fool not to steal all I can." The thought never crosses his mind. To the extent, then, that the test is *this* kind of test, Job passes. He remains as upright as ever. Of course, given his reduced means, his poverty and illness, he has less scope for action; he is actually unable to do many of the good deeds he did in the past, and unable to do many of the evil deeds that one might be tempted to do, had one the resources or power. Moral obligations are obligations on those capable of acting, and Job has been rendered much less powerful. Still, these are my reflections, not Job's; we never hear him say any of this, or hear him lament his inability to steal from his fellow men. Nor does he ever express regret that he has been upright in the past. So it seems to me that we must conclude that Job remains as upright as ever, given his straitened circumstances.

And this means that Job passes the second kind of test, too, the test of the heart—if we construe it in terms of self-interest. The Satan seemed to suggest that Job acted only for reward, to receive God's blessing, and to escape God's punishment. Now Job has been denied any reward; yet he still does not propose to disobey God. He clings fast to his old righteousness. He does not become wicked, and he never laments his righteousness in the past, in spite of the fact that he suffers so terribly (and unjustly). He wishes he had never been born; he hopes for an early death; but he never wishes that he had not been upright, or hopes that he will soon be able to engage in wickedness, even though he claims that the wicked fare as well, or better, than the righteous! It seems clear that *Job's* motive for righteousness is not fear of punishment or hope of reward. He is terribly distressed that his reward does not arrive, that God does not protect him; but, in spite of that, he never offers to desert the path of righteousness!

This means that many readings of the book are at best half-right. The Satan suggests that Job serves God out of self-interest; some commentators agree with the Satan, and say that Job learns only at the end to serve God for God's sake, or for the love of God. We have not yet discussed Job's transformation after the theophany, but it cannot be a transformation from greed, or self-interest, or "fear," in this sense; for we have no evidence whatsoever that Job's motivation was ever purely self-interested. Some commentators say Job moves at the end from egocentrism to theocentrism; but if egocentrism is domination by self-interest, we have no evidence that Job was ever characterized by that. Job never wavers in his righteousness, even when it seems clear that righteousness does not pay. He does not need a theophany, or a transformation, to acquire that kind of loyalty to God.

Other misreadings of the end of the book are related to these. Some commentators say that Job learns that virtue is its own reward. Some say that Job learns that the moral imperative is categorical, and that we have an obligation to do what is right because it is right, and not because we may profit from it. I have not yet explained my alternative reading, or examined in detail the logic of the ending; but if the ending says any of these things, then the book as a whole is quite disjointed. For all of these readings, without exception, assume that the issue is: Why should I be moral? But Job never asks that question. Job knows he should tell the truth, help the weak and defenseless, and so on; and he never, in this work, asks why. What he wants to know is why *God* is doing what He is doing.

This fundamental misinterpretation of the Book of Job, so prevalent in the literature, is easily explained. The reader mistakes the Book of Job for Plato's *Republic*, or for the tradition in moral philosophy that extends from Plato through Kant. Plato and the author of our Job were perhaps nearly contemporaries; our author has been called the most learned ancient before Plato; both had brilliant, cosmopolitan, and moral minds. Their concerns were related. But that is not to say that their concerns were identical. The author of Job was more of a pessimist than Plato; he was to Plato as St. Augustine was to the Stoics: he could entertain and accept the horrible notion that in this world the wicked do sometimes really prosper and the upright really do suffer. What his Job wonders is why that is so, why God allows that to be so. Plato never got this far into empirical honesty; he always believed that it could not be so. Plato asked why a man should be just, and he struggled mightily to show that justice ultimately paid. Job denies the conclusion—denies that justice always pays— but, with a silence that might have shocked Plato, he never asks, "Then why should I be just?" Perhaps the author of Job did not know Ecclesiastes, as Plato of course knew the Sophists. Or perhaps there is some other reason he never raised Plato's question. What is clear is that he did not raise it. And this means that much of what the commentators say about this book is only obscurely relevant to the dialogue at its heart. All the commentary about the love of God, and theocentrism, and the categorical imperative, and virtue as its own reward—all that is directly relevant to Plato's question, a question of moral psychology, or of the justification of morality; but Job does not ask that kind of question. Job asks why God allows the world to be the way Plato denied that it is, why God allows the wicked to prosper and the upright and innocent to suffer. This is a question of theology. Plato believed morality paid; and he asked how. Job sees that morality does not always pay; and he asks why. Perhaps, given his pessimism, he should have gone on to ask another question: Why, then, be moral? Perhaps he should have, but he did not. And so the answers to that question, if they are relevant to this book at all, are relevant only in some indirect way. Their point is not the main point.

To pick up our main thread again: to become immoral is *not* Job's temptation. Even though the wicked prosper, Job never suggests that he is thinking of throwing in his lot with them. What Job *is* tempted to do is stated explicitly but cryptically in the prologue. The Satan tells

God twice (1:11; 2:5) that if Job is tortured he will "curse you [God] to your face." And Job's wife urges him (2:9) to "curse God and die." I propose that we take seriously the strange notion, asserted thrice, that *that* is what Job is tempted to do: he is tempted to curse God.

But what does it mean to curse God? And how does one do that? The Book of Job suggests on its face that there are two ways of cursing God. We hear, even before the Satan episode, of Job's worry that his sons might "have sinned, and cursed God in their hearts" (1:5). (So there are *four* references to cursing God in that short prologue!) Apparently in this book—as elsewhere in the Old Testament—one can sin in one's heart without sinning overtly. Job worries that his sons may have done that; they may have cursed God in their hearts. This is one way of cursing God. Of course, this is not the obvious or paradigmatic way; one normally curses with one's lips. And there are early suggestions that a kind of talk—this mode of cursing God—is on the author's mind. After the first set of catastrophies, the author reports both what Job did and what he said; and he concludes, "In all this Job did not sin *or charge God with wrong*" (1:22; my italics, of course). Then after the second onslaught, when Job's wife says, "Curse God and die," we are told what Job *said* in response; and the narrator comments, "In all this Job *did not sin with his lips*" (2:10). The Qumran Targum adds, "but in his thoughts he already cherished sinful words";[3] Terrien in *The Interpreter's Bible* disagrees, saying, "There is no implication, as the rabbis suggested, that he sinned in his heart."[4] Perhaps not, or perhaps not yet; but the prologue is clearly concerned about talk, and implies that there are two ways of cursing God: with one's lips and in one's heart. The two ways are what we would expect. Generally it is possible to sin overtly and also to commit the same sin in one's heart; Jesus did not invent that distinction. What we can do we can consider doing, we can desire to do, we can be prepared to do; perhaps, indeed, all voluntary action comes in some sense from the heart. So with cursing God.

Now suppose one wanted to curse God simpliciter, with one's lips: how would one do it? Cursing God would be a "speech act," Austin or Searle would say; how does one perform that act? What words does one use to curse God? If *curse* were the only translation of the Hebrew at one's disposal, or if one had been reading Maimonides, one might think it would be virtually impossible to curse

God—that there is a logical difficulty in the concept. For in one standard form of cursing, to curse someone is to call upon some higher power to bring down something untoward upon the one being cursed—as in, "May God damn your life to continual weeping." But when one aims to curse *God*, what higher power shall one appeal to? And shall one say, "Let God damn God to continual weeping"? Could one reasonably expect God to damn Himself to something untoward? (And is there anything untoward, any injury, that can befall God?) So one might think there are logical, or perhaps theological, difficulties inherent in the whole notion of cursing God; one might suspect that it is impossible to curse God without having a muddled head—if one construes it on the model just indicated. Nevertheless—or maybe therefore—Maimonides, following the Mishnah, *did* construe it in just this way.

Maimonides explained very carefully how a court was to determine whether someone had cursed God. Not all the features of his account are relevant here, though I will report that he recorded a controversy over the roles of the several names of God; Maimonides' own opinion was that a curser of God incurs the extreme penalty of death by stoning only when the curser uses one of the proper names of God, not when he uses one of God's attributive names.[5] But the most relevant point for our purposes is the word-model that Maimonides assumed:

> Every day the witnesses are examined by use of substitute names [for God]: "May Yose smite Yose!" Once the trial is done, everyone is sent outside and the eldest of the witnesses is asked, "Say explicitly what you heard"; and he says it. The judges stand on their feet and rend their clothes, which are never to be stitched. The second witness [then] says, "I too heard as he did." If there were many witnesses, each one of them must say, "That's what I heard."[6]

Maimonides presupposed the format, "Let Yose smite Yose"—the odd curse, where Yose is called upon to injure himself; and it would be even more odd if it were God Who were being called on to injure Himself. It could be argued that Maimonides, or the tradition behind him,[7] was trying to define this sin, with its drastic penalty, in such a way that the courts could rarely convict anyone of it. The motive, that is, may have been to ameliorate the apparent harshness of the code.

Now what about Job? Does *Job* curse God? No, not if we construe cursing God on this model. Job never says, "Let God [do something awful to] God"—with or without a proper name of God. But that is only one model, and it is surely the wrong model. There is another way in which I can "curse" someone—I can say very unflattering things about him: "You are a bastard, a son of a bitch, a _____"— and my language may descend into what the *Times* will not print, into "curse words." I curse a man in the first sense (Maimonides') when I call down upon him some injury; I curse a man in the second sense when I attribute to him shockingly unseemly qualities, motives, parentage, or whatever. In the first case, if I have influence with the effective powers, I get them to produce an injury on the man; in the second case, I claim that he already has shocking, degrading features. Job was not muddle-headed enough to curse God in the first sense; indeed, we can wonder whether anyone ever was. One thinks of St. Anselm in such a context; he said that to deny that God existed was to contradict yourself, and so only the fool would say in his heart that there is no God. So here, but more obviously: it would take a terrible fool to curse God in this first sense, and not just because human or divine punishment might be so awful; only a fool would ask God to call down upon Himself any injury. And since laws rarely prohibit what no one is tempted to do, one suspects that the Maimonidean interpretation is fundamentally misguided; the cursing of God awful enough to warrant stoning must have been of the second type. The second type of cursing, when it is cursing of God, is often called *blaspheming*; and the alternate translation of the Satan's prediction is, "He will blaspheme you to your face." This, I suggest, is what the Satan predicts: he says that if Job suffers he will blaspheme God, he will say shocking things about God, he will attribute to God things unseemly. This interpretation is supported by the prologue's defense of Job: "In all this Job did not sin or charge God with wrong" (1:22), or as more literal translations say, Job did not "impute, give, attribute, ascribe to God anything unseemly, tasteless, senseless, wrong." The issue is what Job will "give"—i.e., attribute—to God; will he attribute anything "tasteless," i.e., unseemly? If so, he curses God, in the relevant sense; he blasphemes.

These conclusions are not undermined by the fact that the text literally says, in the key passages, *bless* rather than *curse* (or *blaspheme*). The Hebrews seem to have been so horrified at the notion of cursing God that they found it difficult to even refer to it without a euphemism; so in the Old Testament we sometimes (but not always) find "bless God" where the meaning is pretty plainly "curse God." In the prologue of Job, we get the euphemism all four times; Job fears that his sons have blessed God in their hearts, the Satan twice predicts that Job will bless God to His face, and Job's wife counsels him to bless God and die. Modern scholars do not regard these euphemisms as needed in English,[8] and so in our translations we find *curse* (or sometimes *blaspheme*) instead of *bless*. The use of the euphemism does not affect the logic of the argument: one can "curse" in either of the ways indicated, whether the act is referred to directly or by means of a euphemism; there is a tendency to euphemism when the cursing is cursing of God; and the interpretive issue is: *Which kind* of cursing of God is predicted (euphemistically) in the Book of Job? I have argued against the former sort—the "Let Yose smite Yose" sort; it is too odd logically, and there is no hint in the book that Job is ever tempted to it. It seems more likely that the Satan predicts Job will "eulogize God"[9] —that is, will blaspheme.

Given that this is the temptation: does Job succumb? Does he yield, does he fail the test? To me, though not to many commentators, the answer seems clear: yes, he fails, blasphemes or curses God, just as the Satan predicts. Not that he fails in the prologue; there he blesses God literally—he praises God; there he does not sin with his lips or ascribe anything unseemly to God. But in the body of the work, in the great poetry, in the speeches of the dialogue—there he curses God repeatedly. That is why his friends are so regularly shocked; that is why they say, "your own lips testify against you" (15:6). That is why Job himself provides introductions to parts of his speeches, more blasphemous parts, as if they require preparation: "Therefore I will not restrain my mouth; I will speak in the anguish of my spirit; I will complain in the bitterness of my soul" (7:11). "I loathe my life. It is all one; therefore I say . . ." (9:21–22). "I loathe my life; I will give free utterance to my complaint; I will speak in the bitterness of my soul" (10:1). And that is why, at the end, Job must repent in dust and ashes. What he says in his repentance—"I have uttered what I did not understand" (42:3)—is not the whole truth; for one can utter *praise* of God without understanding it. Job repents because, in speaking beyond his understanding, he has blasphemed, he has cursed God.

Now the blasphemous character of a man's utterances is not, like the color of his beard, evident to the sound natural senses; we must think and judge, and perhaps feel, to determine blasphemy, and people are shaped by different traditions and interpret those traditions differently. Consequently we must expect less than unanimous agreement about *what is* blasphemy. Nevertheless, it seems fairly clear that Job speaks words that he and his auditors are right to regard as blasphemous.

The issue is what Job says *of God*, whether Job curses or blasphemes God. The fact that he curses the day of his birth is not the issue; nor is the fact that he curses his own life.[10] It is not cursing God to wish that you had never been conceived, or that you had died at birth, or that your days would soon end. These may be sins; to some Hebrews, apparently, they were. But sins differ as sins, and not all are blasphemy.

Now Job sometimes describes his miserable state in terms an atheist could recognize—that is, without reference to God:

I am not at ease, nor am I quiet;
    I have no rest; but trouble comes.

                                                                            (3:26)

My flesh is clothed with worms and dirt;
    my skin hardens, then breaks out afresh.
My days are swifter than a weaver's shuttle,
    and come to their end without hope.

                                                                            (7:5-6)

On my right hand the rabble rise,
    they drive me forth,
    they cast up against me their ways of destruction.

                                                                            (30:12)

The night racks my bones,
    and the pain that gnaws me takes no rest.

                                                                            (30:17)

My lyre is turned to mourning,
    and my pipe to the voice of those who weep.

                                                                            (30:31)

None of this, taken on its face, could be blasphemy, for God is not even mentioned in these accounts. But after the opening speeches, Job regularly speaks of his afflictions as the direct actions of God:

> For the arrows of the Almighty are in me;
>   my spirit drinks their poison;
>   the terrors of God are arrayed against me.
>
> (6:4)
>
> . . . [T]hou dost scare me with dreams
>   and terrify me with visions,
> so that I would choose strangling
>   and death rather than my bones.
>
> (7:14–15)
>
> God has cast me into the mire,
>   and I have become like dust and ashes.
>
> (30:19)

There is a shift here. The earlier complaints are like, "A tornado came upon me"; the latter are like, "God sent a tornado upon me." And the violence of some of Job's imagery is startling:

> He set me up as his target,
>   his archers surround me.
> He slashes open my kidneys, and does not spare;
>   he pours out my gall on the ground.
> He breaks me with breach upon breach;
>   he runs upon me like a warrior.
>
> (16:12–14)

Now Job is speaking of God, and not just of his own suffering; and God is portrayed as determined to hurt and destroy him. Nevertheless, I do not believe that this account, by itself, is blasphemous, in the Hebrew tradition. It is not blasphemy to say, simply, that you are suffering horribly and that God causes that suffering. Job portrays God as active, as an agent in the life of a human being; and in this case, as a destructive, terrifying agent. But the tradition itself portrays God this way in the lives of many individuals and nations; God often acts to terrify or to destroy.

Nevertheless, there is an assumption throughout Job's speeches that, if stated, could turn those portraits into blasphemy: and that is, of course, the assumption that Job is "blameless and upright, one who fears God and turns away from evil." In the tradition, God terrifies and destroys the wicked; but he protects the helpless, and he rewards the upright. But Job, believing he is innocent, says God tortures him; when Job's full belief is uttered, the portrait becomes blasphemous. The author of the Elihu speeches recognizes that this is the logic of the issue: "He [Elihu] was angry at Job because he justified himself rather than God . . . "(32:2). And the voice from the whirlwind sees the issue this way: "Will you condemn me that you may be justified?" (40:8) The presupposition in each of these remarks may strike us, at first, as misguided; after all, couldn't Job have justified himself *and* God? Is it really necessary to condemn God in order that Job may be justified? Why do these voices put the issue as an either/or? In other circumstances, of course, Job could have justified both himself and God. But in the circumstances of the drama, at least as Job sees them, (1) God is persecuting him and (2) he is innocent. The implication, however blasphemous, is inescapable: God persecutes an innocent. So God Himself is not "innocent." We really do have here an either/or.

And the implication is not left merely implicit. As Job's rage and despair increase, he loses the ability and the rationale for restraint: he blasphemes explicitly. He speaks of what God is doing in terms that are theologically offensive in the Hebrew tradition (and in most others):

> For he crushes me with a tempest,
>   and multiplies my wounds *without cause*
> [i.e., without justification]. . . .
>
>   (9:17)
>
> . . . [T]hou dost seek out my iniquity
>   and search for my sin,
> although thou knowest that I am not guilty. . . .
>
>   (10:6–7)

Let us acknowledge before proceeding that Job sometimes expresses views that are the opposite of blasphemous; in the book as we have it, Job often voices the "orthodox" view that his friends express. It may be that some, or even all, of these "traditional" expressions of confidence in God's justice have been put into Job's mouth through scribal emendations, or by manuscript conflations of Job's speeches with his friends', or by our own difficulties in determining when Job is quoting a view and when he is affirming it. It is widely acknowledged that the text has been modified over the centuries, is corrupt, and is in any case difficult to interpret. Or it may be that the Job of the drama was always torn between traditional faith and blasphemy. At any rate, the Job that we know would like to believe, wants to believe, what his friends affirm; maybe, with half his heart, he does believe. The Job we have now is a deeply divided soul. At times he does affirm, explicitly and implicitly, the very goodness of God that his blasphemies deny. Of course, the whole point of the drama is lost unless Job had expected something of God other than what seems to be the reality, unless he had expected God to be just. There is no point in Job's many complaints unless he had assumed from the start that a good God rules the world, and consequently that the apparent injustices call for explanation.

Moreover, at least one (though not all) of Job's calls for a trial, a hearing, presupposes that God is just. At least once (23:3–9) Job seems to assume that *if* he could get God to attend to his case he could get justice; he seems to speak as if the attention of Yahweh (like that of the Sumerian deities,[11] and like that of most human rulers) is hard to arouse, but that God would surely see his uprightness and deal with him accordingly, if his case were heard. Now half of that assumption—the half that says God is unaware of the case—may be itself blasphemous in a Hebrew context, and clearly Elihu denies that it is true (34:21), as Job himself does, in other contexts; but it is, if a blasphemy, at least a different blasphemy: it does not impugn God's good will.

Moreover, Job threatens his friends, whom he regards as biased and treacherous, with the punishment a just God has in store for such as are unfaithful:

> Will you speak falsely for God,
>   and speak deceitfully for him?
> Will you show partiality toward him,

will you plead the case for God?
Will it be well with you when he searches you out?
    Or can you deceive him, as one deceives a man?
He will surely rebuke you,
    if in secret you show partiality.

(13:7–10)

This is particularly striking, because of the logical paradox within it. It assumes that God is just, and hence that God will punish those who falsely assert that He is just! Job also says, apparently to his friends:

be afraid of the sword,
for wrath brings the punishment of the sword,
that you may know there is a judgment.

(19:29)

In the book as we have it, Job even praises God's justice at length, in virtually the whole of chapter 27; and the praise sung there is as moving as that in many of the friends' speeches. Job's oath there begins with a reference to God that, while denying His justice, could be taken as a paradoxical affirmation of it, too:

As God lives, who has taken away my right . . .
my lips will not speak falsehood . . .
    till I die I will not put away my integrity from me.

(27:2–5)

Job's final call for a trial expresses a willingness to suffer punishment for any evils that he has indeed committed; and in it he seems to say that God *will* punish wrongdoing:

Does not calamity befall the unrighteous,
    and disaster the workers of iniquity?
Does not he see my ways,
    and number all my steps?

(31:3–4)

And once, after saying his case is hopeless, Job expresses confidence that his audacity is permitted simply because God is just:

Behold, he will slay me; I have no hope;
  yet I will defend my ways to his face.
This will be my salvation,
  that a godless man shall not come before him.

(13:15–16)

The point of these last few pages is to acknowledge that Job often expresses confidence in God's justice—that Job's views, at least as we have them, are often indistinguishable from his friends'. This is not to be denied, however it is to be explained. But these passages of "orthodoxy" are not prominent, much less dominant, in Job's speeches; they are far less than "the other half of the story"; and they are not what motivate the drama or give it its lasting importance. At most—*if* they are genuine—they add further psychological realism to this picture of an obviously tormented soul. The drama really turns on Job's *denials* of these professions of traditional faith, and hence on his blasphemies.

Those blasphemies, as we have seen, include Job's charge that God is persecuting him though he is innocent and though God knows he is innocent. Job emphasizes his frailty, which makes God's persecution even more unseemly; Job is not superhuman:

Is my strength the strength of stones,
  or is my flesh bronze?

(6:12)

Am I the sea, or a sea monster,
  that thou settest a guard over me?

(7:12)

No, Job is little more than nothing, and the hostile attention he receives from God is unseemly:

Wilt thou frighten a driven leaf
  and pursue dry chaff?

(13:25)

Job is pathetic; he pleads for God to leave him alone:

Are not the days of my life few?
    Let me alone, that I may find a little comfort
before I go whence I shall not return,
    to the land of gloom and deep darkness. . . .

(10:20–21)

Job also emphasizes the fact that God is, after all, his Creator; it seems especially unworthy of God to persecute his own creature as He does:

Does it seem good to thee to oppress,
    to despite the work of thy hands . . . ?

(10:3)

Chapter 10 dwells at length on the irony:

Thy hands fashioned and made me;
    and now thou dost turn about and destroy me.
Remember that thou hast made me of clay;
    and wilt thou turn me to dust again?
Didst thou not pour me out like milk
    and curdle me like cheese?
Thou didst clothe me with skin and flesh,
    and knit me together with bones and sinews.
Thou has granted me life and steadfast love;
    and thy care has preserved my spirit.

(10:8–12)

Why then is God treating His own work in this way? The full text here is not clear, but Job seems to say:

Yet these things thou didst hide in thy heart;
    I know that this was thy purpose.

(10:13)

—and some scholars believe Job is suggesting that God's whole purpose in creating him must have been to have a creature to torment!

One interesting tension in Job's rhetoric may be worth mention-
ing here. His complaint sometimes is that God won't leave him alone;
at other times his complaint is that he can't get God's attention. Taken
woodenly, these two charges contradict one another; but I think it is
clear that the two kinds of language should not be pressed toward
literal specificity. Job is suffering horribly; and God is supreme. One
way to put this double point is that God (the source of affliction)
won't leave him alone; another way is that God (the protector of the
innocent) will not attend to his case. God has many traditional attributes, and different attributes underlie these different modes of
rhetoric. There is insight behind the later, paradoxical claims that Job
appeals to God to save him from God; and that, for Job, there are
two[12] "persons" in the Godhead; but some scholars dislike this kind
of talk, so I will not insist on it. I would insist, however, that religious
language be allowed a little flexibility and subtlety.

At any rate, Job does put his point in these rhetorically antitheti-
cal ways. Sometimes God is too intimately present:

> Surely now God has worn me out. . . .
> He has torn me in his wrath. . . .
>
>   (16:7, 9)

At other times, God seems totally absent:

> Behold, I cry out. "Violence!" but I am not answered;
>   I call aloud, but there is no justice.
>
>   (19:7)

At times, these two modes of speech are linked, with God's hand
oppressively present, and God's face or ear hidden:

> . . . withdraw thy hand far from me. . . .
> Why dost thou hide thy face,
>   and count me as thy enemy?
>
>   (13:21–24)
> I cry to thee and thou dost not answer me . . .
>   with the might of thy hand thou dost persecute me.
>
>   (30:20–21)

The silence of God, the unresponsiveness of God, God's failure to come to Job's aid when he calls for relief from his affliction, is formulated in varying ways: God will not listen:

> If I summoned him and he answered me,
>> I would not believe that he was listening to my voice.
>>>> (9:16)

God does not change:

> I have not departed from the commandment of his lips;
>> I have treasured in my bosom the words of his mouth.
> But he is unchangeable and who can turn him?
>> What he desires, that he does. . . .
> Therefore I am terrified at his presence. . . .
>>>> (23:12–15)

God makes the innocent guilty:

> Though I am innocent, my own mouth would condemn me;
>> though I am blameless, he would prove me perverse.
>>>> (9:20)

> If I wash myself with snow,
>> and cleanse my hands with lye,
> yet thou wilt plunge me into a pit,
>> and my own clothes will abhor me.
>>>> (9:30–31)

God just does not care about guilt or innocence:

> If I am wicked, woe to me!
>> If I am righteous, I cannot lift up my head. . . .
> And if I lift myself up, thou dost hurt me like a lion,
>> and again work wonders against me. . . .
>>>> (10:15–16)

All of these statements are blasphemous, are "cursings" of God.
So far I have focused on Job's own case and on what he says

about it. I have claimed that much of what he says about God's dealings with him is blasphemy—sometimes implicit, but often explicit. Job regularly attributes to God, in His dealings with him, things that are unseemly. But Job's blasphemies are wider than that, for he believes, and says, that God deals *generally* with the weak and upright as He deals with Job; he says that God fails to punish—and even rewards—the wicked; and he says that God thwarts *human* justice.

As God does not care whether Job is guilty or innocent, He does not care whether other men are:

> he destroys both the blameless and the wicked. . . .
>
> (9:22)

God's actions are indiscriminate:

> One dies in full prosperity. . . .
> Another dies in bitterness of soul. . . .
>
> (21:23–26)

Or worse, God actually favors the wicked:

> The earth is given into the hands of the wicked;
>   he covers the faces of its judges—
>   if it is not he, who then is it?
>
> (9:24)
>
> The tents of robbers are at peace,
>   and those who provoke God are secure. . . .
>
> (12:6)
>
> Have you not asked those who travel the roads . . .
> that the wicked man is spared in the day of calamity . . . ?
>
> (21:29–30)
>
> Does it seem good to thee to oppress,
>   to despise the work of thy hands
>   and favor [derive radiance from, beam on, derive pleasure from]
>   the designs of the wicked?
>
> (10:3)

As for the poor and weak—those whom God, or even an upright
man, is supposed to help—God neglects them in their hour of need:

> Men remove landmarks;
>   they seize flocks and pasture them.
> They drive away the ass of the fatherless;
>   they take the widow's ox for a pledge.
> They thrust the poor off the road. . . .
> They [the poor] lie all night naked, without clothing,
>   and have no covering in the cold. . . .
> From out of the city the dying groan,
>   and the soul of the wounded cries for help;
>   yet God pays no attention to their prayer
>   [God thinks nothing amiss].
>
> (24:2–12)

God does worse than ignore the sufferers:

> he mocks at the calamity of the innocent.
>
> (9:23)

And, as Job is but a driven leaf, dry chaff, so is man; the unseemliness of God's treatment of man is heightened when one thinks
of what a wretch man is anyway. Job parodies Psalm 8 (or 144):

> What is man, that thou dost make so much of him,
>   and that thou dost set thy mind upon him,
> dost visit him every morning,
>   and test him every moment?
>
> (7:17–18)

It would be best for man if God would forget him:

> Man that is born of a woman
>   is of few days, and full of trouble. . . .
> look away from him, and desist,
>   that he may enjoy, like a hireling, his day.
>
> (14:1, 6)

God, however, is relentless:

> But the mountain falls and crumbles away,
>   and the rock is removed from its place;
> the waters wear away the stones;
>   the torrents wash away the soil of the earth;
>   so thou destroyest the hope of man.
>
> (14:18–19)

I think that all of the above constitutes a strong case for the new interpretation of the book I am proposing here: that in the great speeches—as contrasted with the prologue—Job does blaspheme or "curse God," repeatedly and in manifold ways, just as the Satan predicted. This great work of literature is, in large measure, a work *about words*;[13] and Job's words are blasphemous. In later chapters I utilize this idea to throw light on most of the theological and psychological turmoil in the book. To the extent that the idea does illuminate the rest of the book, the case for this interpretation becomes even stronger.

Chapter 5

Bitterness

So Job does curse God after all. Does Job also curse God *in his heart*, as he had feared that his sons might have? To answer, we need to decide how we will construe the *heart act* (to coin a phrase, to parallel *speech act*) of "cursing God with one's heart." (Or *is* it an act? Is it, rather, a state?) There are two basic ways to approach this, I think, though each way admits of many variations. The easy way, "the safe and stupid way," to quote Socrates, is to say that cursing God in your heart is affirming in your heart, or mind, the words for cursing God with your lips. One can think blasphemous words or can utter them; and so one can blaspheme covertly or overtly. In this sense, of course Job curses God in his heart; for from his heart come the words that he utters. We can construe this, in turn, in a more casual, or in a deeper sense; in a casual sense, almost all one's words come from the heart—unless there are very special circumstances, like lying, or acting in a play, or talking in one's sleep, or making a slip of the tongue (and even in these last two circumstances, one often speaks what one thinks). In a deeper sense, only one's most earnest words come from the heart; only what is heart-felt; only what speaks from the depths. And Job's speeches are from the heart in this sense; indeed, that is why they are so moving. They are a deep cry of the soul, of the soul in distress.

However, this last interpretation of "cursing God in one's heart" pushes us, I think, toward an alternative understanding of the phrase, toward a different approach to the issue. I do not object to the "safe and stupid" approach; it is "stupid" only in the sense that one would be stupid to deny its obviously safe conclusions. And its conclusions may be more than safe; they may even represent what the author of Job intended, or what he might have replied had he been asked what it meant to curse God in one's heart. Cursing, after all, is paradigmatically a speech act; so cursing in one's heart may simply be affirming in one's heart the words one utters when cursing out loud.

But there is another interpretation we should try. When Jesus spoke of committing adultery in the heart, he did not speak of having words in the heart; he spoke of lusting (Matt. 5:27–28). In that famous New Testament passage, one commits adultery in one's heart when one has the passion, the emotion, the psychological state (the state of one's heart) that can quite naturally lead to adultery. Now of course adultery is not a speech act; one can commit adultery without speaking at all, and in any case what one says is not what constitutes adultery. So the parallel with cursing is not perfect. Nevertheless, Jesus' saying is suggestive, and it may have had—like most of his sayings—a long tradition behind it. My interpretation of this saying, generalized, is as follows: doing an act in one's heart is having (in one's heart, where these things are located, metaphorically) the psychological state that is the natural motive for doing that act. When I say "natural motive," what I mean is this: normally one who does the act is motivated by that state; and that state has a tendency to lead to the act, unless something intervenes and interferes. This is the relation between lust for your neighbor's wife and adultery with her. I do not address here the normative issue of whether the psychological state is as bad as the act; Jesus seems to have meant that it was, in some sense. All I am speaking to here is the natural connection between some states and the acts they motivate: certain states of the heart naturally motivate certain acts.

Now given this understanding, cursing God in one's heart would be having (in one's heart) the state that naturally leads to cursing God. But what is that state—that passion, or emotion, or mood? Now as we have noted, adultery is not essentially verbal, whereas cursing God is. So it may be that for a full account of cursing in one's heart we need an account of the words in one's heart. But what lies behind the words? Job says, with his lips, that God hates His own creatures; presumably Job *thinks* those words, too; but out of what state of the heart? In what state is he when he utters such words? What sort of man thinks things like this? Or what condition of heart leads him to?

The answer I propose here is not totally drawn—as most of the above is—from reading the Book of Job; it is drawn partly from there, especially from attention to what Job himself says of his heart. But partly I go beyond the text, for concepts and theories not implicit in the text, to argue that the text justifies their use in this case. I go beyond the text in the sense, somewhat, in which Ernest Jones did when he applied Freudian categories to *Hamlet*. Obviously Shakespeare had never heard of Freud or of any of the concepts Freud invented, and yet the Freudian concepts do apply, with some degree of success, to some of Shakespeare's characters. The main concept I will appeal to is, to some extent, my own "invention"; it is influenced directly by John Rawls's psychology of morals, and Rawls in turn is indebted to Wittgenstein and to the climate in philosophy created by the impact of Wittgenstein.

Our question was: What is it in Job's heart that leads him to curse God? The answer I propose is *bitterness*; or, more specifically, *moral bitterness*. Job speaks of his own state in terms (from the root *mr*) appropriately translated as "bitterness":

> . . . he will not let me get my breath,
>   but fills me with bitterness.
>
> (9:18)
>
> I loathe my life; . . .
>   I will speak in the bitterness of my soul.
>
> (10:1)
>
> As God lives, who has taken away my right,
>   and the Almighty, who has made my soul bitter . . .
> my lips will not speak falsehood. . . .
>
> (27:2–4)

The root meaning of the English word *bitter*, the *Oxford English Dictionary* (O.E.D.) conjectures, may be "biting, cutting, sharp"—and hence, as applied to taste, "obnoxious, irritating, or unfavourably stimulating . . . ; disagreeable"; and hence, in a transferred sense, as applied to "anything that has to be 'tasted' or endured: Attended by severe pain or suffering; sore to be borne; grievous, painful, full of affliction." Job is filled with bitterness; he undergoes "deep sorrow or anguish of heart" (O.E.D.), "sore to be borne." The problem with this account, so far, is its generality; for one can be bitter about many things without having Job's kind of bitterness. We remember that Job is not merely suffering; he is reflecting on his suffering, and on that of others. "Upright men are *appalled* at this" (17:8), he says: "*When I think of it* I am dismayed, and shuddering seizes my flesh" (21:6). And, as I argued above, he is reflecting in the light of moral principles, principles of how the world ought to be, as judged from the moral point of view. He not only suffers; he judges his suffering unjust. He judges his own condition, and that of other men, to be unjust; what is bitter to Job is not *simply* losing his health, but the injustice of its loss. What is bitter to him about others' prosperity or unhappiness is the injustice of it all. Job suffers from *moral bitterness*.

There are sharp, biting, cutting sensations that we can feel without reflection; tastes can bite, and physical injuries can produce bitter pain. In addition, there are states of affairs that, *when reflected upon*, produce bitter anguish—because of the ways in which we interpret them. This is one of the half-truths in Stoicism: the doctrine that it is our "judgments" of things, and not things themselves, that are good or evil. For example, a cattleman loses in his attempt to save his herd from disease; and he reflects, bitterly, that the loss will lead to the end of his career as a rancher. This bitterness is dependent upon the handle by which he tries to grasp it; but still, in this case, the handle is not yet a moral handle, and so we do not yet have the bitterness of Job. Job's bitterness is moral; it cannot be explicated without appealing to moral concepts and moral principles. Job believes the wicked should not prosper; he believes the upright should be rewarded; he believes the weak should be protected. These are moral principles (perhaps wrongly applied). His anguish is moral, dependent upon moral judgments he makes; Job is *morally bitter*.

Many of us have heard of the psychological "experiment" in which lumberjacks were promised a certain pay for a certain amount of work and then not paid as promised; the experimenters wondered how they would respond. The lumberjacks tore the camp to pieces.[1] The psychologists—who labored, probably, under the illusion that appeals to moral concepts are not "value-free"—labeled this experiment a study in *frustration*. And of course the lumberjacks were frustrated. But it was not merely frustration that the lumberjacks could not tolerate; they could not—or perhaps would not—tolerate the *injustice* of the thing. If you want to be value-free here, say they would not tolerate what they believed was unjust; but do not neglect their moral judgment about the way their experimenters treated them. People will tolerate a lot more of what they think they deserve than of what they think they don't deserve. People care what's right and wrong, at least in this sense.

Animals experience physical pains like those we call bitter, and they seem to experience some psychic anguish, too, as when they lose a mate or a master. It is not so clear how many judgments they make about these matters; clearly they are incapable of sophisticated judgments. A dog can mourn his dead master, but cannot know—and hence regret—that the master's death means the farm will be sold. Nor can a dog know that his master has suffered a wrongful death, or that creditors are seizing the farm through dishonest and immoral means. A dog may protect his master, and may discriminate between intimates and strangers; but a dog cannot distinguish between one—for example, the sheriff—with a right to take his master and one—such as a kidnapper—who has no such right. So, though some argue that dogs are capable of primitive guilt, it seems clear that they do not suffer much moral anguish. Moral bitterness, like other moral emotions, presupposes intellectual and moral development at least comparable to that of human beings.

People vary in their conceptions of justice—indeed, my reader may have a conception of justice so different from Job's that he wonders why I speak throughout of "justice" rather than of "Job's conception of justice." I speak this way for economy of language only; everything could be rephrased in the more cumbersome way without loss of any essential point. Job's conception is that the weak should be protected, the upright should be rewarded, and the wicked should be punished; and this is, to be sure, only one conception of justice, not *the* concept of justice. I find that many academics, at least qua academics, lack this conception of justice. They believe that the scholarly (or the good teacher, or whatever) should be rewarded, and that the unscholarly (or the poor teacher, or whatever) should be punished (or at least not rewarded). They wonder not, "Why do the wicked prosper?" but "Why do the incompetent—or maybe the tacky—why do *they* prosper?" And artists wonder why the mediocre, or trashy, prosper, while the brilliant and original suffer. I may do academics and artists some injustice of my own, for they may share Job's conception in parts of their lives that are not so narrowly professional. But the general point stands: people vary in their conceptions of justice.

People also vary in their *concern* for justice. Mature people— excluding only psychopaths, perhaps, and some mental defectives— have some concern for justice, especially as it touches themselves and those they care about. Indeed, as John Rawls argues,[2] there is something puzzling about claiming that you love someone but do not mind if that person is treated unjustly. There are paradigmatic expressions of love, and one of them—in humans—is resentment of wrongs done to the loved one. A love without that feature would be a subhuman love, a love such as animals are capable of, but not quite what a normal human knows. And most of us love ourselves enough to resent injustices to our own persons and powers. But even though almost all of us care about justice, we differ in the extent to which we care. Some people rather expect the world to be somewhat unjust and do not particularly mind; others become enraged or indignant whenever they sense an injustice. Some of us will let ourselves be cheated in a restaurant rather than raise a fuss; others will start a fight before we will pay a penny more than is due. Some are "pragmatists," some "make it a matter of principle." A recognition of this kind of fact was crucial to Stoicism, which recommended a way of life closer to the pragmatic. A revolution is typically led by the second sort of person— by the man who insists on justice, by the type of Camus' Rebel.[3] Michael Kohlhaas, in Kleist's story, was of this second type, though he had a long fuse, and though he wound up doing injustice himself.

Nothing could be clearer than that the Job of the poetry was this second sort of man; he was a man obsessed with justice. When such people suffer great injustice—or, perhaps, see great injustice about them—they cannot tolerate it for long. (Necessarily, I am speaking of injustice by their lights, as they understand it.) And when, in addition, the injustice cannot be effectively attacked and removed; when it is intractible, without remedy, against which no appeal is possible—they regularly are thrown into deepest bitterness, *moral bitterness*. If the injustice is widespread enough, they sense that the whole sorry scheme of things is a cheat, and they become bitter not just about some portion of life, but about life in general. The animals cannot experience this, for they have no sense of justice, or none worth notice; some people cannot, for though they sense that the world is a cheat, they do not deeply care; the Job types are thrown into bitterness toward life itself.

However: as lust for a neighbor's spouse does not necessarily lead to adultery, so moral bitterness, even about life in general, does not necessarily express itself in cursing God, or blasphemy; indeed, for blasphemy to be a serious temptation, a specific kind of theological orientation is required. A morally bitter man will be tempted to curse God only if (1) he believes in God, and (2) he believes that this sorry scheme of things is, in a strong sense, God's doing. First, I think it obvious that an atheist, however bitter, will not curse God—unless saying that there is no God is another form of blasphemy. There seems little reason to defame, or say unflattering things about, or attribute things unseemly to a God you do not believe in. There is no sense in a modern farmer's cursing Demeter, nor in an atheist's cursing God—however bitter either man may be. (I rely here upon common sense. I set aside the very sophisticated question, going beyond common sense, of whether an atheist can reasonably be bitter about *life,* or the *world,* and so curse *it.* Is the world or life enough of a unity, without God, to make it reasonable to have *any* attitude toward it? And is it reasonable to expect justice in a world without God, and so to be bitter when we fail to find it? One might argue that theism is, in some subtle way, a presupposition of general bitterness in the first place, and that a self-proclaimed atheist who is bitter is an atheist with only half his heart. I confess that bitter atheists often strike me as incomplete atheists. But the issues are too complex for development here—and in a sense they are irrelevant. My substantive point is that a morally bitter atheist has no rationale for cursing *God*; this remains true even if the point is vacuous, even if, in the last analysis, there can be no morally bitter atheist.)

Second, a morally bitter theist will perhaps not curse God, either, for he may hold to a sharp separation between God, whom he trusts, and the world, which causes bitterness. So he may curse the world and still praise God. Epicurus had a jaundiced (though not morally bitter) view of the world and yet urged his followers to emulate the gods; his gods were not in control of the world and did not care about it. A Manichean may hate the world and its Satanic ruler while still loving God, Who is battling the forces of darkness. A pantheist, however, does not have this option; it makes no sense to hate the world and love God Who *is* the world; or to hate *natura naturata* while loving *natura naturans*. A theist of the Hebrew or Christian sort is in a less clear-cut position, a position more susceptible to alternative interpretations. To the extent that he emphasizes his belief that there is only one God, and that God rules the world, to that extent it becomes difficult to love God and hate the world; to that extent, then, moral bitterness over the world becomes bitterness toward God; it becomes a cursing of God, at least in one's heart. But traditional Hebrew faith was two-sided, not simple; God creates and rules, but there are powers (human, at least) that oppose the Creator and Ruler. God created the world and found it good, but there is now much evil in it. So in this biblical faith there is soil in which can grow a sense of a fallen world, and of the transcendence of God, and even of dualistic Manicheism. Orthodoxy has always condemned Manicheism; duality of cosmic powers is too far from the norm to be tolerated. There is only one God, and God and the world are related; but biblical thinkers disagree about the intimacy of the relation, or about the degree of God's transcendence. So I think we should say that, for a Hebrew, moral bitterness has a *tendency* toward blasphemy; but the force of the tendency varies with the degree to which God and the world are intimate. The closer the intimacy, the nearer the blasphemy.

This brings us back to Job. In his bitterness Job maintains his belief in God;[4] he never even considers atheism. But he does curse God; and the predisposing factor, the presupposition which makes blasphemy such a powerful temptation, is that Job sees God as omnipotent over the world and as intimately implicated in all the world's ills. We have already seen this: for we saw that Job complains not just of the evils of life but of the evils that men suffer *at God's hand*. Job regularly describes the ills of life as God's work. A philosopher might say that Job feels and sees the evils and then *infers* that God is responsible; and a modern courtroom lawyer might ask Job to limit his testimony to what he witnesses, and to avoid making inferences that go beyond what he actually experiences. But Job is not this kind of witness; he tells his stories of woe almost as if he *saw* God's agency in

the woes. To the modern mind, this is one of the most striking features of Job's speeches: Job never doubts that his sufferings, and the
sufferings of others who are innocent or upright, are the direct results
of God's actions—indeed, *are* God's actions. Job may be, in this
sense, the most God-intoxicated[5] individual in the Bible; commentator after commentator has remarked on this feature of his thought:

> Job does not doubt for an instant that God is directly responsi-
> ble for his plight.[6]

> The disasters which follow are nevertheless attributed by Job
> as well as by the friends to God Himself. There was no ultimate
> dualism in the Hebrew mind. There was no knowledge of "sec-
> ondary causes" . . . no nice distinctions between "absolute will"
> and "contingent will." There was no theory of chance either. . . .
> The universe, in "the strange world of the Bible," belonged to
> God, and it belonged to him from top to bottom.[7]

> [W]e would have to seek quite vainly in that antique poem [of
> Job] for a trace of the grand Grecian idea, which was born in Ionia
> and destined to become in modern times the basis of all philoso-
> phy: we mean the idea of the laws of nature. In the former the
> miracle is everything; everything breathes that facile admiration
> (the joyous gift of infancy) which peoples the world with marvels
> and enchantments. . . . Even in our own day the Muslim pos-
> sesses no clearer ideas of the laws of nature than did the author
> of the book of Job; and the principal motive of reprobation the
> sincere believers in Islam raise against European science is that
> the latter ignores the power of God, by reducing the government
> of the universe to a play of forces that are susceptible of being
> calculated.[8]

> *The Lord took.* Did Job say anything except the truth, did he use
> an indirect expression to indicate what was direct? The word
> ["The Lord took"] is short . . . ; it naturally occurs to us to repeat
> it after him, since the expression has become a sacred proverb;
> but do we just as naturally link it to Job's thought? For was it not
> the Sabeans who fell upon his peaceful herds and killed his ser-
> vants? . . . Was it not the lightning that destroyed the sheep and

their shepherds? . . . Was it not a windstorm from out of the desert that overturned the house and buried his children in the ruins? . . . Yet Job said, "The Lord took."[9]

These nineteenth- and twentieth-century accounts of Job are quite accurate; Job almost speaks as if there were no agency other than God's. Over and over he describes the ills of the world as God's direct acts. If we wanted to be completely accurate, we would note that there are a few exceptions to this. He does describe the actions of the wicked, and his faithless friends, and his family and servants and neighbors, as if they were genuine actions; he complains about what these *people* do. So apparently some people, and not God alone, can act. But even human actions are seen as dependent upon God's:

> He has put my brethren far from me,
>   and my acquaintances are wholly estranged from me.
>
>   (19:13)
>
> God gives me up to the ungodly,
>   and casts me into the hands of the wicked.
>
>   (16:11)
>
> The earth is given into the hand of the wicked;
>   he covers the faces of its judges—
>   if it is not he, who then is it?
>
>   (9:24)

Or, if the actions of men are not dependent upon what God does, they are dependent upon what God fails to do:

> Men remove landmarks;
>   they seize flocks and pasture them. . . .
> From out of the city the dying groan,
>   and the soul of the wounded cries for help;
>   yet God pays no attention to their prayer.
>
>   (24:2, 12)

The last passage, like many similar ones, suggests that God neglects many things a good God would not; and, if that be true, then in a sense some people do have derivative autonomy from God. God leaves them alone to work out disasters. And in another group of passages Job urges God to leave him (and man generally) alone; the presupposition there seems to be that God might give man a little more autonomy, and let him secure some wretched comfort without God's active persecution. So it is a slight exaggeration to say that Job conceives of all agency as God's.

Nevertheless, he does conceive of most agency as God's; and what is not God's *could have* been God's—for whatever we creatures do or achieve, we do or achieve only by God's influence, or permission, or neglect.

It is in the context of this kind of implicit theology—a theology in which nothing happens against God's will—that Job can ask his friends, "As for me, is my complaint against man?" (21:4) It is in this context that he can say:

> Who among all these does not know
>   that the hand of the Lord has done this?
> In his hand is the life of every living thing
>   and the breath of all mankind.
>
> (12:9–10)

And this passage, which follows an account of the prosperity of the wicked, leads naturally into a statement of the presupposition of the whole theology—namely, that God is omnipotent:

> If he tears down, none can rebuild;
>   if he shuts a man in, none can open.
> If he withholds the waters, they dry up;
>   if he sends them out, they overwhelm the land.
> With him are strength and wisdom;
>   the deceived and the deceiver are his.
>
> (12:14–16)

At the end of the book, just after God's speeches from the whirl-wind, Job repents; and his first words there are, "I know that thou canst do all things, and that no purpose of thine can be thwarted" (42:2). Later we must consider the point of the whole repentance speech. But one thing should be clear already: it was not from God's speeches that Job learned that God was omnipotent. God's omnipotence is the presupposition of Job's complaints throughout. It is only because Job understands God to be omnipotent that he can complain so mightily against God's management of the world; it is only because God can do "all things" that it makes sense to ask why God is allowing or perpetrating so much injustice. Consider: A freshman senator can be very little responsible for the miseries of his nation; the chief executive can be greatly responsible. But there are calamities that not even the president can prevent. God, however, has no limitation; He can do what He wills—or so Job believes. This is what makes the drama of the book possible; it is not a secret revealed at the end, or a new principle that solves the puzzle. It is what underlies the puzzle. Almost all of Job's speeches presuppose this view of God's omnipotence, and in several speeches Job explicitly articulates the view.

Though we are interested primarily in Job here, and the logic of his blasphemy, it may be worth pointing out that the friends, and Elihu, and the author of the prologue all share Job's conception of God's omnipotence. One should not be misled by the appearance in the prologue of a Satan figure; this Satan proposes, but God disposes. The author speaks of *the* Satan—like "the accuser," or "the spy"; this figure holds some sort of office in the divine court, probably modeled on an office in the courts of human rulers. *Satan*, in this book, is not yet a proper name, which is one reason scholars do not favor a very late date for the work. We are far, far from a Zoroastrian combat of cosmic forces. All of the friend's speeches, and Elihu's as well, presuppose that God has the power to do as He pleases. They could hardly argue as they do without presupposing God's omnipotence; for unless God were omnipotent, there might very well be wickedness He was unable to punish, goodness or innocence He was unable to protect. They agree with Job that all of Job's ills, and the other ills that he complains of, come from God; they only disagree about whether God has a rationale for the ills—and Elihu disagrees with the friends, perhaps, about what the rationale is.

Let us return now to our analysis of Job's temptation to blasphemy. *Moral bitterness* is what dominates Job's heart. For that kind of bitterness to erupt in blasphemy, two presuppositions are required: Job must believe in God, and he must believe God to be intimately implicated in the world that arouses the bitterness. But Job never even considers atheism; and he has one of the most thorough-going conceptions on record of God's agency in the world—he believes that God *could* do whatever few things He does not directly do. The trap is set. One thinks of the remark of the man born blind in the Gospel of John: it would have been a miracle if Job had not cursed God.

Widespread injustice—unjust suffering and prosperity—tempts the Job type of man, the man passionate for justice, to world-bitterness, and given the appropriate theology, it tempts him to curse God. Job was so tempted and he yielded to the temptation. The brilliance of the portrait of this man is much of what makes the book great. However, one should not overlook the portraits of the friends. Elihu's case is more complicated; but the friends *are* Job's friends, or at least his spiritual brothers. Their conviction of the world's justice is analogous to Job's passion for justice; for them, indeed, the injustice of the world is literally unthinkable. Their praise of God for His protection of the innocent, His punishment of the wicked, and His reward of the upright—their praise is the obverse of Job's curse; and the author makes them express their dedication with speeches whose beauty often rivals that of many of the psalms. And, of course, they share Job's conviction of God's omnipotence. It has become a cliché that Job "wins" the "debate" with them, that the friends are mistaken, and that the author was on Job's side. Without denying the fundamental truth in this view, I want to suggest again that only one who wanted to believe what the friends do believe could have uttered Job's curses. The friends share Job's conception of justice and his conviction of God's omnipotence. They avoid Job's bitterness and blasphemy by dishonesty, by failing to see the world for what it is; their "orthodox theology" distorts, or expresses a distortion of, their sense of reality. Perhaps behind that dishonesty lie other failures and other differences from Job. But much of their theology, and many of their psychic yearnings, are his.

Chapter 6

A Yes to Bitterness and Blasphemy

Given that the book is about bitterness and blasphemy, we are in a position to conjecture how it came to be written, and to understand why it needed to be written. Suppose the prose tale, or the legend behind it, is older than the poetry, as most scholars believe; it tells of a Job who does not blaspheme, of an upright Job who praises God and is thankful, in spite of calamities that would shatter other men's fidelity even in the telling of them. The world is not perfectly just; and there are individuals who suffer horribly without, as far as we humans can see, any moral cause; Job became famous as one such victim of the world's inhumanity. But there are many victims of what can seem the divine cruelty, and if the prologue is faithful to the legend, Job was famous not merely for the disasters that befell him. Job became emblematic of the upright sufferer, victim, calamity-stricken man *who praises God in his suffering*; for in this strange world there are even such types as this. The greatness of Job's acceptance, of his patience, of what Nietzsche might have called Job's kind of yes-saying, is what made the traditional Job famous. He became representative of a virtually superhuman dignity and self-overcoming, a type of man who praises this world and its Lord while torn on the rack of the world's injustice.

Now let us suppose—in our imaginative reconstruction—that a

great poet, a man of learning and sophistication, a man of honest realism and great psychological subtlety, begins to meditate on that story, somewhat as the Greek dramatists meditated on stories in their tradition, or as Shakespeare meditated on chronicles that he read. Like many in the Near East, and like the greatest Hebrew prophets, he has a passion for justice, or at least knows intimately other people who do. He meditates on the story of the Job figure, the man who is "tried" by suffering, and who is, in the end, faithful to God. The poet begins to imagine what such a soul would undergo, not just in his suffering, but in his heart, and he introduces a profoundly new element. He places in the heart of Job a passion which the tradition fails to mention—that very passion for justice of which we spoke—and an understanding of God as obligated to help the weak and the upright and to bring down the wicked. He thereby introduces into Job's psyche a moral and theological crisis that was not present in the traditional story.

Job remains at the center of the poet's creation, and it is he who suffers and undergoes the crisis; but the moral and theological presuppositions of the crisis were not peculiar to Job—they were the community's. So the poet articulates them not only through Job but also through the friends, who speak as the voice of the community. "No doubt you are the people,"[1] as Job says. I say "the" community, knowing that there are problems implicit here; was the community the Hebrew community, or some other? Or was it international, the wider community of many Middle Eastern peoples who shared presuppositions which give rise to Job's moral and theological anguish? These questions are not answerable fully by modern scholarship, but I think that two reasonable conclusions can be stated briefly. This Hebrew book belongs in the Hebrew Bible; it clearly deals with problems an ancient Hebrew needed to face—problems relevant to much of the Torah, the Prophets, and the Sacred Writings—problems other Hebrew scriptures address and should address. But its relevance is also international, as its widely educated author must have known. It presents a spiritually compelling portrait of a justice-obsessed man— inheritor of a tradition that believes in God's justice and power— floundering in the real, unjust world. Or, in religious terms, not just floundering: sinning, blaspheming, cursing God with his heart and his lips.

Let me make this hypothetical account of the origin of the book somewhat more detailed. Probably a majority of scholars now think that the prose story antedates the central dialogue, as I assume here. What I conjecture is actually a four-stage history of our present book: I imagine that there was first a folktale, or many versions of a folktale, about an upright sufferer who was heroic in his acceptance, his patience. There was (and is still today) an archetypical image of the patient Job, spoken of and admired in many cultures. I imagine, second, that our poet found (or even partly created) the particular version of this archetypical tale that we find in the prologue and epilogue today. I imagine, third, that our poet then wrote the great dialogues and something like the speeches from the whirlwind. And then, as everyone agrees, there were added later many minor modifications, perhaps including the Elihu speeches, composed by other persons.

The point I want to argue here is that, if the prose or the folktale really does antedate the poetry, then someone *should have* written a book in response to that tale. The folktale Job is heroic; he was admired widely, and even today some of our finest spirits admire him so much that they find it hard to see what is really in this Book of Job, whose poetry presents such sharp contrasts with the folktale. But the folk portrait, like most simplicities, is intellectually inadequate. The folktale Job is heroic in his acceptance or patience and admirable in that respect. But though he has a strong back, and can bear much, he has an undeveloped mind—I'm almost tempted to say, a weak mind. He bears, but he doesn't think; he doesn't ask questions, not even questions about righteousness and suffering, which are (besides patience) two of the three features that distinguish him.

Yet questions clamor to be asked. How can a case like Job's occur in a just universe ruled by a just God? How does a thing like this happen? The folktale Job has the "practical virtue" of patience; but unless he asks questions like this, he has very little intellectual curiosity. These are not questions that you have to be a modern man, or an intellectual, or a philosopher or theologian to invent; these questions are demanded by the folktale itself. The story would not have been told, there would have been no folktale, if Job's case had not violated the expectations of the teller and hearer. The teller and hearer are quite aware that Job's case should not occur; that is what makes such a story worth telling. It is essentially a story of a prodigy: an upright man suffering catastrophe. And, even more marvelous, this man praises God in catastrophe. The story has built into it two tensions that make it worth remembering (and an ideal of patience perhaps worth honoring). But the Job of the folktale never reflects on the tensions of his own story.

If we accept my hypothesis of a four-stage sequence, then by the time our poet was on the scene someone may have begun to reflect on one of the tensions, the suffering of the upright; for the prologue may present an explanation of this tension. It says that the suffering was proposed by the Satan as a test. I argued previously that the poet of the theophany rejected that, as explanation. But aside from the weakness—or blasphemy!—of the explanation, there remains a dramatic weakness: the prose author has not let Job be nearly as reflective as he, the author, himself is. The prose author seems to answer the question, but his Job is still too unreflective to even ask it. The author does not let Job share in his own degree of thoughtfulness. The scandal is not that his Job does not know about the scene in the royal court, where the Satanic challenge occurs; for authors often know things their characters do not know. The scandal is that this character—the prologue Job—does not even wonder. As a consequence, his portrait is psychologically flat; along with his failure to question goes some failure to feel. He seems not to have been tempted at all; only his wife, the Eve-figure, thinks of cursing God and dying—and it is not clear whether even she sees the moral/theological difficulty in the case. Some kind of Book of Job needed to be written. So our poet wrote the great central dialogues. He made Job into a human being. Now Job has a mind; now he feels, anguishes, and is tempted; now he is spiritually complex and convincing as a character.

The Job of the dialogues is not only psychologically convincing; he is also, at least for many modern readers, admirable. The Job of the tradition was respected for his patience; some of the finest minds of the era since romanticism have honored the poetic Job for his impatience, his bitterness, and his blasphemy. Job has been seen as a kind of Prometheus, who defies a tyrant god in order to benefit mankind; and though the comparison is faulty, its acceptance shows a deep

modern admiration for the "rebellious" Job of the dialogue. A friend
of mine who teaches Job in college courses tells me that her students
love the dialogue but hate the ending, and one reason is the modern
bias in favor of defiance. We moderns hate tyranny; and if God is a
tyrant, an unjust tyrant, we admire the man who has at least the
courage to say so. Some of us believe, with Camus, that the world is
absurd; and, with Camus, we respect the man who can face the moral
absurdity of things honestly, and not be taken in. And even if we do
not actually endorse Job's bitterness, we at least encourage self-
expression, encourage people to talk out their feelings; we fear that
what is not said stays inside to disrupt the psychic life. We hate
psychological repression; so we may actively welcome Joban blasphemy and not just tolerate it.

And the modern reader may have trouble seeing anything wrong
with blasphemy anyway—or, like Oscar Wilde, he may find that
blasphemous is not "a word of his."[2] The modern reader may not
believe in God; and even if he is a believer, he will be influenced by
ideals of freedom of speech and religion, and so he will be tempted to
see nothing wrong with saying anything that one truly believes. We
modern democrats and liberals believe the state should leave us free
to say whatever we think, especially in matters of religion; so we see
no crime in anything Job says. If a modern Job were *arrested* for his
speeches, Amnesty International would take up his case and defend
him. Now many people are tempted to think of religious issues in
political terms; the temptation may have been stronger when there
were many earthly kings as well as a heavenly King, but it is not dead
yet. So many moderns, who see no crime in blasphemy, may see no
sin, either; even if they believe in God as a King, they will tend to
think that He cares only about behavior, not about language. Only
Job's words are bad, and talk is only talk.

The book itself does not take this casual a view of blasphemy.
Blasphemy is probably regarded as sinful by Job himself—his pref-
aces (noted previously) to some of his worst accusations already suggest that he does—and clearly it is so regarded by his wife, the
friends, Elihu, the Satan, and even God—God in the prologue, and
God in the theophany. Job has to repent at the end, and it is his *words*,
and the state of heart behind them, that he repents.

If blasphemy, then, is sinful in this book, why is it sinful? What is it that is so wrong with cursing God? Before the theophany, we see hints of answers along two related lines, but the hints are quite obscure.

One suggestion which might be relevant is that we humans cannot help or injure God. If this be true, then our cursing God cannot really injure Him; and it would probably follow either that whatever is wrong with blasphemy is intrinsically wrong—cursing God is just inappropriate, unfitting in itself—or else that the harm blasphemy does is harm to humans, that we harm ourselves when we curse God. So we may have here the beginning of an answer to our question: we should look to human life, or to the blasphemy itself, to see what is wrong with it. This conclusion might be seen as harmonious with the slighting of ritual and cultic matters in the book and the stressing of moral concerns.

The human characters in the drama do seem to say that we cannot help or hurt God. Of course the strong assertions of God's omnipotence throughout the book—which we have already discussed—might be taken to imply this; but in addition the characters seem to raise this issue explicitly. After stressing his own insignificance, Job asks, "If I sin, what do I do to thee, thou watcher of man?" (7:20) Maybe the import is debatable, but Job seems to suggest that he cannot harm God. Eliphaz asks later:

> Can a man be profitable to God?
>   Surely he who is wise is profitable to himself.
> Is it any pleasure to the almighty if you are righteous,
>   or is it gain to him if you make your ways blameless?
>
> (22:2–3)

Eliphaz seems to say here that a man cannot help God. Elihu appears to make both points, and even more clearly:

> Look at the heavens, and see;
>   and behold the clouds, which are higher than you.
> If you have sinned, what do you accomplish against him?
>   And if your transgressions are multiplied, what do you do to him? . . .

> Your wickedness concerns a man like yourself,
> and your righteousness a son of man.
>
> (35:5–6, 8)

Now the scholars disagree about the implications of some of these passages; but Elihu, Job, and Eliphaz seem to believe in a God we cannot help or harm; and they and the other two friends all stress the power of God and the insignificance of man. My conclusion is that this is one of the major themes of the Book of Job, before the theophany. An implication is that sin is sin not because it harms God but for some other reason. A strong suggestion in some of these passages is, so to speak, humanistic: what is sinful about sin, and hence about blasphemy, is that it harms man—in some way to be specified. But this is terribly vague. It does not carry us very far.

Another difficulty is that we are relying upon hints in the speeches of the human characters, and later God rebukes the friends for speaking falsely (42:7) and rebukes Job—and implicitly all of them—for "darkening counsel by words without knowledge" (38:2; 42:3). God clearly rejects much of what they had said; perhaps He rejects this notion, too, the notion that men cannot help or harm Him. Perhaps the "High God" of the dialogues is too high; or perhaps the dialogues are caught in a misunderstanding of what divine "height" really is. Though theologians for centuries have affirmed the doctrine of God's transcendence in the sense in question, it might in fact be mistaken, and some modern theologians believe that it is, or that it is basically unbiblical; and some Christians believe it is inconsistent with the trinitarian conception of a suffering Christ. Terrien even says (of 7:20) that Job's "wish" "for a Deity who would be impassive and insensitive to human conduct . . . constitutes his real blasphemy":

> Should not the God of the universe be far beyond any reach of man's capacity to hurt him? The hero portrays himself as if he were a theologian intent upon the seemingly noble task of purging his conception of the Deity from any stain of anthropopathy. But such a god is an idol, the product of the mind of man.[3]

Terrien is wrong to single out the assertion of God's impassivity as Job's one "real blasphemy."[4] I believe I have shown in chapter 4 that

blasphemy is at the heart of this book, and that Job blasphemes repeatedly and in multifarious ways, not (just) in this way. But Terrien
and his allies may be right in their claim that the impassive God is an
idol; God's stormy rebuke of Job and his friends could be interpreted
as implying that. We must raise that question again later, when we
examine the theophany in detail. For now, we must note that it is
risky, at best, to rely upon the theology in the dialogues—for at least
some of it is rejected by the theophany. So all we have found so far is
a terribly vague suggestion that we are not yet sure we can rely upon
anyway.

There is another set of passages which might help us, which also
suggest vaguely what may be wrong with blasphemy. At several
points, some character or another hints that cursing God is connected
with other sin, so that the blasphemer must also be a sinner of a more
ordinary type or that he must be somehow in league with such sinners. There are two conversations in the prologue in which blasphemy is predicted. God says that his servant Job is "blameless and
upright, one who fears God and turns away from evil." I have argued
for interpreting this as praise of the high morality of Job's conduct
and character. Apparently the Satan grants this point but predicts
that in adversity Job would curse God to His face. Now what is the
logic here? Is it that in adversity Job would still "fear God" (i.e., be
deeply moral) but would (nevertheless) curse Him to His face? Or is it
that in adversity Job would curse God instead of "fearing" Him? I
think the second interpretation is more plausible. The Satan seems to
be saying, "Yes, Job fears God now; but once he suffers, he won't;
then he'll curse God instead." The Satan seems to pose an oscillation
between extremes: at one extreme, Job fears God so thoroughly that
his case merits divine notice; but after he suffers he may swing to an
opposite extreme, no longer fearing God, but actually cursing Him.

If this is meant, then the Satan sees a connection between cursing
God and other sin; it may be implied that cursing God is an extreme
form of sin, a form one might reach after passing through other sins,
or a sin bringing with it many other sins. This interpretation would
square with the special horror the Hebrews felt for blasphemy, and
with the terrible penalty—death by stoning, as several texts specify
(though, interestingly, nothing in the Book of Job mentions a penalty).[5] Now we, the readers, do not see this Satanic connection man-

ifested in the book itself; in it, Job curses God but continues to be (otherwise) blameless. And we are never told the basis of this supposed connection, the reason blasphemy is supposed to be connected with other sins. Nevertheless, there may be in the prologue an assumption that there is a connection.

Eliphaz, too, may think that there is some kind of connection. He asks whether a man should "argue in unprofitable talk, or in words with which he can do no good" (15:3). His next remark (15:4), difficult to translate, probably means that Job's talk is actually harmful: "But you are doing away with [undermining, subverting] the fear of God [religion, the sense of reverence—"fear" is the literal translation], and hindering [diminishing, depreciating] meditation before God [communication with God, devotion toward God]." Does Eliphaz simply mean that Job is not being very reverent in his charges against God? (That is certainly true.) Or does he mean that Job's irreverence undermines practical, moral religion, in some way unspecified? Perhaps he does. He continues (15:5): "For your iniquity teaches your mouth, and you choose the tongue of the crafty." The last words are those used for the snake in Genesis 3:1; so maybe we have here the suggestion that Job's words will lead to other sin. But these suggestions, like the Satan's, are terribly vague and brief.

We cannot do much better with the words of Elihu, the other character who seems to see a connection between blasphemy and other sin, and who speaks of it at least once and maybe twice. The second passage is quite unclear, but the Gordis reading is as follows:

34:36a Would that Job were tried to the end
  36b   because of his confidence in evildoers,
  37a for he adds constantly to his sins,
  37b   he increases impiety among us
  37c   as he multiplies his words against God.

If we accept this translation, there may be suggestions in both 36b (to be discussed later) and 37b of connections between blasphemy and other sin; but other interpreters, like Pope or those of the RSV, seem not to see such suggestions at all. So one hesitates to rely heavily upon Gordis's reading here.

For 37a the RSV reads "For he adds rebellion to his sin," and

Gordis himself says that the word he translates as *impiety* in 37b
"carries its original connotation of 'rebellion against higher authority,'"[6] human or divine; so there may be in 37a or 37b the suggestion
that Job's words either constitute or encourage *rebellion*. This word
presents us with an alternative interpretation of what is wrong with
blasphemy—it is, or it leads to, rebellion against God. Many scholars
speak of Job as a "rebel" and call his attitude "rebellion against God,"
and here we find a little textual support for this language. For my
own part, however, I am uncomfortable with this particular slant.
The textual support is weak, and the idea seems to me to involve
difficulties. Job might be seen as rebelling *against orthodoxy*, but that is
different from rebelling against God, I would think. And how does
one rebel against God? Think of the political analogue in the background of this metaphor. If one rebels against Caesar, one takes up
arms and tries to overthrow his rule. But God's rule cannot be overthrown (certainly no one in this book would think it could be); and
how would one take up arms against God, how would one even try to
overthrow His rule? Perhaps the notion is that Job is defiant, refuses
to say he is guilty, and deliberately blasphemes; but that would make
him closer to the critic and the conscientious objector than to the
rebel. Political critics state publicly that the government is bad; some
of them claim that the government treats them unjustly; and if criticism of the government is outlawed, a conscientious objector may
speak out anyway and wait to be punished. History and literature
display many courageous individuals who tell the king to his face that
what he is doing is wrong. These parallels with Job are fairly close,
whereas the political rebel seems engaged in activities that have no
clear analogue in the man-God relationship, at least as it is construed
in the Book of Job.

Generally, 34:36–37 is intriguing, but it is too obscure in meaning
and too short on detail to allow us to base much of an argument upon
it. However, the other Elihu text is much clearer and seems to elaborate what Gordis's 34:36b only suggests:

34:7   Where is there a man like Job,
          who laps up blasphemy like water,
    8   who is in league with evildoers
          and consorts with wicked men?

9 For he has said, "It does a man no good
      to be in favor with God."

(Gordis)

Job does indeed lap up—or rather spit out—blasphemy or mocking words; and now Elihu suggests what is wrong with that. He says that Job is "in league with" or "consorts with" the wicked. In what sense? Perhaps in the sense of the following verse (34:9): Job "has said, 'It does a man no good [does not profit a man] to be in favor with God [to take delight in God].'" The comment Terrien makes seems apropos:

> Vs. 9 refers to another saying of the hero which is not found verbally in the present text of the poetic dialogue. But Job has often spoken of the suffering of the innocent (9:22–24; etc.) and of the prosperity of the wicked (21:7–13; etc.), and therefore of the lack of due reward or punishment upon the earth. Such a line of reasoning is in effect equivalent to declaring, "It profiteth a man nothing that he should delight himself with God" [as the King James Version translates this]. . . .[7]

Is this, then, what is wrong with blasphemy (of Job's sort)—that it gives aid and comfort, so to speak, to evildoers, by implying that they are leading prudent lives? Is this the sense in which a blasphemer like Job "consorts with" or "is in league with" the wicked? Might this even be what Eliphaz means in the obscure 15:4 quoted above? Is it that blasphemy of Job's sort gives a theoretical justification to wickedness?

My reader may remember that in chapter 4 I distinguished sharply between Job's question and Plato's. The Greek sophists (and most moral philosophers after them, until Kant) assumed that the ultimate reason for doing anything is that in the long run or ultimately it pays, it profits a man. And because Plato believed that the virtues had the support of reason, he labored mightily to show how justice (which, among the virtues, poses perhaps the most difficult problem) is indeed profitable. But Job never asks how it pays to be upright; he sees (or believes he sees) that it does not. What he asks is why God allows such a state of affairs. Now we see that Elihu, in 34:7–9, may be close to seeing the issue as the sophists would have seen it; for if Job's conclusion is accepted, then a sophist would have gone on to say that it was unreasonable to be "blameless and upright" as Job is. This conclusion would certainly give aid and comfort to the wicked; and this may be what Elihu means.

However, I would not exaggerate the importance of this passage (34:7–9), read this way. There are other ways to read it; for example, 34:8 may just mean that Job is also an evildoer and wicked—since he blasphemes in the way indicated. Or v. 9 may connect with ("for") v. 7, rather than v. 8; and the meaning of v. 8 may simply be the point Elihu and all the friends make—that Job is a sinner of the ordinary sort (as well as being a blasphemer, as vv. 7 and 9 say). So we have a very thin reed to lean upon if we wish to interpret Elihu as seeing a connection between Job's problem and Plato's. And I see no unequivocal suggestion in the whole book that anyone else makes this connection; so I would be most reluctant to give up the sharp distinction, insisted upon above, between what is at stake in the Book of Job and what is at stake in the *Republic*. In this book, before the theophany, we have suggestions that blasphemy is connected with other sin. There are even intimations that it is an extreme, a relationship to God at an opposite pole from being a "servant" who fears Him and turns away from evil. But these hints are left vague, and the suggestion that Job's blasphemy will be connected to other sin seems not borne out in the book itself. Moreover, we must remember that all these hints occur before the theophany, and hence are suspect; they are suggested by the Satan, or by the human characters, each of whom—not just Job, it seems to me—"darkens counsel by words without knowledge" (38:2).

Moreover, we know that the God of the theophany does not quite share the friends' view of Job's blasphemy. They never see anything noble or admirable in it; for them it is an evil (of some sort) without any redeeming qualities. But though God humbles Job and silences his blasphemies, nevertheless it is this (otherwise) upright, intrepid blasphemer who calls God forth, whom God takes seriously enough to speak to out of the whirlwind. As the initial Job is so upright that God takes special notice of him in the prologue, so the blaspheming Job in the drama receives a healing vision, and God's word that *in some sense he had "spoken of me what is right"* (42:7); and after repentance he even receives restoration of his fortunes. The romantic and modern admiration for the blaspheming Job is, at least in part, warranted by the text; the poet himself admires this character. As we will see later, the message of the theophany, acknowledged by Job, is clearly that his blasphemies were ill-founded and must be repented; but the theophany and the sequel make equally clear in their own ways that Job was somehow justified in his cursing. In Shakespeare we sometimes see a subject showing an extreme loyalty by telling the king to his face that he is wrong—when he *is* wrong; here, it is as if the most loyal subject tells God to His face that He is wrong—when He is not! Blasphemy of Job's sort has, in this book, a kind of paradoxical status: it seems a form of sin God honors, or one God honors while He rebukes. Apparently this man who quarrels with God, who curses God even, is somehow closer to God than God's would-be defenders are.

Chapter 7

A No to Job's No

I have conjectured how, and why, the Book of Job came to be written. I have argued that the simplicities of the folktale, of the patient Job of tradition, cried out for artistic development, for something like the poet's response, which allowed expression of the tensions and emotional concreteness left implicit in the legend. And I have noted how Job's consequent fall from patience is seen by many of us, and even in part by the poet, as a kind of fortunate fall, as a fall into honest, heroic realism. The poet took a character admired for his patience and turned him into one awesome in blasphemy. The camel, able to bear many burdens, became a lion, with a clear-eyed independence and a No.[1] Many modern readers, following the lead of the poet himself, see this transition as an elevation; we admire this weakling who can reject orthodox lies (or half-truths) and complain against the Almighty Himself.

But the poet did not stop with this defiance; he went on to write speeches from the whirlwind that bring that rage to an end, that return Job to silence and to an acceptance analogous to his traditional patience. In this chapter I will argue that in this, as in the earlier development, the poet's instincts were right; he was right to try to undermine the bitterness he had allowed Job to express. The book should not have ended with the blasphemous Job. However admirable that new Job may be, however heroic, however honest and in his way faithful to God unto death—he should not have had the final word in this drama. This is what I want to argue here, against the Promethean spirit of much of our age.

Now of course tradition gave the poet one reason to undermine Job's defiance. If the epilogue, or the New Testament, or the testimony of Bishop Theodore of Mopsuestia can be used as evidence, the folktale already had an ending: Job humbly accepted what God sent, and finally he was rewarded. Unless the poet could restore Job to his former patience, unless what made the legendary Job admirable in suffering could somehow be reestablished, then the tradition would have been assaulted in a way that is difficult to make plausible to the reader. This new Job and the old Job would seem incompatible, would seem at war. The poet would not have just developed the old story; he would have taken it in an opposite direction. Tradition demanded that the poet somehow work out a new reconciliation between Job and the world (or God).

Indeed, even the book as we have it, which includes the God speeches and Job's repentance, has shocked some readers. Bishop Theodore thought the book did not belong in the canon, and his reasoning suggests that it was the clash with tradition that provoked his criticism. Theodore accepted the "popular story of Job as the true account, dismissing the biblical book of Job as a mere literary product written by a man anxious to parade his learning and to gain repute. The speeches attributed to Job by the biblical author Bishop Theodore thought unbefitting a man 'who mastered his life with great wisdom and virtue and piety.' "[2] Theodore seems to have thought that letting Job blaspheme at all went too far; how much more scandalous if the book had ended with Job's blasphemy.

Moreover: in my judgment, which I will partly defend here, more than tradition demanded a reconciliation—there is wisdom, insight, in the tradition. Whatever the honesty and grandeur of Job's complaint, what satisfaction can be found in the morally bitter life? Given Job's theology, it leads to blasphemy; but theology aside, I believe that Job's bitterness represents a kind of psychological or spiritual illness, a lack of psychic health; and I suspect that underneath it are philosophical presuppositions that are untenable.

The honest rage of Job represents a giant step forward from the insensitivity or dishonesty of the friends, the credulity of those who themselves are fortunate, "the wisdom of the well";[3] and from the psychic numbness of the Job of the preface. If we were psychiatrists and our patient made that progress, or if we were philosophers and our student came that far into honest insight, we would believe that together we had traveled far in a healthy direction. But we would also believe that we were only halfway home, that a sound intellectual or psychic stance had not yet been achieved. The poet who created this flesh and blood Job—this mind and heart Job—had more on his conscience than merely a break with tradition; he had created a new spiritual problem when he solved his old one. He had created an honesty and a moral sense that are unbearable, an honesty and a moral sense at war with reality—whether God or the world be the ultimate reality. So not only tradition but also reason demanded that the drama not end with Job's silencing of the friends; a reconciliation with reality, an acceptance, needed to be achieved somehow. Bitterness should not have had the last word.

Some commentators who admire blasphemy more than patience think that the poet himself was their kinsman in spirit, and that he appended the theophany and epilogue somewhat cynically, only to pacify the tradition, and that his "real message" is in the blasphemy, not in the reconciliation. To some extent such claims are unverifiable; for what can we know of our author beyond what he wrote (to the extent we can determine that)? But in a sense we can appraise these claims, when we reach the theophany; for we can see whether it has any cogency as a solution to the problems in the dialogue. And before we reach that point, before we consider the voice our poet gave the whirlwind; and apart from the demands of tradition; we can ask whether there were reasons for writing something more, to end Job's bitterness and to restore him to an acceptance of the world. I believe that there were good reasons.

I am not asking only whether the book as a work of art needed to make *something* of the debate between Job and his friends, of Job's heroic defiance, and of his final call for a trial. Almost certainly it did. All of these features of the book called for response, denouement, resolution. We needed to see what came of all this, and perhaps some of the ending needed to be in prose, to match the prose of the prologue. What I am asking is not that, but whether, in the denouement, the poet should only have honored Job's blasphemy, or whether he should also have humbled it, shown its limitations, displayed its dark side—as he did. I believe he should have if his book was to be wise, was to show balanced insight into the serious problems with which it deals.

In what follows now, I may seem to be giving Pollyanna more than her due. However, if we take the drama's dialectical nature seriously, countervailing views to a defiance like Job's must be entertained and fully explored. To study it aright, to honor its complexity, we must give all represented viewpoints their just weight. Moreover, since Job himself and his complaint are spotlighted, we will have to exercise imagination and judgment to illumine the dialectic's opposite side.[4]

Given that one is bitter, perhaps blasphemy is therapeutic, and even heroic; but how desirable is it to be bitter? One way to evaluate bitterness is pragmatic or utilitarian, to ask what good bitterness does, and what harm. Granted, we don't want to ask only that kind of question—unless we want to endorse every kind of self-delusion, every kind of "bad faith," every fantasy that makes a person "feel good." I assume that concern for truth, fundamental honesty, is a virtue; it is one of Job's virtues; still, an honest person can ask himself which of his honest attitudes are helpful and which are harmful. Everyone recognizes in his own life that some of his attitudes are self-destructive, or not conducive to his own best interests; we sometimes must struggle with our own inclinations, for the sake of goods they threaten. Most of us recognize, also, that our moods and attitudes are sometimes harmful to others. And these psychic states that present problems often have a cognitive base: we are angry (or whatever) *because of* what we know or believe. This means that not all truth should be dwelt upon. The Stoics spoke of everything as having two handles, one by which it can be borne, and one by which it cannot. They did not mean to recommend dishonesty; they did not mean that people should invent pleasant lies and dwell on them instead of unpleasant facts. They meant that, given the many truths one can consider, one should (often, at least) focus on, dwell on, emphasize those which promote peace of mind and right relations, rather than the opposite. This remains good advice, provided it comes after and does not undermine what Job has already achieved: honesty, self-understanding, and purgation; and provided it does not cripple efforts to change the world where it can be changed. It may be that some of Job's insights need to be focused on for purposes of reform: maybe, for example, some of those judges whose eyes are covered can be removed from office; maybe we can stop some of the exploitation of the poor; certainly some theological orthodoxy needs reform; and in any case we do not want Job to save his peace of mind by self-deception. But, without lying, there may be attitudes it is better not to cultivate and not to express too self-indulgently.

Moral bitterness toward the world (or toward God, conceived of as intimate with the world) is such an attitude, I believe. Bitterness might be compared somewhat with envy, of the sort that makes a person willing himself to suffer if only the envied person does not prosper. No one enjoys being envious, or feels better off for being envious; envy is in itself an emotion we would rather not feel. Similarly for moral bitterness; no one enjoys being bitter or thinks himself better off for being bitter—even if he would not sacrifice his honesty as a means of escaping bitterness. David Hume based his analysis of morals on a contrast between the immediately "agreeable" and the useful, the *dulce* and the *utile*. He said that some sentiments were praised because they were agreeable and some because they were useful. But envy and bitterness are the opposite of agreeable; they are, in themselves, disagreeable states of mind. And envy and ordinary moral bitterness are attitudes toward individual persons or things, not toward the whole world; so, unless they expand, they poison only parts of our psychic lives; but Job's kind of moral bitterness is an orientation toward the whole structure, the basic fabric, of the world.

Furthermore, this kind of bitterness, like almost any attitude, is contagious; it poisons the atmosphere for others as well. If I am correct in arguing that moral bitterness is an undesirable state, then one has self-interested reasons for hoping to overcome it. But one also has altruistic, social, cooperative reasons: a bitter person makes his friends, family, and associates suffer, and not just himself. (And that means that one has an *additional* self-interested reason to fight bitterness; for if one makes one's friends suffer unduly they tend to abandon ship, or even to seek revenge.) Of course, one's friends have some obligation to respect one's mood, perhaps to indulge it somewhat, to sympathize to a degree; Job is rightly angry that his friends and "comforters" so quickly lose their comforters' role and so completely fail to enter into his bitterness. They came to visit because they sympathized with him in his suffering, and they sat silently with him for a week; and Eliphaz at least began with words of comfort. Suffering they could understand and sympathize with; but moral bitterness was too far to travel into fellow-feeling.

So Job was right to be disappointed with them as friends, to compare their friendship with streams that dry up in the hot sands of the desert (6:15–21). But let us think briefly of Job and his friends as real people, not just as characters in a drama. A real Job would have obligations to his comforters; for bitterness is hard to bear, and Job asks much when he invites his friends into that dark night. The person who asks his friends to bear much of his bitterness—or grief, or envy, or any of the other "disagreeable" emotions—must consider the cost, not require too much, and be grateful for their willingness to sacrifice on his behalf; for entering into such moods is a sacrifice. That is one reason so many friends prove false in times of anguish; they are incapable, or unwilling, to bear the anguish of their friends. A friend in need is a friend indeed; and often we can give money before we can lend a sympathetic ear.

One of the Enlightenment philosophers[5] saw a great problem of social living in the fact that we differ so much in our sentiments; we can share each other's feelings, and we want to, to some extent, but to do so often involves an invasion of ourselves and a dimunition of our private feelings. He thought that good men strove for a kind of compromise with one another. When I visit you in the hospital, I partly feign and partly really share in your suffering; these are my duties as your friend. But you, the patient, also have duties to me, your visitor; you try to put a fairly good face on things; you don't ask me to enter fully into your depths, or ask me to stay too long; and you show some genuine interest in my own less desperate life outside the hospital.

Job was angry with his friends for their failure to enter into his bitterness; he was right: they failed. But throughout the entire book Job never once asks about their lives, never asks how their families are, and never rejoices in their triumphs and good fortune. He never once thanks them, sincerely, for their willingness to visit him in his distress and to sit in silent sympathy for a full week. And even though he cannot honestly accept Eliphaz's assurance that things will get better—that God will not desert him—he never expresses any thanks that Eliphaz is, in his own way, trying to offer comfort. These are humdrum, commonsensical considerations; but if we try to think realistically about bitterness, instead of romanticizing it, we need to think on them.

The issue cannot be merely one of who is right, or most nearly right (as Job is, I assume), on the theoretical question of whether the world is just—and partly because there are a billion theoretical questions that can be addressed, and one is a fool to harp on this one forever. The issue must also be, how are we treating our friends? What are we asking of them? And, behind this, the issue must be, how are we treating ourselves?

I will not go so far as to say that it is always better to light a candle than to curse the darkness. For one thing, we cannot always, or ever completely, control our moods; most of us *will* curse the darkness sometimes. And cursing the darkness, when we really feel a curse in our hearts, can be therapeutic; certainly trying to repress the curse, or failing to acknowledge its existence, is dangerous. And some kinds of darkness (as the saying itself recognizes) can be lighted, and sometimes a curse calls attention to what can be changed for the better. But cursing the basic scheme of things, *cursing the world*, or *cursing the world and its Lord*, is not terribly helpful in any practical way; the bitterness behind such a curse is a bitterness we would be better off without, and a bitterness our friends do not need much of, either.

From time to time I have meditated on one of the stories told of Margaret Fuller. She is supposed to have said to Thomas Carlyle, "I accept the universe"; and Carlyle is supposed to have responded, "By Gad, she'd better!"[6] Now Fuller's "acceptance" must have been at least related to Job's; for behind it was a kind of gripe against the universe, perhaps a moral complaint, like Job's. If so, in what sense is it true that such a person had better accept the universe? Or, if Carlyle had been a character in the book of Job—speaking, say, where Elihu now speaks—and if Carlyle had said to Job, "By Gad, you'd better accept the universe!"—what sense might that have made?

A Russian might say to a dissident that he had better shut up, that he had better accept the Kremlin's rule—or else he will get sent to Siberia, or worse; if he doesn't accept the regime, it will crush him. Similarly, one might say to Job, "Job, you'd better shut up and accept

God's world, or else He'll punish you"—but that seems morally offensive. If Job's complaint is justified—or even honest—do we want
it silenced by force, or by threats? I think not. There would be an
attack on integrity there, and an appeal to force instead of to reason,
and this is not—perhaps Kant would say—treating a man as an end
in himself. So if this is our model for understanding Carlyle, I think
we must side with Job rather than with his critic.[7]

Let's try another model. Some people have great difficulty accepting the fact that all of us must die, that we are all mortal; or they
have trouble accepting their own mortality. Now one might say to
them, "By Gad, you'd better accept it—because there's nothing you
can do to change it. You can live prudently, and so perhaps live to the
biblical three score and ten, or longer; but there is no possible way to
live forever. You must accept your mortality." How *must*? *Must* in the
sense that those are facts that cannot be changed; and dwelling
on what cannot be changed, and lamenting it, and making yourself
miserable in that way, is just that—making yourself miserable. You
have to die, and if you are honest you have to recognize that fact; but
you do not have to let that knowledge make you miserable. You are
stupid—or neurotic—to let the unavoidable truth produce avoidable
misery.

A character in the book might have said something like that to
Job; not exactly that, but something at least like it. He could have
said, "Job, you are right; there is much injustice in the world. And it is
good that you see this. It enables you to help those of us who are
trying to correct some of that injustice. And it shows that you are not
living in a dream world. But no matter how honest we are, and how
much effort we make to correct injustices under our control, there will
remain injustices. There will be injustice in the future; and all the
horrible injustices of the past will eternally remain, for no one can
change the past. But we cannot (i.e., *should* not) let the injustice in the
world poison us; our recognition of the unavoidable does not need to
produce misery of a sort that itself is avoidable." *This* a Carlyle could
sensibly say, and this is what I have been trying to say in the last few
pages.

Throughout most of this pragmatic or utilitarian critique of Job's
bitterness I have assumed that Job's attitude toward the world, like
many attitudes, is to some degree struck, or assumed; that it has the

character of a pose; that in some small measure the Stoics and Sartre are right when they say that we choose these things. And I have been giving reasons for downplaying bitterness, so as to make life somewhat better for ourselves and our fellows. But of course the Sartrean assumption has its limits. Emotions or moods like bitterness do not come or go at will; even if we find powerful reasons for wishing we were not bitter, we may not be able to overcome ourselves. There may be unconquerable depths of passion; and certainly there are states which are extraordinarily difficult to overcome. And people vary in their abilities to get over things even when they know they should. Job himself, in this drama, does not overcome his own bitterness; the voice from the whirlwind overcomes it. In this drama, the victory is a gift, is Grace; it is not an achievement of Job himself.[8] But the main point here, in the structure of this essay, is that Job's attitude is not quite so admirable as some of his modern readers assume; and hence that we have reason—apart from theology or tradition—to be glad that the book does not end in Job's moral bitterness. Of course, not all books have to end well, as comedies, or with victories; but Job is presented in the dialogue as victorious, at least over his comforters; and the dialogue fails to show what I believe I have shown here, that there is a dark side to his victory.

And I think there would be another inadequacy in the book if we left off the ending, the ending after the dialogue. There would be a dramatic weakness: all this talk, unrepented, would come to nothing. Job talks, he reasons, he silences his opponents; shouldn't he act? At least, let us ask what act might naturally follow from the dialogue as we have it. It seems to me that one plausible outcome would be Job's suicide. I know that suicide was hard for a Hebrew to contemplate,[9] and maybe for an Uzite, too; but Job has already shown his theoretical freedom from conventionality; why not go on to this practical freedom? It seems to me that Job has two strong grounds for suicide. One is obvious: his life is miserable. The sufferings of Job are proverbial, and we get list after list of them, in concrete detail and in violent imagery. Is life really worth living under these conditions? Job has already expressed the wish that God would cut off his days. Why not end them himself? Throughout history men in all cultures have seen that a longer life is not necessarily a happier one; in all cultures there are people who express gratitude that horrible suffering—for example, their parents'—has come to an end in death. And in most cultures some men have drawn the conclusion that wisdom dictates taking action to hasten our own death in cases of severe unhappiness. So I think Job had reasons of the sort philosophers call "prudential" (self-interested) for killing himself.

He may also have had moral reasons. Job is a man of the highest moral character, a man obsessed with justice, a man who is outraged at the injustice of the world. Men of little principle can tolerate being a part of an unjust scheme; if the pay is good, a pure opportunist will execute babes or torture saints. But a man of principle will not. Men of deep principle act on their principles, and they refuse to cooperate with schemes they regard as unjust. Men of principle have resigned from business firms, schools, churches, political parties, even nations, to protest injustice. Might a man of principle resign *from the world*, from life, rather than be a part of what he regarded as its injustice? Now of course Job is not being asked to do any of the world's dirty deeds; he maintains his uprightness in this unjust world. But many men of principle have refused to cooperate even with justice when it is connected with injustice; young men in America refused to work *anywhere* for Dow Chemical because Dow made napalm used in Viet Nam. I do not say these protestors were right, but I understand their point. Since Job was a man obsessed with justice, I think that he would have at least considered suicide on moral grounds; he would have asked himself, at least, whether he could in good conscience continue to live in such an unjust world and continue to serve such an unjust God. Job talks about the injustice of the world, but he does nothing about it; just as he talks about the misery of his life but does nothing about it. What he might do is commit suicide. Maybe there are strong reasons why he should not; but if so, we should hear them. Otherwise, Job—if the book ends with the dialogue—is open to the charge of hypocrisy; the reader may ask him to put up or shut up.

Perhaps—though I feel very cautious here—we should consider also the possibility that a Joban bitterness would eventually lead a real Job to murder rather than to suicide, that the destructiveness in Job's heart would express itself against others rather than against himself. Of course, if Job hates and condemns the whole world, he cannot destroy *that*; God, or the world, really is too great for a mere man to

successfully attack. So I see suicide as the most plausible act to express Job's bitterness; if one cannot destroy the world, one can at least
leave it, sever one's ties to it, end it in oneself. But I suppose that a Job
might turn into a Captain Ahab or a Michael Kohlhaas. Moby Dick had
taken Ahab's leg; Ahab sensed that the great white whale was the
source not only of his own injury but somehow of evil throughout the
watery world. Ahab's bitterness turned into a destructive campaign
against that more than human, natural force. Michael Kohlhaas pa-
tiently (at first) suffered grievous injuries but eventually led a destructive campaign for revenge and justice—and is "justice" much more
than revenge, and restoration of one's honor, in these cases? The
authors of these masterworks saw Joban connections; they made allusions to our book.[10] In both of those works we see a wounded sense
of honor and of justice leading to fanatical destruction. In both cases
the obsession is suicidal; but the outward aim, at least, is murder and
revenge. A real Job might become like such later fictional heroes. Of
course the three cases differ. Kohlhaas identifies the source of his
afflictions *in the world*. Kleist wrote in our modern philosophical atmosphere, not in a religious or mythological one. Melville, through his
Ahab character and much more, dramatized and subtilized his own
quarrel with God, nature, religion, and society. In his sprawling
novel he could include more than did Job's author—could include
even his personal rage against publishers, uncomprehending readers, and the plight of a serious artist. If Ahab is more like Kohlhaas
than Job, Melville himself is closer to Job than to Kohlhaas. Despite
such differences, there is much kinship among these three works.
And we know how the wounded, the dishonored, the unfortunate
look for scapegoats; perhaps a real Job would have forgotten that his
quarrel was with God Himself, as he says, not with any man or group
of men, and would have begun a campaign against some Moby Dick
of an enemy, some scapegoat mythologized into a cosmic force for
evil. All of this would require a drastic shift in the way Job sees his
problem; as we have noted earlier, one of the striking features of this
book is the way in which Job fastens *exclusively* on God as the source
of the world's evils, as if he saw little efficacy in the natural and
human forces which—on the surface—caused those ills. So I find it
hard to see what Job would attack, if he were to become a destroyer
like those (other?) fictional characters. Still, perhaps we can count the

psychological subtlety of Kleist and Melville as suggesting an additional problem with Joban bitterness: it can lead to a demonic crusade.

In any event, there is another and deeper problem with Job's stance, as I see it; and that has to do with the theoretical underpinnings of the moral sense, the sense of justice, the morality which has underlain Job's bitterness all the while. I have emphasized throughout that Job's bitterness is moral bitterness, that it rests on and presupposes moral principles. Now we have discussed the misery this bitterness is and produces; we have seen moral bitterness as an unhappy state in itself, a state we would be better off without, a state we would want our friends to be spared. Finally, we have seen that there are connections between this bitterness and suicide. By making us more unhappy, it makes suicide more attractive; and the moral principles underlying it condemn the world, and hence at least raise the issue of whether a man of such principles can with a clear conscience continue to exist in such a world. What is the implication of all this? What does this say about these moral principles of Job, this *Joban moral sense*? It says that this moral sense is a threat to life itself: it makes us less happy and less likely to live. It is hostile to life; it is no-saying; it condemns the real world.

The terms I use here are Nietzschean. Nietzsche, "the old artillerist," as he called himself, carried on a war against the no-saying that he saw in Christian and late Jewish morality. As Job was obsessed with justice and injustice, Nietzsche was obsessed with what he called yes-saying and no-saying. What he meant by *no-saying*, and related expressions, varies somewhat from context to context; but there are three most important meanings, and all three are relevant to his critique of "morality"—or of the dominant kind of Western morality, which derives from intellectual and social forces in the ancient Near East.[11]

One kind of no-saying is living in illusion, in lies, in false optics; it is failing to see things for what they are, or lying to oneself and others about what one does see. Typically, or perhaps historically, the origin of illusion is in suffering, Nietzsche thought; the person whose life is wretched is the one who has a motive for denying the truth, for lying his way out of reality. Nietzsche believed that the fundamental assumptions of Western morality and religion were lies invented by or for sufferers to ease their suffering—that they were compensatory illusions, somewhat like "wish-fulfillment" dreams.

A second kind of no-saying is trying to suppress biological or psychological forces that are actually helpful or essential to life. What forces have this status is, of course, controversial; but it was Nietzsche's view that they include selfishness, lust, and the will to dominate—all of which have been regarded with suspicion in much of Western morality. The first way of saying no is *theoretical*, in traditional philosophical terminology; one denies the truth. The second way is *practical*; a no-sayer in this sense is opposed to or attacks certain forces he recognizes as real but regards as evil. For Nietzsche, a man who denied that our lives end with the death of our bodies would be a no-sayer in the first sense; one who acknowledged the power of the sex drive, but regarded it as basically sinful, would be a no-sayer in the second sense. Actually, this last example requires some clarification for its full understanding, and there may still be some scholarly controversy over the best account. But Walter Kaufmann's lifetime work on Nietzsche stressed what I believe is the correct interpretation of Nietzsche's many formulations of this theme. Nietzsche seems to have believed that there are three fundamental ways of dealing with a drive or impulse: one can express it directly, one can try to eliminate it, or one can cultivate, elevate, and "sublimate" it. Nietzsche was a lifetime critic of the first two alternatives— direct, brute, stupid expression, as well as extirpation, "castration," excision; and he was an advocate of the *use* of the powerful drives to strengthen and elevate life. His *yes-saying* included within it, we might say, a no; he was opposed to a simple yes and to a simple no, but was in favor of a sublimed yes. He thought that classical Christianity and late Judaism taught the simple no, or castration: "If thine eye offend thee, pluck it out"—where it is not exactly the eye that is intended.

The third kind of no-saying involves an attitude not toward a particular element of life, as in the first or second kind, but toward the whole of life or nature. Nietzsche seems to have thought that attitudes toward life as a whole, or judgments of the goodness or badness of life, were not capable of theoretical justification, that there was no way to prove that the whole scheme of things was good or bad; but he thought that *claiming* that life was bad, showing a negative attitude toward life—no-saying in this third sense—was a sign or a symptom of serious trouble, suffering, poor health, weakness, or degeneration. He thought that something impudent and absurd was displayed when a man, himself a part of nature, turned upon the nature that had produced him and called it bad. He believed that a healthy, growing, strong human being had an affirmative attitude toward himself and what was related to himself; and Nietzsche believed that everything was related to everything else. Consequently he believed that a fully healthy man, or a superman, who understood the interrelatedness of all things, would affirm the whole of life and would, indeed, wish for its eternal recurrence. Bertrand Russell once said: "This has been my life. I have found it worth living, and would gladly live it again if the chance were offered me."[12] This seems to have been close to Nietzsche's idea: the superman would desire the eternal return of his life—and indeed of the whole scheme of things. But Nietzsche believed that much of Western morality expressed an opposite attitude, a no-saying to life. He analyzed this attitude in many ways, but the way most relevant here is the following: Western religious morality finds much of the structure of life immoral; it regards the moral evaluation as the ultimate evaluation; and so its ultimate appraisal of life is that life is bad. Nietzsche believed that Western morality has built into it, therefore, a basic-level no-saying to life. As long as this no-saying is accompanied by a belief that this world is not our home—by a belief in otherworldly realities, God and a next life—then religious no-saying is balanced by a yes to these other "realities"; but once these compensatory beliefs collapse, the Western spirit is left with an unalloyed nihilism—the belief that what is, ought not to be, and what ought to be, is not.

Now to return to Job, or to Job as he stands in the great dialogue in the book. Is he really a no-sayer, in a Nietzschean sense? It would be anomalous to accuse Job of being a no-sayer in the first sense, of being dishonest: Job accuses his *friends* of dishonesty, of lying, of not seeing what is before them, of failure to recognize what every wayfarer knows about the evil in the world. Job believes—and proves, most commentators say—that the friends are living in illusion; Job's moral anguish is the result of his honesty, his courageous refusal to be taken in by traditional lies. Job will not lie despite the enmity of his friends, despite the affront to tradition, despite the reluctance of his own heart to accept the blasphemous truth. Nor is he willing, having seen the harsh realities, to posit another life in compensation. He would like to; he says that he could stand his current misery if he thought he would live again and be restored; but he knows that man lives only once and then is gone forever (chap. 14). Job has precisely the kind of intellectual integrity Nietzsche praised, the kind that can be cruel to one's own hopes and that can attack one's own convictions.

Now one could be ultra-Nietzschean here and say that Job still believes in God, and that *that* belief is itself a lie, and so even Job is a no-sayer in this sense; but that seems to me a terribly off-center, literally eccentric, way of understanding Job's character. And it confuses Job's character with the character of the author of the Book of Job. In that book, there is no illusion in belief in God; God IS; and so if a Nietzschean wants to say that every theism is no-saying, then he must say that the author of the book has not achieved full affirmation of reality. But the character conceived by the author has, or has about as fully as one could ever expect. Job is a yes-sayer in our first sense— he is honest—and therein lies much of his greatness, and of his heroic appeal.

I do not think the book has much to say about the second kind of no-saying. I discussed previously the kind of morality presupposed in the Book of Job, the sense in which Job is "blameless and upright, one who fears God and shuns evil." This morality stresses truthfulness, faithful judgment, respect for institutions of property and marriage, protection of the weak, and a rejection of cruelty; it allows a kind of pride in having lived up to these demanding norms; but it sees the self as having to be submissive to these norms and to the God whose laws they express. And given what the drama of the book itself reveals, I think we must say that Job and the author at any rate place a very high premium on intellectual integrity. The relationships between those norms and Nietzsche's are very complex. Job's integrity and hardness with himself suggest Nietzsche's kind of yes-saying, the yes that includes a no; Job's pride suggests yes-saying; Job is something of a desert aristocrat, and this suggests the kind of yes found in Nietzsche's "master morality." On the other hand, Job clearly sees himself as God's servant; he often stresses the pathetic character of his life; and his ethics are largely focused on the protection of the weak, which Nietzsche usually—but not always—

associated with the no of "slave morality." A great part of the problem here lies in the difficulty of deciding what Nietzsche really meant
to say about master- and slave-morality; but much of the problem
stems from the fact that the Book of Job does not investigate the bases
of the morality it presupposes. We are presented with graphic details
of a sheik's ethics, but we do not know how it is to be understood or
explained. What is its *Grundlage*, its basis, its fundamental principle?
What kind of people are served by this morality? What is its fundamental stance toward the natural human drives—affirmative, negative, or both? I do not see how we can answer these questions. We
could speculate about them, but I think we would come up with too
many hypotheses; we would not have evidence in the text that would
allow us to decide among them.

However, it is really Nietzsche's third kind of no-saying that
concerns us here. Nietzsche argued that biblical ethics contained an
implied judgment that life as a whole is fundamentally bad: that life is
immoral, and that the moral question is the ultimate normative question. The Job of the dialogues certainly has a lot of this kind of no-
saying; this is what his moral bitterness, and his blasphemies, really
come to. Job condemns the world on moral grounds; he finds it profoundly immoral. And, of course, moral questions are, for this Job,
the ultimate questions; he cannot say that the world is immoral, but
who cares? He is not, say, a nineteenth-century aesthete who could
say that the *beauty* of the world justifies it.[13] Job says no to life, and it
is an ultimate no; that is why I raised the question of suicide. Job
himself wishes he were dead, or had never lived. His expression of
that wish seems largely self-interested; from the point of view of Job's
own best interests, it would have been better if he had never been
born. But Job also condemns the world from the moral point of view:
the world is immoral, it is not what it morally ought to be. And his
obsession with this issue certainly makes him sound like one for
whom the moral issue is the ultimate issue. It is true that Job wavers
in the *kinds* of moral indictments he brings against God and the
world; some are harsher than others. And, since sometimes he expresses the view that his friends express, we have to say that he is
somewhat unsure whether he should be bringing these terrifying
indictments at all. And he never goes so far as to conclude formally or
explicitly that the world is so throughly immoral that it would have

been better if it had never existed, as he does say that it would have been better if *he* had never existed. So we do not have as full and complete a no-saying of Nietzsche's third kind as we could imagine: a categorical, unequivocal, moral condemnation of the whole of life. But we certainly have strong *elements* of this kind of no-saying, a no to life in its totality, a no based on moral grounds.

And this should make us wonder, I think—as Nietzsche wondered—whether there is something fundamentally askew in the morality that produces such a nay to life. Remember, there is a Joban origin of this indictment: the world is indicted *by Joban morality*. The world does not measure up to Job's standards; so Job condemns the world. But maybe the conflict shows that something is wrong with Job's morality, instead of with the world. This is certainly what we suspect in analogous cases. If a new teacher gives all his students failing grades, or if an art critic never likes anything he reviews, we suspect at least that his standards are too high, or misguided. Job's courage and honesty—and maybe his suffering—lead him to see, as the friends do not, that their common standards condemn the world. But that condemnation of the world gives us a strong reason for suspecting that the standards are somehow awry.

We have already noted that moral bitterness has its undesirable side, that it makes life even harder for the bitter man and for his associates; so we argued—somewhat as a Stoic might—for cultivating other attitudes and downplaying this one in our lives. But we did not there suggest that maybe this dark side of bitterness shows something wrong with the moral sense that generates it; now we make this more radical suggestion. Job is not illusioned about the world; in that lies most of his superiority over his friends. But maybe he and they are illusioned in their moral sense; or, if the word *illusioned* has suggestions too cognitive, maybe Job and his friends are unfortunate in their moral sense. Maybe they would be better off with one that did not lead to Joban bitterness. Remember that in the dialogues, only dishonesty can prevent bitterness; bitterness is the "natural" (we might say), "logical," honest reaction to the world, given the Joban moral sense. And bitterness is not a state we would wish upon ourselves or our loved ones. Doesn't this suggest that there is something wrong with Job's moral sense? Is a moral sense with this natural consequence something we want to fully endorse?

Now of course *any* moral sense will have some tendency to make us unhappy, because every moral sense distinguishes between the good and the bad, the right and the wrong, or whatever; and naturally we will have a tendency to be cast down when the bad or the wrong prevails, just as we will have a tendency to be reassured and strengthened when the good or the right prevails. And both will occur, since every moral sense acts as a guide to real life situations. In this respect a moral sense is no different from love; to love someone is to rejoice in his good fortune, but it also makes us a victim of his misfortunes—for we suffer when he does, because he does. There is no love, no friendship, no caring, without the possibility of pain.[14] But this just means that when we love we make ourselves susceptible to new pain; it does not mean that the natural result of love is essentially pain, when we reflect on the beloved as a whole person. Analogously, a moral sense makes us suffer sometimes; but it does not necessarily lead—one would think—to a suffering, painful, view of reality itself. But *Job's* moral sense does just that. That makes one suspect that something is wrong with it, and not just with his cultivation of the bitterness it evokes.

Now my argument or suggestion here has an assumption which needs to be brought into the open. I'll put the assumption somewhat vaguely, to diminish its controversial quality. The assumption is that a moral sense has a pragmatic or utilitarian aspect, that it is—at least in part—a device, a tool, a means; and that consequently we may criticize it just as we criticized bitterness, on pragmatic or utilitarian grounds. If the moral sense we have makes our lives worse off (I am deliberately nonspecific about who "we" are, and about the criteria for being "worse off"), then we have grounds, I assume, for asking whether our moral sense is askew or needs to be improved. I am not going so far as to suggest that one's moral sense is totally pragmatic or utilitarian, but only that it is so in part at least. In this respect it is different from a sense of natural and mathematical truth, as classically understood; classically and usually people believed that—for example—the effect of the theory of evolution on our happiness is irrelevant to the truth of the theory. A political platform, by contrast, is usually thought to be, at least mostly, an attempt to achieve a happy state of affairs. What I am assuming here is that a moral sense is a device at least somewhat like a political platform, and not totally like a natural science as classically interpreted; that it is reasonable to adopt one moral sense rather than another if—ceteris paribus—the former makes our lives better, fuller, happier, richer than the latter. Freud thought that Victorian morality fostered neurosis, and, so, should be changed; all I am assuming is that this is an appropriate kind of opening argument. It may not be decisive; I do not assume that much. There may be other constraints, including purely theoretical ones, on a morality. But I am assuming that the pragmatic or utilitarian constraint is *at least* one reasonable constraint. Job's moral sense makes him and others less happy; so it needs to be changed or we need to be shown why not. The bad consequences of the Joban moral sense at least raise the question of whether it should be changed. I think I have formulated the assumption weakly enough so that it is virtually noncontroversial; there are deep controversies in moral philosophy over the depth and precise character of this "utilitarian" or "pragmatic" element, but none I think—unless Kant really disagreed—over the idea that this is *an* element in morality. So we have virtually noncontroversial grounds for at least wondering, at the end of the Joban dialogues, whether there is something wrong with the Joban moral sense that underlies them.

None of the argument of this chapter shows, or is meant to show, that the poet handled well the problem of reconciliation, in the theophany and the epilogue. We have not yet examined in detail those parts of this work. What I mean to have shown is that there are strong grounds for thinking that some sort of reconciliation needed to be achieved at the end of the book—or that, in some other way, the poet needed to show the darker side of the heroic defiance that is so attractive in the dialogues. He said yes to Job's no and he should have; but he needed also to say no—and he did.

Transition:
The Apparent Irrelevance
of God's Speeches

The two preceding chapters have been less an explication and more of an independent defense of the structure of the Book of Job. I have argued that the poet was wise to create the bitterness and blasphemy of Job, and that he was again wise to bring an end to them. But *how* did he return Job to his traditional patience? To answer that question, we need to examine in detail the ending of the book, and especially what are most clearly normative in it—the two great speeches of God Himself. After three cycles of the dialogues, Job calls elaborately, formally, for a trial. Next the speeches of Elihu intervene.[1] After these we finally reach the theophany, so-called: "Then the Lord answered Job out of the whirlwind" (38:1 and 40:6).

We expect God's message to settle matters. We have heard from Job and from his critics; surely now God will clarify the issues, or reveal who has been in the right, or explain what must now be done. But God's speeches seem, at least on their face, grandly irrelevant to all the issues of the book. As we have seen, the problem of evil in human life is a central issue; but God does not reveal what happens to the innocent, or the upright, or the wicked. Indeed, He does not even *mention* the innocent or the upright; and it is not clear that He mentions the wicked. He seems grandly oblivious to the fates of all, or almost all, people; instead He discusses the animal kingdom, the plants, the surrounding natural order, and the two larger-than-human creatures, Behemoth and Leviathan. He changes the subject, we might say. Was He not listening? Did He not hear what the argument was about?

Moreover: in the debate in the dialogues, the comforters had accused Job of various sins of conduct, and Job had protested his innocence. Job called for a trial, to set matters straight, and presumably to vindicate himself. When God finally speaks, it is not for a trial, or not for the kind of trial Job had envisaged. No questions are asked about Job's conduct; the Lord takes Job to task, but only for his speeches, not for his actions. Why? Does God's silence mean that Job *was* a sinner of the sort the friends claimed, or that he was innocent, as Job claimed?

In the prologue, God and the Satan had agreed to test Job, presumably to see how he would behave in adversity, and hence what motives he had for serving God before the test. Now when God speaks He does not mention this issue. He does not discuss His service in adversity, or motives for serving Him; indeed, He does not discuss Job's, or any man's, service of Him at all! What became of the issue that initiated the drama? Why is that not the focus of God's speeches?

God's voice seems not just a voice from the whirlwind; it seems a bolt out of the blue, a crashing irrelevance. Or is there a rationale, a logic, hidden in these speeches? Job seems to find one. He says, "I had heard of thee by the hearing of the ear, but now my eye sees thee" (42:5). What is it that Job "sees"? What is the insight that is conveyed in these speeches?

Finally: the two long speeches of God directly challenge Job's knowledge, reveal his profound ignorance, and say that he "darkens counsel by words without knowledge" (38:2; see also 42:3); Job responds by ceasing to speak (40:4–5), and by confessing his lack of understanding (42:3). But immediately afterward, in the epilogue, the Lord chastizes the friends, not Job, and tells them they "have not spoken of me what is right, as my servant Job has" (42:7, 8). So did Job speak "what is right," after all? Was he *not* so profoundly ignorant, as the theophany insisted he was? Does the epilogue contradict the theophany?

There are even more puzzles, but these are enough to let us know that the difficulties are great, that the ending of the book is immensely perplexing. This means that our analysis of that ending— from God's speeches through His rebuking of the friends—must be careful and in great detail, if we are to see what is said or suggested there. Let us return then to the text.

Chapter 8

The Lord's First Speech

The Lord's first speech from the whirlwind, whatever else it may be, is a rebuke to Job, a put-down, a humbling. Its mode of address is sarcastic or ironic. It stresses the great contrast between Job and the God who addresses him; and it stresses the littleness of Job in the grand spectacle of God's creation. Job responds appropriately to this message: "Behold, I am of small account" (40:4).

If we are ever to make sense of the theophany, we must explore the precise character of this humbling, to be clear what it is that God says to and asks about Job. Some details are obscure; but most of this speech is quite lucid. The clear points are interrelated, and together they form a complex network of insinuation that Job is indeed quite "small," in various ways, in relation to God and to the nonhuman domains of God's world. God takes Job out of the human scene almost altogether, and asks him about his place in the natural order, the order of beings that are not human. And though it is one man, Job, who is addressed, what is insinuated of him could equally well have been suggested of any man, or at least of any man of Job's time. Job's limitations in this speech are not the peculiarities of one individual named Job; they are the limitations of any human being, or they are meant to be. So the implicit contrast is between man and the rest of God's creation, between the human and the nonhuman order. The message is that man is quite small in God's cosmos. Job might well have responded, "Behold, we are of small account."

But what sorts of "smallness" does man show? How is man "small" in relation to the natural order? The first way is ignorance; man is small in understanding. The very first words of the speech sound this theme:

> Who is this that darkens counsel
>   by words without knowledge?
> Gird up your loins like a man,
>   I will question you, and you shall declare to me.
>
>   (38:2–3)

God asks, "Do you know . . . ?" (38:33; 39:1, 2) where the intended answer is, clearly, "No, I do not know." God says, "Tell me, if you have understanding" (38:4); "You know" (38:21), and "surely you know" (38:5)—where the meaning in the divine sarcasm is, plainly, "You do *not* know, you do *not* have understanding." The questions that God asks Job are so patently unanswerable, so obviously what a man cannot answer, that perhaps we need no confirmation from Job himself; but Job probably does acknowledge his ignorance: "What shall I answer thee? I lay my hand on my mouth" (40:4); and certainly at the end of God's second speech Job confesses his ignorance (42:3):

> "Who is this that hides counsel without knowledge?"
> Therefore I have uttered what I did not understand,
>   things too wonderful for me, which I did not know.

Job confesses more than that, but at least he confesses that. The theme of man's ignorance is touched on tangentially throughout the book, but here in the theophany it is made central and hammered home. This theme is an important aspect of God's speeches. And if we assume, as I do, that the theophany is normative, then we must conclude that the book as a whole is profoundly skeptical, agnostic; its message is largely a counsel of silence. What we know best is that we do not know; at least, we do not know the sorts of things God asks about in this speech.

What does God ask about? A few of His points of inquiry seem unimportant, at least to human life, and to the basic order in the cosmos:

> Do you know when the mountain goats bring forth?
>   Do you observe the calving of the hinds?
> Can you number the months that they fulfil . . . ?
>
> (39:1-2)

But in many cases, God seems to be asking about fundamental structures of reality. He begins:

> Where were you when I laid the foundation of the earth?
>   Tell me, if you have understanding.
> Who determined its measurements—surely you know!
>   Or who stretched the line upon it?
> On what were its bases sunk,
>   or who laid its cornerstone . . . ?
>
> (38:4–6)

We have five questions here. Now we might attempt to trivialize the issue, and say that most of these questions can be easily answered. Where was I? Answer: I didn't exist then. Who determined the measurements, stretched the line, laid the cornerstone? Answer: God did. But these surface answers only point to the absence of deeper answers. If I did not exist when the earth was founded, I do not understand what was done then—at least if I cannot understand what I do not witness (an assumption we might question).[1] And if "God did these things" is the surface answer to most of these questions, hovering about are more searching questions: *How* did God? (How did God lay the foundations, etc.?) And what *are* the foundations that God laid, what are the measurements, the line, the cornerstone? God's penultimate question makes explicit that this is the issue: "On what were its bases sunk?"—not merely, "Who placed them there?"

And perhaps the poetic language here suggests an even deeper mystery, the mystery of our inability to even speak literally of such matters: for surely the earth does not have, literally, a "foundation," a "cornerstone." The poet uses architectural images; but surely these are *merely* images or metaphors. We are speaking of the natural order as if it were one of man's works, so we describe it in the vocabulary of man's works. But the earth is not a house, and the vocabulary of architecture applies to it, if at all, only metaphorically. We not only cannot answer God's questions; we cannot even hear them except as they are translated into metaphors.

Similar remarks apply to God's second set of questions:

> Or who shut in the sea with doors,
>   when it burst forth from the womb;
> When I made clouds its garment,
>   and thick darkness its swaddling band,
> and prescribed bounds for it,
>   and set bars and doors,
> and said, "Thus far shall you come, and no farther,
>   and here shall your proud waves be stayed?"
>
> (38:8–11)

A simple answer is available to Job: "God, You did all this, as You Yourself say [in v. 9]!" But how did God do all this? And what are the bars and doors that contain the sea? And surely all this talk of doors, and of birth from the womb, and so on, is metaphorical—borrowing language from several areas of human life to describe what is independent of human life. Do we even understand enough of God's creation to ask nonanthropomorphic questions about it, much less to answer such questions?

God is asking in these early questions about the most basic structure of the earth—the "foundations," the division between sea and land, and the like. God implies that Job did not exist when these were established and that (consequently?) he does not understand them. A later passage strikes the same note:

> Where is the way to the dwelling of light,
>   and where is the place of darkness . . . ?
> You know, for you were born then,
>   and the number of your days is great!
>
> (38:19, 21)

God means, of course, that Job was *not* born then, and his days are *not* great, and (consequently?) he does not understand these things.

However, some of God's speech implies that Job's problem is not merely that he is a latecomer; Job has not visited, and (so?) does not understand, a great deal of what exists about him in his own time:

> Have you entered into the springs of the sea,
>   or walked in the recesses of the deep?
> Have the gates of death been revealed to you,
>   or have you seen the gates of deep darkness?
>
> (38:16–17)
>
> Have you entered the storehouses of the snow,
>   or have you seen the storehouses of the hail . . . ?
> What is the way to the place where the light is distributed,
>   or where the east wind is scattered upon the earth?
>
> (38:22, 24)

Again we hear questions Job cannot answer; and again, I suspect, the metaphorical language domesticates these mysteries only ironically—for literally, such terms as *storehouses* must be out of place. The natural world is removed from the human by a great gulf.

The next passage introduces, or makes explicit, new themes in this great symphony of man's smallness in the world:

> Who has cleft a channel for the torrents of rain,
>   and a way for the thunderbolt,
> to bring rain on a land where no man is,
>   on the desert in which there is no man;
> to satisfy the waste and desolate land,
>   and to make the ground put forth grass?
>
> (38:25–27)

Of course, this is another of those questions Job can answer at the simplest level: he can reply, "You, Lord, did this, not I." But that answer raises all the old questions that Job cannot answer. More important, this question contains a new idea, and maybe two. Not only is God's action in creation beyond man's comprehension—that theme we have already seen—but also: much of God's activity has no relevance to human life. He brings rain "on a land where no man is, on the desert in which there is no man."[2] Moreover, God's reason for this activity, it is perhaps suggested, has to do with His other creatures, not with man: "to satisfy [not man but] the waste and desolate land, and to make the ground put forth grass." Before this passage man's limits have been stressed: Job, a man, did not always exist; he was not a party to the creation; he does not understand God's world. But now it is also suggested that the creation is not wholly for his sake. God makes the waste land put forth grass where no man is. There is probably the suggestion that God actually cares for the waste land, that His purposes include plans for land where no man is. That is: It is clearly implied that God *acts* upon lands where no man is; it is at least suggested that God has purposes for such lands.

The next passage returns to more general questions about weather phenomena:

> Has the rain a father,
>   or who has begotten the drops of dew?
> From whose womb did the ice come forth,
>   and who has given birth to the hoarfrost of heaven?
>
> (38:28–29)

Now God speaks of His creativity in images not of architecture, or housekeeping, or commanding and obeying, but of sexual genera-tion: has the rain a father, has the ice a mother? Perhaps again these are questions that can be answered at their simplest level: "No, they have no parents; You made them"; or perhaps, "You are their Father and their Mother"—but, especially if we supply the second answer, we see vividly the metaphorical nature of the question, and the irony in the domesticating anthropomorphisms. The shift from metaphor to metaphor underscores the inadequacy of all these metaphors; and the use of the mother and father metaphor, with their inherent con-tradiction—can God be both Mother and Father?—forces this issue to the surface.

The next passage introduces, or makes explicit, another new theme: Job's weakness. It asks about Job's knowledge of, *and power over*, the stars:

> Can you bind the chains of the Pleiades,
>   or loose the cords of Orion?
> Can you lead forth the Mazzaroth[3] in their season,
>   or can you guide the Bear with its children?

> Do you know the ordinances of the heavens?
> Can you establish their rule on the earth?

(38:31–33)

I want to make a few comments about the relations between power and knowledge here, with some suggestions about their relations elsewhere. Later, I will discuss the relevance of Job's weakness and of his ignorance to the issues of the book; it seems that they are relevant in very different ways. After all, Job's ignorance implies that he cannot say much that is sensible, about some subjects; but does his weakness imply that? One would think not. A weak man might still, perhaps, sensibly argue the case for his innocence; whereas an ignorant man might need the help of the more knowledgeable. An ignorant man might not be capable of discussing the problem of evil; but it is not obvious how his *weakness* would incapacitate him for that discussion.

Nevertheless, in this passage we have the two questions about Job blended: Can Job bind, loose, lead, guide the stars? And does Job know the stars' ordinances? The author seems to regard these questions as intimately related. Gordis says, "God knows the laws governing heaven and earth, because He has established them; does Job?"[4] But shouldn't we divide the questions here? When Newton discovered his laws of motion, he said that he was thinking the thoughts of God after Him; but Newton never imagined that he had established the relations he discovered—God had done that. Couldn't Job know the ordinances of the heavens—indeed, don't we know them?—without having created them, without being able to maintain them, without being able to change them? One would think so. We tend to distinguish these issues; we can "know that" without "knowing how," we can understand the principles of something we cannot control. But our poet connects these issues intimately; he moves easily from "Can you bind . . . ?" to "Do you know . . . ?" And verse 33 moves quickly in the reverse direction:

> Do you know the ordinances of the heavens?
> Can you establish their rule on the earth?

Or, as Gordis translates,

>   Do you know the laws of the heavens;
>   Can you establish order on the earth?

The main difference between these two translations has to do with
whether stich b, the second half of the verse, refers simply to the
earth or to the influence of the stars upon the earth. But in either case
we see the poet move quickly from ignorance to impotence, as above
he moved in the opposite direction. In this book, regularly, not to be
able to do is not to know, and vice versa. Knowledge is power; knowing is knowing how to and being able to—fairly often for this poet.
Earlier we saw the assumption that only he who witnesses something
knows it; now we see the assumption that only he who can do something knows how it is done. God created, God witnessed creation,
God knows; Job did not create, Job did not witness, Job does not
know. The modern mind may have trouble with these inferences. We
may wish to distinguish issues, and to allow knowledge that transcends witnessing and power; but the author of this book seems not
to—at least fairly often. (Not always: what Job knows in his confession, 42:2–6, his creaturely insignificance, is certainly not something
he created.)

Since 38:22 God has been asking Job about the elements of the
weather, unless verses 31–33 are an interruption, which they may not
be, for the stars were often thought to be involved with weather. The
next few verses continue the weather theme:

>   Can you lift up your voice to the clouds
>   that a flood of waters may cover you?
>   Can you command the lightnings . . . ?
>   Who has placed wisdom in the ibis
>   or given understanding to the cock?
>
>   (38:34–36, Gordis)

Again, at least in the first two of these three verses, Job's impotence is
stressed; the implication is that God, not man, can do these things.
Verse 36, with uncertain meaning, is especially interesting if this
translation is accurate. I give here Gordis's reading, favored by others, so that the verse refers to the ibis, believed to foretell the rising of
the Nile, and the cock, who forecasts the dawn and perhaps was

believed to forecast the rain.[5] This interpretation gives some of the birds more knowledge than men have, about some matters! This fits the overall thrust of the speech as a rebuke to Job's pretence to understanding. However, it also runs counter to the theme just mentioned, of the power/knowledge intimacy; for surely these birds do not *control* the phenomena that they "understand," that they have "wisdom" about. Perhaps we should say (if this translation is appropriate) that the poet presupposes a distinction between shallower and deeper understanding; these birds have the shallow ability to forecast, but they do not have deep understanding. Perhaps the poet would even say something similar about a Newton—who did, in fact, think there were mysteries closed to him—or about the modern assumption that we understand much that we cannot control. The poet might claim that *our* understanding is shallow—perhaps even that it amounts to nothing more than the ability to predict, an ability these birds possess! And some philosophers have argued that science *is* like that. This issue has received much attention in recent philosophy, and the majority opinion is probably that our understanding is more than a forecasting ability; but the issues are quite complex, and the view that we only predict, or in some other way are inherently shallow, has been defended by many minds who seem, by ordinary standards, far from shallow.

With 38:38, almost immediately after the references to the two birds, the discussion of the weather comes to an end. In the next verse, the poet has God begin a series of questions and remarks that focus on the animal kingdom. We are still far from the human realm; we certainly are not speaking of good men or bad, or of how they fare in this world. But at least we have moved up to the animals. The questions still stress Job's unimportance:

> Can you hunt the prey for the lion,
>   or satisfy the appetite of the young lions,
> when they crouch in their dens,
>   or lie in wait in their covert?
> Who provides for the raven its prey,
>   when its young ones cry to God,
>   and wander about for lack of food?

(38:39–41)

Now of course Job does not do these things. But who *does*? One
answer might be, "Those animals do these things for themselves."
The lion finds its own prey, and satisfies the appetite of its young;
and the raven finds its own prey, and either the raven parents, or the
young themselves, secure food for the young ravens. Or the answer
might be, "God provides the prey for these animals and the food for
their young." Most commentators read the passage in this latter way.
The young ravens, after all, "cry to God" (v. 41). In the Psalms the
young lions seek their food from God (104:21), and He gives food to
the young ravens (147:9). Regardless of which way we read the passage, these creatures can get along nicely without Job.

Next God asks Job about three other animals that have nothing to
do with man. Job is asked what he knows of the mountain goats—of
their pregnancies, of their calving, of the maturation of their young
(39:1–4). The implication is that Job does not observe (39:1) these
things and so does not know (39:1, 2) them. In the other two passages, God stresses the independence of these creatures—their independence from man, that is:

> Who has let the wild ass go free?
>> Who has loosened the bonds of the swift ass . . . ?
> He scorns the tumult of the city;
>> he hears not the shouts of the driver.
>
>   (39:5, 7)

Some of these creatures are permanently, not just normally, wild;
they cannot be domesticated:

> Is the wild ox willing to serve you?
>> Will he spend the night at your crib?
> Can you bind him in the furrow with ropes,
>> or will he harrow the valleys after you?
> Will you depend on him because his strength is great,
>> or will you leave to him your labor?
> Do you have faith in him that he will return,
>> and bring your grain to the threshing floor?
>
>   (39:9–12)

These animals, like the ravens, do not need man; but God is pointing out that they cannot even be made to live with man. Their lives are inherently alien to man's life.

After these passages God mentions three other creatures—the ostrich, the horse, and the hawk (or some similar bird). The relevance of the ostrich and horse passages has been troubling to some commentators. The account of the ostrich is very obscure in the Hebrew, and the translators of the Septuagint omitted it altogether. One of many attempts to make some sense of it in English is Gordis's:

> Do you know the wing of the ostrich beating joyously?
>   is her pinion like that of the stork or the vulture?
> For she leaves her eggs on the earth
>   and lets them be warmed on the ground,
> forgetting that a foot may crush them
>   or a wild beast trample them.
> Her young ones grow tough without her;
>   that her labor may be in vain gives her no concern,
> because God granted her no wisdom,
>   and He gave her no share in understanding.
> Now she soars aloft
>   and laughs at the horse and his rider.
>
>   (39:13–18)

Assuming that something like this is what the passage says; what is its relevance? What makes it suitable here? Perhaps it implies that the nonhuman world is strange, weird, alien to human expectation—and not only, as we have seen, alien to our knowledge and control. Perhaps it implies (also?) that the animal kingdom is remarkably diverse. Earlier God mentioned "wise" birds that knew things men do not know; now we have a bird with no wisdom.[6] Above we had a creature (the lion) that cared for its young, and now we have a creature who leaves its eggs to be crushed (or so it was thought). If 39:13 really contrasts the ostrich with two other birds, as many scholars think, then we may have two kinds of contrasts introduced there. The vultures and the stork fly, of course, while the ostrich cannot. ("Soars aloft," which Gordis reads in 39:18, cannot be a description of *flying*, if the ostrich is the subject.) And the ostrich is (in popular thought) a poor parent, the vulture [falcon?] is an ordinary one, and the stork exemplary. Or perhaps the overall point is that the ostrich, for all its real and imagined faults, is still under God's care; its amazing speed—greater than the horse's—shows that. Or perhaps all of these implications are in the text. None of them is incompatible with the general sense we see here, and they all expand the pertinence of the passage.

The passage on the horse is quite striking. Here is a plausible translation:

> Do you give the horse his might?
> Do you clothe his neck with strength? . . .
> He paws in the valley, and exults in his strength;
> he goes out to meet the weapons.
> He laughs at fear, and is not dismayed;
> he does not turn back from the sword. . . .
> When the trumpet sounds, he says "Aha!"
> He smells the battle from afar,
> the thunder of the captains, and the shouting.
>
> (39:19, 21–22, 25)

The brief questions in 39:19 are of course to be answered, "No, Job does not do this; God does this." But how is the horse portrayed? He is represented as strong and fear-inspiring; and above all, as loving war, loving the war of man with man. Here we have our first animal with a genuine connection to man, the first "domesticated" animal, not at all literally the "wild" horse, as Gordis says once;[7] and what is this animal, which man "breaks," like? He loves war. He loves weapons, the sword (and the quiver, the spear, the javelin, 39:23), and the trumpet and the shouting of warfare. The first—the only—"tame" animal God describes turns out to be the wildest of the lot, the one man uses to fight against other men.

What are we to make of this portrayal? If we think of war as evil, then in the horse we find a lover of evil. Under that interpretation, we have moved in this speech from a nature beyond man to a nature alongside man but alien, and now to a nature man uses to heighten the evil in human life. God created this part of nature, too—unless we say that God created the *wild* horse, and that only when man puts that wild animal to human use does it become such a force for evil. Either way, the horse seems to be a creature *not* intended for man's benefit. Job's horizons continue to be expanded.

On the other hand, it is not clear that war per se *is* an evil in this book. Of course being killed in war is an evil, and one that righteousness protects against, according to Eliphaz:

> In famine he will redeem you from death,
>   and in war from the power of the sword.
>
>   (5:20)

But "evildoers" in this work are not described as warriors, nor are the righteous portrayed as pacifists or peacemakers. Nor is participation in war represented as a reward or a punishment. Of course war was and is a fact of life, and ancient literature often gloried in it, and in the horse's prowess in war; the warrior ideal, and man's own near-animal exultation in battle, seemed acceptable. If we read the passage in this light, then the horse heightens the goodness, not the evil, in human life, but it is a dangerous goodness, a warrior goodness, in a realm of heroic virtues and the violent harnessing of natural strength. This is not the realm of respecting boundaries and property rights or of helping the widows and orphans—not the realm of righteousness as this book understands it. When nature enters man's world in the figure of the horse, it does contribute to the goodness of man's life, but in a way beyond what the dialogues represent as good and evil. So in this interpretation, as in the earlier one, we find God expanding the horizons.

The next passage concludes God's questions in His first speech. God asks:

> Is it by your wisdom that the hawk soars . . . ?
> Is it at your command that the eagle mounts up . . . ?
> . . . [H]e spies out the prey;
>   his eyes behold it afar off.
> His young ones suck up blood;
>   and where the slain are, there is he.
>
>   (39:26, 27, 29–30)

(The words translated *hawk* and *eagle* in the RSV may be synony-mous; or the first may be a genus term including the second.) Of course the answer to God's questions remains, "No, Job does not do that; *God* gives these creatures their wisdom/power." These birds are not man's creatures or servants. We may have further references to war; these birds feed on the slain, or corpses, perhaps after the war-fare the horse loves. We may have here, then, another creature re-lated to man through warfare; he does not like the fighting itself, as the horse does, but he loves the carnage. He loves death, even hu-man death; he eats human flesh and feeds his young on it. This is a creature that God has made.

In the first speech, then, we have a picture of God's creation, the nonhuman world, in thorough foreignness to man. Man did not create it and does not control it. It existed before man; man has not visited much of it; man does not understand its principles or even many of its details. Many of its animals live their lives without any reference to man; many of them cannot be domesticated; some, when brought into man's world, love his warfare; some feed off his corpses. These creatures are different from man and different from each other. The picture, in this speech, of God's creative activity in the nonhu-man world, and of Job's "smallness" in relation to it, is coherent, well-organized, and smoothly integrated—if I have interpreted it fairly.

There is an important, general point I need to add. This picture of the nonhuman cosmos is *praise*. The world described is alien, un-known, even hostile to man, or at least to man as the dialogues understand him; but it is beautiful, or awesome, or wonderful, or *somehow* good. God recounts His creative acts with pride. These acts transcend man in many directions, but not primarily in the directions of horror, or evil, or ugliness. The poet does not intend Job to reply, "No, I didn't create all that, and I'd be ashamed of it if I had." God's questions to Job are about a world that is somehow glorious. In spite of the harshness in the portraits of the last three creatures, the lan-guage is the language of praise, of celebration. The witnesses of cre-ation rejoice: when the bases of the earth were laid, "the morning stars sang together, and all the sons of God shouted for joy" (38:7). It is perhaps not *crystal*-clear, but it is fairly clear, that Job acknowledges the glory of the creation in his responses to each of God's speeches. I have mentioned Job's laying his hand on his mouth, at the end of

God's first speech, and I have noted that this is a gesture of silence, which is appropriate for ignorance that knows itself as ignorance. But it is also, as Pope notes, an appropriate, ancient expression of *awe*: "This gesture is graphically represented on a Mesopotamian seal cylinder of the late third millenium B.C. depicting Etana mounting heavenward on eagle's wings while one of the gaping onlookers holds his hand to his mouth."[8] In the Book of Job, it seems a gesture of respect. In 29:9, as Job tells of his good life in the old days, he mentions that "the princes" had "laid their hand on their mouth" out of respect for him. After God's second speech, Job confesses that he had spoken of things "too wonderful" for him (42:3). I think it is implied throughout not just that God's work is too powerful and complex for Job, but also that it is somehow a good work, a work meriting Job's awe, reverence, praise. Clearly, when Job says that he is of small account (40:4), he acknowledges his ignorance and weakness, and the small place of man's world within the encompassing cosmos; but he seems to also acknowledge the grandeur of that natural world. The world beyond man (and beyond man's righteousness) has its own immense value.

In the Genesis 1 account of God's creativity, man is created only on the sixth day; but in that account, long before man arrived, God saw that His world was good. God saw "that the light was good" (1:3); that the separation of the earth from the seas, and the vegetable productivity of the earth, were good (1:13); that the astronomical lights were good (1:18); that the birds and the moving creatures of the water were good (1:21); and that the animals of the land were good (1:25)—all before man was created. The Lord's speeches in the Book of Job continue this praise of nature, by which I mean the nonhuman creation.

I do not think, however, that how, or in what sense, nature is good can be explicated very easily from the Joban theophany. There are writers who think that the theophany praises the "beauty" of the creation, and in a few passages the poet does seem to emphasize the beauty of the natural order; but in many passages this does not seem to be the point at all. The poetry is beautiful, but not everything it describes is.[9] There are writers in the Rudolf Otto tradition who believe the theophany expresses a peculiar, uncanny "numinous" awe, one seen by Otto as distinctive of religious experience and supposed to be indefinable in nonreligious terms;[10] as if the creation were

shown to be uncanny and attractive-and-forbidding in some distinctive way. Now a part of the Otto analysis is clearly correct: the theophany does have two aspects in tension—Job is humbled, rendered
small in his own eyes, and silenced, while at the same time the
creation and God Himself are glorified. The theophany does present a
world both attractive and daunting. What is not clearly correct is the
claim that this doubleness of the message involves some unique,
indefinable category or quality of experience. The theophany, like
Genesis 1, is vague about the kind of goodness it reveals; it does not
follow that the revealed goodness is sui generis. And, as I show here
and in the following chapters, the senses in which Job is humbled are
definable.

Moreover, when God discusses His living creatures (not the
stars, rains, etc.), he seems to indicate a kind of providence for them,
and so a part of the goodness of the natural order may be that in it
God meets the needs of His creatures. We have already noted the
passage (38:25–27) that suggests that God waters the waste places so
that they may bring forth life—or "grass" (38:27) at least. And when
God discusses the birds and beasts, He mentions, in at least most of
the passages, how their needs are met. The young lions (38:39–40),
ravens (38:41), mountain goats (39:1–4), and hawks/eagles (39:26–30)
all seem cared for; references to the young, who are basically unable
to care for themselves, heighten the suggestion that God's intentions
are provident. Also the wild ass (39:5–8) and the adult ostrich (39:18),
at least, are provided for. The horse is presented as more than compe-
tent in battle (39:19–25). The eggs and the young of the ostrich seem
poorly cared for (39:14–17), however, though that passage may be an
addition; and God does not mention the needs of the wild ox (39:9–
12). But by and large the picture is one of providence for the living
creatures. The creation is not just beautiful; it is an order in which the
needs of the creatures are met, at least to a considerable extent.

Of course, there is a problem if we stress this providential theme.
God shows His concern for the lions and ravens by providing them
with prey. But how does He show His concern for their prey? By
providing lions and ravens to prey upon them? The speeches do not
address this question, which would seem to call for some answer.
There may be an answer; as environmentalists and sportsmen con-
tinually tell us, there is a sense in which predators can be good for a

species, or a genetic group, by eliminating the relatively unfit and so by strengthening the stock. But it is not clear that our poet knew this. And anyway this account presupposes a somewhat hostile environment, so that the stock needs to be strengthened, and it is not obvious how this fits a picture of provident care. Nor is it obvious that this approach speaks to the issue of how God cares for the "actually existing individual" animal who is preyed upon. It may be good for the herd that he is killed, but is it good *for him*? Always? Maybe there is a sensible answer here (too); I do not say that there is not. What I am arguing is that the theophany's account of the prey-predator relation is one-sided, if it is meant to indicate God's active benevolence; if that is the aim, the account needs to be broadened. As we have it, all it indicates is that God meets a considerable number of His creatures' needs—not that He meets all their needs, or the needs of all of them, or any optimal combination of their needs. The theophany reveals a natural order that is good; part of its goodness lies in its provident character; but nothing is said about its being perfectly provident, or of its being the best of all possible provident orders.

Before concluding this discussion of the first speech of God, I must mention three brief passages in it I have ignored up to now. Each of them may pose an objection to the interpretation I have presented so far. The first occurs in God's introduction to the speech, to be translated perhaps as follows: "Who is this that *darkens counsel* by words without knowledge?" (38:2) Now I have emphasized the point that Job spoke "without knowledge"; that theme is insisted upon in the first speech, and is acknowledged by Job in his responses to both speeches. But what does it mean to "darken counsel"? What is Job accused of, in that expression? Is it man's counsel, or God's, that Job darkens? And what is it to darken that kind of counsel?

The commentators present a good deal of evidence that the word translated *counsel* refers to *God's* counsel, rather than man's, and that His *counsel* is something like His plan, purpose, design, or scheme in His creation and control of His world. Job *darkens* that design in some sense—perhaps he declares God's design to be dark or obscure, as Gordis says.[11] Or perhaps he speaks in such a way as to make the design *become* dark or obscure, hard for man to see. However we read *darkens*, God seems to imply here that He *has* a counsel—a plan or design for or in the world. But we should not see more in this implication than the text allows. God has a counsel; but if we ask what that counsel *is*, what we are told of it—then we must go to the rest of God's speeches themselves for an answer. There—at least throughout this first speech—we are repeatedly told that His counsel in the world cannot be understood by men. True, God says that Job darkens His counsel; but God Himself insists that His counsel is largely dark to men—men cannot understand it. Terrien comments, "The counsel of the ruler of this universe operates in full light."[12] Interpreting these words in their most natural sense, it is hard to find a more wrong-headed commentary; *we* see, at any rate, only as in a glass, very darkly—*that*, not the opposite, is in large measure the burden of God's speech. I do not think it justifiable to interpret one obscure phrase, "darkens counsel," in such a way as to contradict the clear, elaborately reiterated message of the speech it introduces. I do not know quite what the phrase does mean; but surely we must interpret it in its context. And its context clearly opposes any "full light" interpretation.

How, then, could Job be "darkening" what is already obscure? Perhaps we should distinguish two ways God's counsel could be obscure: it is intrinsically obscure to us, for we cannot understand it; but we can understand that, and not let our thoughts of it be twisted, darkened, by the untenable speculations of a Job. Socrates thought that recognition of ignorance was wiser than pretense of knowledge; and clearly the author of this book agreed; perhaps this is the point here, in this (itself obscure) phrase.

Or perhaps *obscures* is the wrong sense of *darkens* anyway. In some O.T. passages (Job 22:15; Ps. 26:4) with apparently related adjectives, the sense is nearer to *evil* than to *obscure*. So perhaps God means that Job *villifies* His counsel, which Job surely does. That is what his blasphemies come to. Or perhaps the translators should reconsider the possibility that the phrase refers to *human* counsel, not divine; for if Job speaks without knowledge then he may darken (obscure) human counsel. And obviously Job darkens (villifies) the orthodox human counsel. At any rate, the point of the passage cannot be that God's plan is plain to us, or that only Job's rantings keep it from being plain to us. That interpretation runs counter to a main theme of the entire speech.

A second passage I have hurried over, so far, is 38:12–15, near

the beginning of this speech. God has asked Job about the foundations of the earth, and the limits to the sea; He is about to question Job
about the gates of death, about darkness and light, and then about
weather phenomena. In between there is a lovely bit of praise to the
dawn, which might be translated in this way:

> Have you commanded the morning since your days began,
>   and counseled the dawn to know its place,
> that it might take hold of the skirts of the earth,
>   and the wicked be shaken out of it?
> It is changed like clay under the seal,
>   and it is dyed like a garment.
> From the wicked their light is withheld,
>   and their uplifted arm is broken.
>
> (38:12–15)

Terrien comments on the last three verses,

> Dawn lifts up the darkness as a veil under which the earth has
> been asleep and shakes the wicked out of it like parasites (vs. 13).
> When the earth awakes, the sunrise sharply accentuates and
> reddens its configurations (vs. 14); and the evildoers desist from
> their deeds, for the light of day banishes their own false light (vs.
> 15).[13]

This is a plausible commentary if the translation is correct. But either
one—this translation, or this commentary—ruins the neatness of my
interpretation of God's first speech. The dominant theme in that
speech is man's "smallness"—his ignorance, his impotence, his mar-
ginality to much of nature. We have not yet explored the relevance of
this theme to those issues the rest of the book addresses. One of those
issues is, of course, the problem of evil in the life of man; remarkably,
God's speeches do not seem to address that problem. God hardly
mentions men at all, except to indicate their insignificance; he does
not mention innocent men or righteous men; and aside from this
passage, in His first speech He does not mention the wicked or evil-
doers. The theophany ignores, almost totally, the three kinds of human beings who figure so prominently in the debate of the dialogue;

and its effect would be greatest, clearest, most forceful, I think, if it *totally* ignored them. Evildoers are virtually ignored: why mention them so casually now? Why not keep the canvas completely free of them; why not change the subject completely?

But here we have the wicked scattering with the dawn, because their deeds are evil and they hate the light. Now it is clear that this is not a main point, even in this passage; the main points have to do with the ignorance and weakness of Job, the greatness of God, and the grandeur, the power, and the beauty of the dawn. The reference to the wicked is a mere detail among other details. But it spoils the effect. The subject of the fate of the wicked is too big, too important a subject, in this book, to be brought up casually. The wicked should be completely ignored, as they are largely ignored. Bringing them in suggests that we have here a partial solution to the problem of evil: God takes care of them by scattering them with His dawn. But this is a pathetic solution; it is so partial a solution as to be ridiculous. So the evil cannot get away with everything; so the light causes problems for them; is this all God has to say for Himself? What of all that the wicked get away with in the dark (24:13–17)? And what of the things they still get away with in the light? A proposal like this reduces a grandly sublime speech to an absurdity—if this really is a good translation.

I think we have here only three tenable alternatives. (Regarding this as a significant contribution toward solving the problem of evil is not tenable.) We can conclude that the great original poet did not write these embarrassing lines. Or we can say that the poet, great as he was, still made an unfortunate mistake, a lapse in judgment, which he failed to correct. Or we can say that these lines are not translated correctly. They *are* extremely difficult to translate. Some interpreters believe that they really refer not to the wicked but to the stars—as 38:31–33 does, a little later. The New English Bible, for example, under the influence of G. R. Driver's erudition, renders the passage as follows:

> In all your life have you ever called up the dawn
>   or shown the morning to its place?
> Have you taught it to grasp the fringes of the earth
>   and shake the Dog-star from its place;

to bring up the horizon in relief as clay under a seal,
  Until all things stand out like the folds of a cloak,
When the light of the Dog-star is dimmed
  and the stars of the Navigator's Line go out one by one?[14]

This kind of reading has its supporters and its detractors, and I am
not qualified to add much to the learned debate between them. But I
prefer this reading to the other one. If the poet did not write lines like
these, he should have; the poem is better this way. A great issue in
this book concerns the prosperity of the wicked; much of the force of
God's first speech comes from His sublimely ignoring that issue; but
if He is going to ignore it, He should ignore it completely. This is one
of those cases in which a word or two is far worse than total silence.
There are issues that should never be trivialized; if they are dealt with
at all, their difficulty and solemnity demand that they be treated
subtly and in depth. The prosperity of the wicked is such an issue. It
is crystal-clear that the poet's overall strategy in the Lord's speeches is
to bypass that problem, to be silent about it. To mention it in passing,
or to seem to mention it, in the passage in praise of the dawn, and to
present there such a flimsy contribution, would be a terrible mistake.
I prefer to think that the original poet did not make this mistake; but
even great poets make mistakes, in terms of their own projects; and
this may be one. The Lord's speeches are 99 percent silent on the fates
of the wicked, the upright, and the innocent; I would read them as
totally silent. If this decision requires amendment of the text, I
amend; but it seems to require only a learned and subtle translation—
and the appropriateness of this translation to the overall argument is
one piece of evidence that it is the correct translation. In the rest of the
present study, I assume that it is correct. The reader may want to note
that this is a premise in some of my arguments to follow.

Finally, I must note that Gordis believes that there is an additional reference to the wicked in this first speech. God asks Job:

Have you entered the storehouses of snow,
  have you seen the storehouses of the hail,
which I have reserved for the time of trouble,
  for the day of battle and war?

                                        (38:22–23, Gordis)

Gordis comments:

> The snow and the hail are both kept stored for the day of
> retribution against evil-doers (Isa. 28:17; Ezek. 13:13), against
> crops (Ex. 9:22–26; Hag. 2:17), or in battle (Jos. 10:11) . . . . The
> poet is not glorifying the powers of nature *per se*; they are instru-
> ments for a moral purpose.[15]

Gordis makes a narrower and a broader claim here. The narrower one
is that this passage implies retribution against evil-doers; the broader
one is that overall the glorification of nature in the theophany is "for a
moral purpose." Eventually we will consider the broader issue; here
let us look at the narrower claim. If Gordis is right, we have two
references to the wicked, not one, in the Lord's first speech. I have
discounted the reference in the dawn passage; it is, or at least should
be, a reference to the stars, not to the wicked. Many scholars believe
that the text is mistranslated to refer to the wicked. But the present
passage does not even arguably mention the wicked; Gordis sees an
overtone of such a reference because in other O.T. texts God uses hail
(not snow) to punish or to warn the Hebrews or their enemies. I would
argue here as above: the contribution that hail makes to the solution
of the problem of evil is ridiculously flimsy. I can well imagine the
sarcasm of the Job of the dialogues if the friends had claimed that the
wicked were punished by hail, and the innocent and upright were
saved from hail. (In his wilder moments, he would argue that exactly
the opposite is the case.) And I do not think we want God to offer
arguments even weaker than those the friends offered. So, as before,
I prefer to ignore this possible reference; after all, the text does not
mention the wicked here—and it should not even hint at their destruction by hail. If other scriptures connect hail with retribution, that
does not entail that the Book of Job does; this book is, after all, a
critique of the doctrine of retribution. We must be very cautious about
introducing into it overtones from books that it criticizes.

Chapter 9

The Lord's Second Speech

The second speech from the whirlwind can be divided readily into three parts: there is an introduction; then an account of Behemoth, "the first of the works [or ways] of God" (40:19); and finally a poem in praise of Leviathan: "Upon earth there is not his like"[1] (41:33).

The first two of these three parts are nearly equal in length, running to nine and ten verses, respectively; but the Leviathan section, containing thirty-four verses, is almost twice as long as the other two combined. One would expect it, therefore, to be the most important of the three. As we have already seen, the Lord's first speech is a highly well-organized and coherent address; we have not yet interpreted its relevance to the main issues of the book, but in itself it seems a carefully wrought work of art. The Leviathan section, as I shall explain in the present chapter, fits fairly nicely onto the picture drawn in the first speech; the other two sections do not fit so smoothly. It is difficult to determine the pertinence of parts of them, given the context provided by the first speech (and continued in the Leviathan passage); and some parts of them actually seem to clash with the overall context. All of this leads me to think it best to begin our discussion of the second speech with the long Leviathan passage, even though it comes last in our text.

Leviathan

The identity of Leviathan has been debated throughout the recorded history of Joban interpretation. He is obviously some kind of well-protected animal, or animal-like being; man's weapons, and man's implements for capturing wild creatures, are useless against him. He has a "double coat of mail" (41:13), "rows of shields" (41:15), "immovable" "folds of . . . flesh" (41:23) that make him secure against man's attacks. He is frightening in appearance, and it is quite dangerous for a man "to stir him up" (41:10), to approach him to do battle, or to attempt to capture him. He seems at least partly aquatic: he cannot be drawn out "with a fishhook" (41:1) or filled "with fishing spears" (41:7); he "spreads himself . . . on the mire" (41:30); and he has some connection with the ocean:

> He makes the deep boil like a pot;
>   he makes the sea like a pot of ointment.
> Behind him he leaves a shining wake;
>   one would think the deep to be hoary.
>
> (41:31–32)

Apparently he has a formidable mouth: "Who can open the doors of his face? Round about his teeth is terror." (41:14) Startlingly: he is fire-breathing:

> His sneezings flash forth light,
>   and his eyes are like the eyelids of the dawn.
> Out of his mouth go flaming torches;
>   sparks of fire leap forth.
> Out of his nostrils comes forth smoke,
>   as from a boiling pot and burning rushes.
> His breath kindles coals,
>   and a flame comes forth from his mouth.
>
> (41:18–21)

Now given that passage, especially considering its length, one might say it is obvious what Leviathan is: he is a fire-breathing dragon, or at least a fire-breathing dragon-like creature. This is what I would say. This makes him quite different, in our eyes anyway, from the creatures in the Lord's first speech: they were all actual beings, whereas Leviathan is a being of story and song only. This does not entail that the poet knew that. He could have heard of such a creature and believed that it existed. But he could not have seen one. So even for our poet, then, there is probably a difference between Leviathan and (at least most of) the creatures in the first speech: he had seen them, or at least he could have; whereas he either invented, or utilized stories of, Leviathan. Or to put the contrast in the least controversial way: the poet probably had seen the first-speech creatures doing much of what he said they do; if he had seen an animal he calls Leviathan, he had not seen it breathing fire, smoke, and sparks. He is embellishing, or trusting reports of others, or else speaking metaphorically about fearsome and vaporous breathing.

Beyond this—that Leviathan is or seems fire-breathing—what kind of beast is he? From the time of early rabbinic sources, many readers have interpreted him as a kind of whale, or as some other sea monster or great fish, because of his powers in the sea; but much (though not all) of his description fits the crocodile quite well, and a majority of scholars today, probably, stress the crocodilian motifs— which are even more obvious to the learned than to the general reader. Now whether he be whalelike, crocodilian, or of some third character, evidence has been accumulating that this Leviathan has cosmic and mythic overtones. There are a few O.T. passages and some apocalyptic and rabbinic sources in which Leviathan seems to be some great cosmic force, and his flesh is promised as food for the righteous in Paradise. In Ugaritic literature, a marine monster Lotan (*ltn*) and perhaps some related monsters, some with more than one head, are slain or conquered by Baal and/or his companion 'Anat. In the Ugaritic literature this Lotan is a serpent or is associated with one, and there are biblical and rabbinic sources that make Leviathan or his associate a serpent. So, for many commentators, Leviathan in the Book of Job should be understood as some larger-than-life beast, perhaps a serpent, having powers like those of a cosmic principle, not an animal on the scale of ordinary crocodiles or whales. This cosmopolitan book echoes non-Hebraic Near Eastern myths in many ways; the Leviathan passage may involve allusions to, or appropriations of, more such myths.

The poet, of course, is fundamentally a monotheist: there is one God, one Lord. Some commentators argue that this tells against the cosmic and mythic interpretation of Leviathan, but their argument seems to me confused. The partly-parallel Behemoth passage opens with the line, "Behold, Behemoth, which I made as I made you . . . " (40:15). If God made the related creature, it is natural to assume that He made Leviathan. There is no hint in the Leviathan passage that Leviathan is uncreated. And the poet's silence should be decisive. Not only does it count in favor of the analogy with Behemoth, but also we must remember the overall context: this whole book is monotheistic, and the Hebrew tradition it enters is monotheistic. To present Leviathan as uncreated, primordial, would involve jolts to both contexts. Certainly, in these contexts, without careful, elaborate preparation of the reader, the poet could not present a being other than God as uncreated. This is not a point one can just assume or assert *en passant*. So Leviathan, it is virtually certain, is meant to be a creature, a creation of God, not a primordial rival God has to subdue or come to terms with. But none of this entails that Leviathan is just another "flesh-and-blood," natural-scale creature. Creature, yes; ordinary, maybe not. After all, the Lord's first speech tells of some creatures with cosmic power; the sea, for example, was created—it "burst forth from the womb" (38:8)—and yet it is an awesome power. I see nothing impossible in the view that Leviathan has cosmic powers, like Lotan in the Ugaritic myths, while still one of God's marvelous creations. However, in the text at our disposal, the poet does not unambiguously attribute to him any such power. Most of his powers seem *local*, so to speak, connected with his immediate body—his ability to repel spears and to shatter bronze, for example. An exception might be his ability to make "the deep boil like a pot," to make "the sea like a pot of ointment" (41:31); but that could well mean that he makes the sea *in his vicinity* "boil" in this way. So, though his fire and smoke are the stuff of myth, and though his description may be influenced by international cosmogonic myths, there is not much in our text to suggest more than an ordinary (!) fire-breathing sea serpent. If I had to bet, and the poet could somehow reappear to resolve the issue, that is how I would wager.

Now, regardless of all this: what is the point about Leviathan?

What is the message? And how does it fit the message of the first speech? It seems clear that we have here a continuation of the basic line of argument in the Lord's first speech. There we saw many creatures God provided for who had no connection with the life of man. Two were described that enjoyed man's warfare. One mentioned could not be tamed. Now we have one who cannot be tamed and whom we had better not *try* to put to our uses. "Will you play with him as with a bird, or will you put him on leash for your maidens?" (41:5) This creature, unlike the wild ox (in what is said of him), is dangerous to any man who tries to do battle with him, a creature we cannot even see without terror. This is the point, whether we interpret Leviathan as a whale, a crocodile, or a serpent, cosmic or localized. This point is certainly true of the great serpents of the myths; and, with pardonable exaggeration, it is true of the crocodile (which was sometimes captured) and the whale (which, with modern equipment, can be killed, and sometimes even captured). It would be easy to think of any one of these as armored, untamable, and most dangerous to do battle with.

The discussion of Leviathan fits nicely into, extends neatly, the first speech; the theme of man's puniness in the world is continued and heightened. We do not have here any explicit emphasis on man's ignorance; Job is not asked whether he understands various powers of Leviathan. But we do have the weakness theme; and now the theme is heightened into terror. And we still have the prominent note of praise, of celebration. In the first speech, the wonders of creation are presented as glorious, awesome, making the morning stars rejoice; now this frightening creature is presented as glorious. The praise, the celebration of creation is continued into celebration of the terrifying.

Perhaps we should note that there is a formal or poetic difference between the account of Leviathan and the accounts of the creatures in the first speech: Leviathan gets a much, much longer treatment than any creature got in that other speech. He gets a full thirty-four verses (all of chap. 41), whereas in the first speech only the horse got as many as seven verses, and most creatures had to make do with a three- or four-verse treatment, often sharing their few verses with some other creatures. The Lord seems to warm to His subject when

He gets to Leviathan, and so to go on at length; whereas in the first speech He seemed to have innumerable creatures He might consider and so did not grant any of them much more than brief mention. Perhaps this difference weighs in favor of interpreting Leviathan as a cosmic force rather than as a localized monster; in the first speech even the sea received only a four-verse treatment (38:8–11), with a half-verse echo a little later (38:16). Perhaps this difference counts against the authenticity of the Leviathan passage; but the content certainly fits well onto the first speech, and we know that our poet employs many, many styles before he finishes this complex book. So I do not think we can draw either of these conclusions with any security. It may simply be that with well-known creatures a brief reference is sufficient, but with a creature outside the experience of the reader, or of the average reader, it was necessary to be explicit about whatever details one wanted to emphasize. If one wishes to terrify with an unknown (and unknowable?) monster, one must paint an elaborate picture.

It is never said that Leviathan is malicious, or a man-hater, or that he is bent on destruction to man or to things generally. He is said to be dangerous to one who "dares to stir him up" (41:10), who would "lay hands on him" (41:8); he is "without fear" (41:33). It is not said that he goes about doing harm. On the other hand, it is not said that he doesn't. Gordis says that the poet "underscores the paradox that these massive beasts [Leviathan and Behemoth], ordinarily peaceful, are possessed of extraordinary strength."[2] This is false. The poet does not say, much less underscore the statement, that Leviathan is "ordinarily peaceful"; maybe the crocodile (which is what Leviathan is, Gordis thinks) is ordinarily peaceful, but our poet does not say so. Furthermore, the poet does not simply say that Leviathan has strength, though he does say that; he says that Leviathan is dangerous to those who lay hands on him.

Gordis plays down the dangerousness of Leviathan in another way. After saying that Behemoth is "liable to capture by hunters (v. 24)"—which, again, is not what the text says—Gordis adds, "Leviathan too may be taken captive (vv. 25ff) and be eaten by mortals (vv. 30,31)."[3] But the clear implication of the text is that he cannot be captured: "Indeed, he who attacks him loses all hope, since at the mere sight of him, he is laid low" (41:9, Gordis translation). We could say, I suppose, that the poet is being hyperbolic, and means only that very few (not *no one*) can capture Leviathan; and if Leviathan really is the crocodile, as Gordis thinks, that claim is true. But even so, the poet's point is not, as Gordis says, that "Leviathan . . . may be taken captive"; what the poet says or seems to imply is just the opposite. Nor does the passage say that Leviathan may be "eaten by mortals (vv. 30,31)." The verses Gordis refers to here say, in his own translation,

> Will traders bargain over him?
>   Will they divide him up among merchants?
> Can you fill his skin with harpoons
>   or his head with fishing spears?
>
> (40:30–31)

And if there is any doubt that the intended answer is no, the next verse removes it:

> If you dare lay your hand upon him,
>   not long will you remember the battle!
>
> (40:32, Gordis)

Gordis is far off base, and curiously so, in these remarks. Probably he was thinking of what is true of the crocodile rather than what the poet actually says about Leviathan. But the upshot is that Gordis stresses man's power over Leviathan, whereas our poet stresses the creature's power, and the danger he presents to men who attack him—and the poet celebrates that dangerous power.

Gordis makes another mistake about (Behemoth and) Leviathan. He says that in God's first speech, creatures alien to man are nevertheless beautiful to God; whereas in the second speech the monsters are "unbeautiful,"[4] "repulsive"[5] to man, and that part of the point has to do with this: that God creates and sees as beautiful not only the nonhuman (first speech) but even what is "repulsive" to man (second speech). But again there is nothing in the text that says that Leviathan (or Behemoth) is unbeautiful or ugly. Gordis may find the crocodile unbeautiful; but the poet does not say that Leviathan is. The point in this passage is not that what is ugly to us is beautiful to God, but the passage does involve a contrast. The contrast point is that what is terrible to us, what we cannot do battle with, is still wonderful, majestic, good in the eyes of God—and in the eyes of the poet, for his language remains language of celebration. Gordis sees that the poem is a poem of praise, just as God's first speech was;[6] and he sees that the first speech's creatures are easier (for us) to celebrate than Leviathan and Behemoth are. In the second speech the poet has given the screw another turn. But the problem with Leviathan is not that he is ugly; it is that he is awesomely dangerous (to those who approach him). (I do not quarrel so much with Gordis's related notion, his idea that these creatures are beautiful to God. They are praised by some standards, one would think; though, as I argued in the preceding chapter, it is not very clear what the standards are. One might claim—but I have not seen this argued—that whereas in the first speech we have the beautiful [in part], in the second speech we have the sublime—in which terror may be an ingredient, as some aestheticians have said.)

I have not yet discussed in detail the two verses 41:10–11. In one translation, what they say about Leviathan is the following:

> No one is foolhardy enough to stir him up,
>   for who can stand up to him in battle?
> Who has confronted him and emerged unscathed?
>   Under all the heavens—no one!
>
>   (Gordis)

If this is a correct reading, then these verses fit smoothly into the rest of the Leviathan passage, and into the pair of speeches from the whirlwind. However, some scholars translate them very differently, so that instead of continuing the theme of danger, these verses explain the relevance of that theme and of the whole theophany. In the next chapter I will consider that other interpretation and comment on the explanation it offers. But if we take them in the sense the quoted translation provides, then they require no special comment: they say basically what the rest of the Leviathan section says—that Leviathan's awesome powers make him secure against human attack, and even dangerous. And this fits smoothly onto the message of man's smallness in the Lord's first speech.

Behemoth

Controversies about the identity of Behemoth parallel those concerning Leviathan. Many interpreters believe that Behemoth is some more-than-natural monster, perhaps a great bull familiar to the poet from stories in other Near Eastern traditions and echoed in some Hebrew sources. Others think he is some natural beast—perhaps the hippopotamus, as many today believe; some have thought he was the elephant; and the New English Bible, following G. R. Driver, regards him as the crocodile (and Leviathan as the whale).[7]

The details of this controversy are interesting, but I do not see that much hangs upon it for the interpretation of the Lord's speeches. *If* Behemoth was familiar from myths, and if he had some cosmic role, it is quite clear that the poet has Hebraicized him—or at least made him a creature of Yahweh. As we have noted, in 40:15 God says pointedly, "Behold, Behemoth, which I made as I made you. . . ." (The Septuagint omitted "which I made," but the meter and syntax seem to call for it.) And then 40:19 says "He is the first of the works/ways of God," which probably repeats the idea that God created him. Given that Behemoth is some sort of creature—in the root sense of that word—he could be either a creature with local power, that is, a powerful "natural" creature like a hippopotamus, or a being with cosmic powers, a primary force of some sort in the universe. The poet could move, I think, quite easily from the ordinary animals of the first speech to grander animals, or even to super-animals, in the second speech.[8] The scholars that I have read do not reveal any importance that the issue of Behemoth's identity has for the interpretation of the speech; or, when they try to, they mistakenly assume that if the beast is of more than ordinary power he must not be a creature—which is clearly false.[9]

As I have noted, the section on Behemoth precedes the one on Leviathan in our text; I discuss them in the reverse order because the Leviathan passage is longer and its points clearer. Some scholars doubt the authenticity of the whole second speech; some accept the

Leviathan passage but reject the section on Behemoth. Terrien, expressing this latter view, writes:

> In all probability this section (40:15–24) has been added to the original text by a wise man of the Joban school who interpreted Leviathan . . . as a crocodile of mythical proportion and thought that its Egyptian counterpart, the mythical hippopotamus, was unfortunately absent. Both figures are found side by side or fighting together on many frescoes of the Ancient Egyptian Empire . . . and even on the late tomb of Petosiris. The Behemoth passage is not written in the style of questions as is the first discourse . . . or the section on Leviathan. . . . It will be observed also that vs. 19 refers to "God" in the third person—a strange procedure in the mouth of Yahweh.[10]

This view may be correct. I prefer, however, not to start with an assumption that the passage has been "added." Let us take the text as the tradition has delivered it to us and see what it seems to say.

Now we cannot proceed without any assumptions at all; our explications here occur within a context of our other work. We have already examined the first speech, and also the Leviathan passage. We found in both a clear message. Given that background, if we now ask whether the Behemoth section has a similar meaning, we might well conclude that it does. Clearly Behemoth is being celebrated, as Leviathan was, and as the other creatures were; his power is one focus of emphasis; and perhaps, like Leviathan, he is praised in terms of his power to withstand human attack. The passage ends with a verse (40:24) that probably strikes that note: "Can one take him with hooks, or pierce his nose with a snare?"—in the RSV interpretation. (The language here, quite obscure, is suggestive of, and perhaps is borrowed from, that in the Leviathan section.) It may be, also, that a verse (40:19) in the middle of the passage sounds this theme: "He is the first of the works [or ways] of God; let him who made him bring near his sword!"—again, if the RSV is roughly right; and the preceding verses (16–18) praise the creature's strength, and a later verse (23) praises his calm, his confidence, in troubled water. So maybe the poet intended a message similar to the one about Leviathan. That is: if we know already what the Leviathan message is, and then look for that in the Behemoth passage, perhaps we can find it there.

However, this power/danger interpretation of these verses is not without its internal difficulties; the texts cited do not unambiguously support it. Moreover, parts of the Behemoth section seem to strike other notes—and notes whose relevance is not obvious. Let us consider these two problems in that order.

Consider the first text cited above, 40:24, which seems to ask about Behemoth the sort of question asked about Leviathan: "Can one take him by hooks, or pierce his nose with a snare?" Now the Hebrew actually speaks puzzlingly of capturing Behemoth "in/by/with his eyes," not "by hooks"—and various suggestions, many quite interesting, have been made about how one might take a creature in or by or with his eyes, or what the Hebrew might have been before some possible corruption occurred. Another source of difficulty is that the first half of the verse in Hebrew is short, and the verb lacks a subject, so scholars typically insert what they think is missing—perhaps "Who is he (that)?" or something similar. But this means that they read into the passage the sort of question we find in the Leviathan section; they do not quite *find* that sort of question there. Still, the line does speak of *taking or capturing* the creature, so we have some parallel with the Leviathan section in any case. And what else could the question be? The scholars seem to vary only on the details of their conjectures; they agree on the overall thrust of the verse. So perhaps we should regard the general point here as secure—though we might be more radical and reject the whole verse, as the Septuagint editors did—"as out of place and a partial duplication of vss. 26 and 28," Pope conjectures.[11]

The other verse I quoted, in support of the power/danger interpretation, was 40:19: "He is the first of the works [or ways] of God; let him who made him bring near his sword!" The first half of the verse is somewhat unusual, with its "ways of God"; but Proverbs 8:22 and other sources use *ways* to refer to wisdom as the first of the creations of God. So the scholars usually think "ways of God" means "works of God"; a first of God's *ways* might be a "primordial production" (Pope)—or *first* might mean *best*, perhaps hyperbolically.[12] The second half of the verse, more important to our problem, is quite difficult to read—"corrupt beyond recognition," Terrien says;[13] but scholars generally agree it has something to do with bringing a sword near. So we have some evidence, but not evidence as good as we would like, that Behemoth is described, like Leviathan, as dangerous to do battle with. It is odd that the point is not any clearer here, when it is *so* clear about Leviathan; but at least the point *seems* to be made.

There are another two verses that praise the beast for his strength:

His bones are tubes of bronze,
  his limbs like bars of iron.

(40:18)

Behold, if the river is turbulent he is not frightened;
  he is confident though Jordan rushes against his mouth.

(40:23)

Now these two verses do not mention his use of his strength in battle, to defend himself and to present danger to his (human) attackers; but perhaps we can take it for granted that such strength could be used in battle. In that case, again, we have evidence for interpreting the Behemoth section as we interpreted the one on Leviathan. I conclude, not so confidently as I would like, that this is the correct interpretation, or rather, part of the correct interpretation. There is a power progression here, from the first-speech creatures, through Behemoth, up to Leviathan—meant to terrify.

The other problem in the Behemoth passage is that it seems to introduce additional themes, themes we do not see in the Leviathan passage, which are not easy to connect with the well-integrated set of motifs in the first speech and the Leviathan sequel.

For one thing, there is a strong sexual theme in the Behemoth passage—so strong that some medieval Christians thought of Behemoth as a symbol of sexuality or sensuality. The text reads:

See, his strength is in his loins
  and his power in the muscles of his belly.
He can stiffen his tail like a cedar,
  and the sinews of his thighs are knit together.

(40:16–17, Gordis)

Though the translations do not usually reveal this clearly, three of the terms in 40:17 are sexual in meaning or implication, and one (maybe two) in 40:16. Leviathan's sexual power is not mentioned at all, nor is that of any creature in the first speech (though most of the animals there are described as having offspring); but the sexual theme, concerning Behemoth, is about as clear as the danger theme—maybe clearer. *Why?*

The creatures in the first speech, and Leviathan in the second, are discussed in their relationship, or lack of relationship, to Job, or to man: what does Job know of, what can Job control of, what did Job give to these creatures? But the sexual power of Behemoth seems described for its own sake. Does the poet (perhaps a later poet) intend some connection, or lack of connection, with us? If so, what might it be?

The sexual power of the beast would not seem to have any relation to his danger to a man who attacked him—unless we think that the beast might defend himself by raping his adversary, or might defend himself and then rape his adversary. Is this an extravagant hypothesis? Perhaps. But maybe not; some scholars believe that Job's own speeches make two references to homosexual rape. Job says to his comforters,

> Have pity on me, have pity on me, O you my friends,
>   for the hand of God has touched me!
> Why do you, like God, pursue me?
>   What are you not *satisfied with my flesh?*
>
> (19:21–22)

In his final set of oaths, Job tells of wrongs that deserve punishment and calls for a trial on those kinds of charges:

> If I rejoiced at my foe's misfortune,
> Exulted when trouble befell him,
> Or let my mouth offend,
> Seeking his life with a curse;
> If males of my household ever said,
> "O that we might *sate ourselves with his flesh.*"
>
> (31:29–31, Pope)

These expressions about being sated with someone's flesh are subject to numerous interpretations, but some scholars make them refer to rape. If we interpret them this way, then the meaning must be meta-

phorical in the first passage. No one has *literally* raped the suffering
Job. Moreover, "To *eat* the flesh of" someone means to slander or
calumniate in Akkadian, Aramaic, and Arabic; also sometimes in Hebrew (Ps. 27:2; Dan. 3:8, 6:24).[14] Pope claims that "there is no reference here to calumny,"[15] but the friends do slander Job throughout
their speeches, so a reference here to calumny would certainly fit the
context. Still, Job is given to violent rhetoric; the Job we know from
the dialogues would be capable of saying that he was being raped.

In the second passage, Job could be denying that he ever allowed
his men to even think of sexually abusing their enemies; such abuse
was known widely in the ancient Near East, and Job has just denied
that he took other extreme ways of dealing with his "foe"—why not
deny this way? Earlier in this speech Job has mentioned sexual sins—
once (31:9–10) and maybe twice (31:1); so it makes sense for him to
mention another. But other readings are possible; in particular, v. 31
may go with the following verse, not with the preceding verses about
the enemy; if so, perhaps Job is offering to suffer if his men have not
fed the guest:

> if the men of my tent have not said,
>   "Who is there that has not been filled with his meat?"
> (the sojourner has not lodged in the street;
>   I have opened my doors to the wayfarer). . . .
>
>   (31:31–32)

So there *may* be references to sexual abuse in these speeches, but
there may not be. If there are, then it would be less extravagant to
suppose that sexual vigor in the Behemoth passage is meant to have
threatening overtones, that the danger in the Leviathan passage is
partly paralleled by sexual danger in the Behemoth passage. This
would be more plausible if we knew that, apart from our book, the
hippopotamus or the great bull of the myths (or whatever Behemoth
is) had a reputation for rape in the lore of the ancients.

Of course, we can think of sexual power as a function of, and
sign of, power generally; there is some biological warrant for this
view, and it is a view accepted in many cultures, including those of
the ancient Near East. So maybe Behemoth's sexual power is men-

tioned as a sign of his general power; and maybe his power is important in any human attempt to capture or to fight with him. In either of these ways we could connect the sexual vigor theme with the danger theme, thereby solving two problems at once: we would have strengthened the modest evidence that the danger theme is present in the Behemoth section, as it is in the Leviathan section, and we would have made sense of the new note of sexual vigor, which, as presented in the text, is not brought into connection with the basic question behind all the theophany—viz., What is man in relation to the nonhuman cosmos?

So far we have attempted to interpret Behemoth's sexuality in the context of combat because the Leviathan section focused on battle, and some of the Behemoth section involves battle imagery. We might give up this direction of our effort. Perhaps the beast's sexuality is insisted upon for other reasons. Perhaps it is implied that Behemoth has a sexual power greater than man's, and that Job's sexual inferiority is humbling to him in its own right, not because it is a sign of inferiority in battle. This interpretation would make both beasts in the second speech superior to man, but not just in Leviathan's way; Behemoth would be superior in sexual and in other powers, with only a hint of danger; Leviathan would be dangerous. But in the praise of Behemoth for his sexual powers it is not *said* that those powers exceed man's; this would be a point that we have to read in, to make tighter an analogy with Leviathan.

We could give up even more of the influence of the Leviathan section and say that the sexual magnificence of Behemoth is insisted upon for its own sake, not in any comparison with man. We know that the first speech celebrates God's creation, and has the morning stars rejoicing at its wonders. Leviathan and Behemoth are celebrated in the second speech. Maybe Behemoth is celebrated for his own sake, and maybe his sexuality is part of his grandeur; perhaps the speech simply praises him for what he is, or for what he was thought to be in the lore of the time. And if the Lord's speeches are to catalog the great powers of nature, and to celebrate them, then sexuality belongs somewhere in the list; perhaps this is the poet's way of introducing it. He has already had God mention the processes of gestation and birth (39:1–3); the sea is portrayed as a newborn babe, bursting from the womb; and most of the first-speech creatures are described with their young, usually caring for their young. The sexual drive itself certainly deserves some notice. We cannot come to terms with nature without taking account of that.

Perhaps in one of these various ways we can make sense of the sexual theme in the Behemoth section. Clearly it could fit into the second speech in more than one way; it is also clear that whoever wrote this or left it in the form we have it has not given us enough clues to be certain how it was intended to fit—at least if we rely only upon the theophany itself. Later (in chap. 12) I will return to questions about sexuality in the book, and there I will make a few more suggestions. The issue, I believe, is more important than most scholars seem to see.

Before we leave Behemoth, however, we should note a few other problems in this section. In the very first verse (40:15), it is said that Behemoth "eats grass like an ox." Now perhaps he does; perhaps he is some natural creature who eats grass like an ox, or perhaps he is a legendary beast who is reputed to eat grass like an ox. But why does the poet mention this? Why is this important, here? We have a problem analogous to that with the sexual theme; it is hard to see the relevance of what is said here. Perhaps this passage counts in favor of the mythological interpretation of Behemoth; in a fragmentary Ugaritic text designated *BH*, Baal and El are associated with some bull-like, buffalo-like monsters called *Eaters* and *Devourers*;[16] also, as Pope notes,

> The Bull of Heaven in the Gilgamesh Epic apparently had a mammoth appetite and intake, for when Ishtar browbeat her father Anu into creating the monster Anu warned that there would be seven years of food shortage . . . (ANET, p. 85, l. 101–10).[17]

So perhaps this line is the poet's way of saying that Behemoth is the great ox-like Grass Eater (of the myths). In that case, the line does not so much make a point about Behemoth as identify him, so Job will be clear which Behemoth is being described: the Great Eater. Otherwise, it is not obvious why the poet thought Behemoth's diet, or eating habits, deserved mention in the theophany.

Another troubling verse is 40:20; in this case, the meaning of the first stich is unclear, and so is the relevance of either half of the verse. The RSV translates:

> For the mountains yield food for him
> where all the wild beasts play.

The rendering of the second stich is secure. In 20a, *produce* would be a little closer to the difficult text than *food*, and Gordis suggests *tribute*; Pope rejects this whole approach and argues for "The beasts of the steppe relax." If the reference really is to *food*, then 20a might imply whatever 15a implies—perhaps that Behemoth is the Great Eater, who needs the produce of whole mountains to satisfy him. Gordis, fighting the mythological interpretation of Behemoth, suggests that the tribute might be the water from the mountains, in which the beasts play (20b)—and we are about to have other references to water (40:21–23).[18]

In other readings, the first stich refers to the beasts as singing or relaxing, as the second stich clearly refers to their playing. But what is the point of that? Why does the poet mention that? In "Home on the Range," the deer and the antelope play, and the buffalo roam; all these details help to explain what kind of home the singer wants, and what he finds so attractive about that home. But why should the theophany pay that kind of attention to this peaceful scene? One would expect Behemoth, not his habitat, to be celebrated here—if *where* (or *there*) in 20b does refer to his habitat. *There* sometimes refers to the land of death (see 1:21; 3:17); the Septuagint rendered the verse, "And having gone to a steep mountain, he causes joy to the quadrupeds in Tartarus."[19] Clearly the meaning and the import of this verse are insecure.

The next two verses are also uncertain in import. A plausible translation is:

> Under the lotus plants he lies,
> in the covert of the reeds and in the marsh.
> For his shade the lotus trees cover him;
> the willows of the brook surround him.

> (40:21–22)

The great problem here, I think, is again one of relevance: Why does the poet mention all this? Why is all this supposed to be important? An answer is not easy to come by. But we might try to link these verses to the following one, which says something like this:

> Behold, if the river is turbulent he is not frightened;
>   he is confident though Jordan rushes against his mouth.
>
> (40:23)

Then perhaps the set of three verses all speak of the beast's calm, and hence of his power, as clearly v. 23 does. That would connect all three with the power theme, and hence perhaps with the danger theme, in the Leviathan passage.

Gordis notes that Behemoth is presented as "peacefully" lying in the rushes, and claims that "The poet then underscores the paradox that these massive beasts, ordinarily peaceful, are possessed of extraordinary strength. . . ."[20] As I have noted, I do not see this paradox in the Leviathan section, but it could be seen here in the Behemoth section. It is not terribly paradoxical, however. Why shouldn't Behemoth be peaceful? He has nothing to fear. His bones are like bronze, his limbs like iron (40:18); he is confident in the river (40:23); no one, or no one but his maker, can do battle with him (40:19) or capture him (40:24).

Let us sum up. The Behemoth section includes ten verses (40:15–24). Two of those verses (19, 24) seem to echo directly the power/danger theme in the Leviathan section. One other verse (18) praises the beast's strength, another (23) probably does, and two others (21–22) may be associated with this latter verse. The other clear theme is sexual: two verses (16–17) refer to the sexual power of Behemoth, which may be related to his general power or may be important in some independent way. One verse (15) introduces the creature, probably says (as does 19) that he *is* a creature, and perhaps identifies him as the Eater—or, if not, says something about his eating habits. Another half-verse (20a) may also speak of his prodigious eating. The remaining half-verse (at least) tells of beasts at play, a subject whose relevance is not obvious. The Behemoth section, I conclude, can be interpreted as belonging in the theophany, especially in its power-and-danger progression, but the "fit" is not totally smooth.

The interrelated points in God's first speech clearly belong together; the Leviathan section, though far longer than one would expect, after the survey of creation in the first speech, nevertheless has a point, a unity, and a clear relevance to the first speech; but we have to work hard to get all of the Behemoth section to fit this context. I conclude that we have somewhat weaker authorial powers here, or ill-advised editorial revisions, or textual corruptions.

Introduction to the Speech

Finally, by a reverse ordering, we arrive at the introduction to the second speech, the shortest (by one verse) of the speech's three parts, and the part (in my judgment) hardest to fit into the rest of the theophany. The full text of it runs somewhat as follows:

> 40:6 Then the Lord [Yahweh] answered Job out of
>   whirlwind:
>   7   "Gird up your loins like a man;
>   I will question you, and you declare to Me.
>   8   Will you deny My justice,
>   put Me in the wrong, so that you may be in the right?
>   9   Have you an arm like God;
>   can you thunder with a voice like His?
>   10   Deck yourself with majesty and dignity;
>   clothe yourself with glory and splendor.
>   11   Scatter forth your furious wrath;
>   look on every proud one and humble him.
>   12   Look on every proud one and bring him low,
>   and tread down the wicked where they stand.
>   13   Bury them all in the dust;
>   press their faces into the grave.
>   14   Then I will acknowledge to you that [or: Then
>   I will render thee homage?]
>   your own right hand can give you victory."

This is my own version of this text, based on several translations. What the text says is not much in doubt; the real problems with it have to do with its import. We will need to consider it almost verse by verse.

The first verse (40:6) is almost identical with 38:1, the verse that introduced the Lord's first speech: "Then the Lord answered Job out of the whirlwind." The only difference is that the article before *whirlwind* (or *storm*) is absent from the second occurrence. One could argue that the line fits the first speech better than the second, since there is much more of Job to be answered when the first speech begins, and since it is hardly necessary to say again "out of [the] whirlwind," because the source of the Lord's voice had already been identified. One might well argue for shortening this line to "Then the Lord answered Job," or just "Then the Lord answered"—which would parallel some of the introductions to speeches in the dialogues. But many of those introductions were more wordy than necessary, too; Eliphaz, Bildad, and Zophar are introduced every single time as "the Temanite," "the Shuhite," and "the Naamathite"—though we know their tribes of origin already, from the prologue (2:11). The poet repeats all sorts of things. So we cannot conclude from the repetition of this one line that the poet did not write it twice or, from the beginning, write two distinct speeches of the Lord.

Verse 40:7 is absolutely identical with the earlier 38:3. So the three-verse introduction to the first speech has been shortened to two verses here. The poet omits "Who is this that darkens counsel by words without knowledge?" (38:2)—though Job himself repeats this, quotes it apparently, in his response to the second speech (42:3a), and he repeats it there almost verbatim. This means that we have, perhaps, another suggestion that the Lord's speeches were originally only one speech, but again the evidence is not terribly strong. The verse which *is* repeated in the two introductions—"Gird up your loins like a man; I will question you, and you declare to Me" (38:3; 40:7)—like 40:6, could be argued to fit the first speech somewhat better than the second, in this case because the first speech is more thoroughly of an interrogative nature than the second. But again, there are plenty of questions in the second speech—except in the Behemoth section, which has only one (40:24)—and the speech *opens* with questions. And Job seems to quote the second half of this verse in his response to the second speech (42:4b). So again we have some evidence, but not overwhelming evidence, that something is amiss in the content or organization when we reach the second speech.

Next, verse 40:8 asks, "Will you deny My justice, put Me in the wrong, so that you may be in the right?" This was not part of the opening to the first speech, and Job does not quote it in his response, but I agree with most commentators in thinking that it is an important verse. We need to be careful, however, in deciding *how* it is important.

Job has, repeatedly, denied God's justice, reduced to nought His righteousness, put God in the wrong (as various translators formulate 8a)—"in his own case and even in the world at large," as Pope says.[21] This is the heart of the Joban blasphemy, his "cursing of God" that we have discussed above. Clearly Job has done this, and this is what outraged his friends and the young Elihu, so it is clearly appropriate for God to take notice of it.

The part of the verse calling for more controversial comment is 8b:

> Will you condemn me that you may be justified?
>   (RSV; see also Pope)
> . . . wilt thou condemn me, that thou mayest be righteous?
>   (KJV)
> . . . put Me in the wrong, so that you may be in the right?
>   (Gordis)

What are we to make of *that*, or *so that*, in this line? I look for a reading that best fits the rest of the book. Now Job *is* justified, righteous, or in the right—except for his blasphemy, and the state of heart that leads to it. He has been singled out in the prologue as the rarest of the rare, God's exemplary servant, blameless and upright, fearing God and turning away from evil. So in my judgment the line must mean, "Will you conclude from your own righteousness [and your suffering] that I am *not* righteous? Will you let being in the right, being justified [and yet suffering], lead you to condemn Me, to say that I am in the wrong?"

This half of the verse seems to involve the kind of either/or that we discussed in chapter 4 above; if Job is innocent, then God is not, for God is persecuting an innocent man. This is the logic behind the Joban blasphemy, a logic Elihu grasped: "He was angry at Job because he justified himself *rather than* God" (32:2). Now God seems angry for the same reason, though His anger is expressed ironically, in a question. For Job to justify himself, see himself as righteous, as in the right, he must condemn God, "put [God] in the wrong"—*given the background theology*, given the assumptions operating throughout the dialogues. In those dialogues, God has an obligation to protect the righteous; Job is not being protected; but Job himself (he says, and the prologue says) is righteous; so God himself is in the wrong. Part b of verse 8, then, in this interpretation, nicely summarizes the bind that Job's righteousness and traditional theology have produced: together they entail blasphemous claims about God. God is angry with Job for putting Him in the wrong, for blaspheming, for cursing Him—which the Satan had predicted Job would do.

Some commentators see more than this in this line, but I think they are mistaken. God asks, ". . . wilt thou condemn me, *that* thou mayest be righteous?" (KJV)—and some commentators read *that* (or *so that*) as *purposive*, and then interpret Job's purpose as an effort to achieve or to maintain righteousness or even self-righteousness. At least, I think this is what Terrien means. Terrien speaks here of "an existential blow which will strike at the hero's spirit rather than at his mind."[22] Now I agree that a spiritual problem is present here—viz., bitterness—but the hero's mind, the theology in his mind, has created that bitterness. *That* spiritual problem can only be attacked by undermining the intellectual error giving rise to it, and the Lord's speeches address the relevant issues of the mind. Terrien says that Job chose "to declare God to be wrong in order to maintain his own self-righteousness."[23] This suggests that Job was self-righteous, wanted to remain so, and condemned God as a means of achieving that end. But the text does not mention *self*-righteousness, which, I assume, is a kind of sin; a self-righteous person is, perhaps, one who is *not* righteous but who poses as righteous, probably to evade his real responsibilities. He is the man who tithes mint, and dill, and cumin, and who neglects the weightier matters of the law, like justice and mercy. Or he is the man who takes pride in his righteousness, so that he forgets how much his righteousness is not his own doing, and then lords it over his less fortunate neighbors. In the verse at hand,

God speaks of Job's being righteous, not of his being self-righteous. And if Job, or the prologue, can be trusted, Job *is* righteous; he is one of the rarest, an exemplary "servant" of God. He is not merely posing as righteous; his condemnation of God arises out of his real righteousness, his recognition of it, and out of the background theology, which holds that a righteous God would not allow a righteous man to suffer anything like the torments of Job. The problem lies in the theology, not in Job's failure to be righteous. And nothing in either of God's speeches mentions any sin of Job's, except the sin of his talk. Job blasphemes; but that sin arises out of his (otherwise) sinlessness, not out of an effort to pose as what he is not, as the self-righteous man does.

Nor should we speak here, as Terrien does, of "justification by faith."[24] Job is justified by his deeds, by his "works," and by the devotion to God that lies behind those deeds. We have examined in chapter 3 what this book means when it describes Job as God's "servant," "blameless and upright," "doing good and avoiding evil." Clearly it is abnormally difficult to be as blameless as Job—otherwise why should God single him out for such praise, in the prologue?— but Job *is* the exceptional man. We must not think of Job as a Pauline sinner, trying in vain to live up to the impossible demands of the law. Job *has* lived up to the demands of righteousness. Now he has a spiritual problem; the background theology leads him to curse God. And so he sins. But his sin is a sin against God, not against righteousness. In this respect, Terrien is right: the sin of Job is "not a sin of the horizontal type produced by ethical crimes directed against men, but a sin of the vertical type by which a creature dares . . . to indict his creator."[25] We need to be careful, however, about what this means and what it does not mean.

So far we have looked at the first three verses of the introduction to the second speech. There is nothing in them that is surprising; they are more or less what the dialogues, and the introduction to the first speech, would have led us to expect here, and they are truly introductory. With the next four verses, however, God begins the challenge proper: He asks Job about his power. As we have seen, Job's weakness is one of the emphases of the first speech. The first two of these next verses are fairly similar, in content at least, to some of the first speech verses:

Have you an arm like God;
   Can you thunder with a voice like his?
Deck yourself with majesty and dignity;
   Clothe yourself with glory and splendor.

(40:9–10)

It is perhaps a little odd that the Lord speaks of himself in the third person, in 40:9; but if we take *thunder* to be the key word here, and so interpret all of this as asking about the lightning and the thunder—as most commentators read it—then these verses resemble some of the weather verses in the first speech. The thunder and lightning are *God's* "voice" and "clothing," not Job's. So these verses continue the power/weakness theme of the first speech—as the Leviathan section surely, and the Behemoth section partly, will continue it and heighten it into terror. But the language here suggests more than power: God clothes Himself with *majesty, dignity* or *grandeur* (Pope), *glory, splendor*. This is one of those passages that tempt one to agree with Otto's followers: here we *do* seem to have something numinous, something awesome, something specially attracting and forbidding. Clearly God *is* asking about Job's power—for He asks "can you?" And He speaks of His own "arm," which is regularly a symbol of His power.[26] But the power He asks about is spoken of indirectly, for the most part, and in especially regal, glorious language.

If we look again at these two verses, we see that the question form of verse 9 changed very smoothly to a challenge form in verse 10. The challenge continues in verses 11–13, but the content now is puzzling:

Scatter forth your furious wrath;
   look on every proud one and humble him.
Look on every proud one and bring him low,
   and tread down the wicked where they stand.
Bury them all in the dust;
   press their faces into the grave.

(40:11–13, my version)

Here we find another, the last, of those rare spots in the theophany in which the wicked may be mentioned, in the text as we have it. God challenges Job to crush the wicked, in verse 12b; and if the "proud one" in 11b and 12a (Gordis reads "proud sinner" and "arrogant one") is the same wicked one, then the three verses involve a sustained challenge to Job to crush the wicked.

There are three problems with this three-verse passage. One is the difficulty we noted earlier in other contexts: the overall strategy in the theophany *seems* to be to ignore the problem of evil in human life; but here it appears (briefly). We still have in the theophany absolutely no reference to the righteous, and no reference to the innocent weak; but God does seem to refer here to the wicked, the third group whose fate was debated by Job and the comforters. A second problem is that the logic of the challenge shifts radically in these three lines. Throughout the first speech God reports elaborately on what He does, and contrasts His power (and knowledge, and omnipresence) with Job's weakness. But here He asks Job about power that even God does not clearly have. In the first speech, Job did not set limits to the sea, whereas God did. But here: Job cannot crush all the wicked, either—but can God? *Does* He? If we say yes, to gain parallelism with the other challenges, we have to assume that the comforters are right and Job wrong in the dialogues. Why should we assume that? There is nothing else in the theophany to suggest that; Job seems to most readers to have won the debate with the comforters; and in the epilogue God says that Job has spoken truly, and the friends have not. Surely the plainest reading of this book is that the wicked are *not* always crushed—and that the weak and the righteous are not always protected. So here in the present verses, 40:11–13, God is challenging Job to do something even God does not do. This is not like any of the preceding challenges. Why does the logic shift here?

(There is the same shift of logic between verses 9–10 and 11–13. Rhetorically the two sets of verses seem to belong together; the poet moves smoothly from the question-challenge in vv. 9–10 to the challenge in vv. 11–13. But v. 9 asks Job whether he has "an arm *like* God," whether Job can thunder "with a voice *like* His." Both questions suggest that we are about to contrast what God can do or does with what Job cannot do. But we don't continue that contrast; instead, we wind up with no contrast—or no clear one. We ask about things Job cannot do—but then God does not do them either.)

This brings us to the last verse (40:14) of the introduction, which presents itself as a conclusion from the preceding:

> Then I too will render you homage [will praise you],
>   when your right hand will have brought you victory.
>
> (Gordis)

Or:

> Then I will acknowledge to you
> that your own right hand can save you.
>
> (Pope)

Or:

> This will I also acknowledge to you
>   that your own right hand can give you victory.
>
> (RSV)

The scholars[27] convince me that the *praise* (or *render homage*) version of stich a is better; God says, then, that He will honor Job when Job has crushed all the wicked. Gordis believes[28] that here God "tacitly concedes" that He Himself has not done that. This may be correct; but if it is, it reinforces my point that the logic of this challenge is quite different from the logic of the other challenges. And it seems—to me at least—strange (and artistically weak) for God to slip in such a monumental concession so quickly, when the rest of the theophany ignores, or virtually ignores, the issue, leaving Job and the reader to gather the import indirectly. There is nothing in principle wrong with changing the logic within the theophany; but I think that a major change would best be introduced carefully, with a full development. I do not see such a development here.

The second half of the verse refers to Job's saving himself, or bringing victory, with his own right hand. If the line only sums up the preceding, then the victory in question must be the complete crushing of the wicked (see vv. 11–13). Gordis thinks that the "victory or salvation referred to in our passage would be Job's success in obliterating all evil and 'instituting perfect justice in the world' (Kraeling)."[29] If that is the meaning, then the line generalizes from the preceding; that kind of victory would involve, I think, the crushing of the wicked, and also the protection of the innocent and the upright, all of whom figured in the debate in the dialogue.

Some scholars see overtones here that are more nearly Christian. Pope says, "If Job could do what he charges God has neglected to do, then he could save himself."[30] And Terrien, who claims that this verse "may be considered as the pivot of the book," comments on the second stich:

> Man is aping God whenever he attempts to save himself, i.e., whenever he tries to be a man without God (cf. Gen. 3:5; cf. also Mark 15:31), the master of his own destiny, the author and fulfiller of his own salvation. The poet is anticipating here the N.T. analysis of justification by works.[31]

This strikes me as an odd reading of the line. Of course, there are richer and poorer "anticipations" of doctrines, and in at least a thin sense the Book of Job does anticipate much of the New Testament. It certainly is related to N.T. themes. But some of Terrien's language is counter-intuitive; if it is apt, it is apt in an obscure way that needs explication. I have argued that Job is one of the most God-obsessed, God-intoxicated men in the Bible; it is odd to be told that Job tries "to be a man without God"! And Job does not seem to want to "save himself"; he wants God to save him, as (he thinks) God is supposed to save the upright. And the problem in this book, after all, is not how to justify Job; Job is just, righteous, upright, from the opening of the prologue; the problem is how to reconcile Job's justification with his wretched fate—and how to deal with the other violations of what Job and his comforters expect from God.

So I prefer a reading of this verse that is less Christian and more dependent upon the text before us for its inspiration. I am attracted, therefore, to the readings I suggested earlier, so that the "salva-tion"/victory here is a victory over the wicked, or perhaps a victory over all injustice. But even with one of these readings, the line is odd: For why should the Lord suggest that Job himself could accomplish such a victory with his own "right hand"? Job never suggests that he himself could institute "perfect justice" in the world, or in his own case; his bitterness is over God's failure to institute justice. He believes that God is supposed to save men like Job, and to crush the wicked, and to protect the innocent. He stresses throughout his own weakness. Why does God now emphasize what Job had already doubted, or suggest that Job cannot do for himself what Job never said he could do for himself?

As I read the book, then, most of the introduction to the second speech fits poorly into the context provided by the prologue, the dialogues, and the first speech. The first verses, as we have seen, fit perhaps too well; it is strange that God should shift later to questions about Job's power over the wicked. All sorts of puzzles are presented by that maneuver. I am inclined to believe again that the power of authorship is lower here—either in the original poet himself, or in a transition to a new author. We saw above some grounds, though weak grounds, for doubting that two of the first three lines were originally part of the book; now we have modest grounds for thinking the book is weakened by the last five lines.

To conclude: the Leviathan section in the second speech is different in length, and in form somewhat, from what appears in the first speech; but its content is clear and fits and nicely expands the content of the first speech. The rest of the second speech presents a good many puzzles. The introduction to it and the Behemoth speech fit loosely into the overall context, but not so well as we would like, and their meanings are less than perfectly clear. In the concluding chapters of the book I will emphasize the parts of the theophany that clearly belong together—the whole of the first speech and the Leviathan section. I will have a little more to say about Behemoth; but for the most part I will play down the two short parts of the second speech that fit this context less well. Sound scholarly method, I think, requires that our interpretations be built mainly on what is elaborately developed and clear, and that we rely as little as possible upon short passages whose meaning or relevance is uncertain.

*The Meaning of
the Book of Job*

Chapter 10

Job's Ignorance—and Knowledge

As we have seen, one theme of the Lord's first speech is Job's igno-rance: God repeatedly asks Job questions he cannot answer. "Tell me, if you know"—but Job does not know. After the first speech, Job lays his hand on his mouth (40:4) and resolves to talk no further (40:5). After the second speech, he confesses that he had uttered "what I did not understand, things too wonderful for me, which I did not know" (42:3). Clearly a message of the theophany, as we can read it on the pages before us, and as Job himself hears it, is that Job—indeed, *man*—is profoundly ignorant. The response, the proper response, is intellectual humility and silence. The most plausible interpretation of the whole book is that the theophany is normative in it; surely we must take God's own words more seriously than the words of mere men. If so, then the message of the whole book is deeply skeptical, agnostic, suspicious of man's claims to insight into the highest mysteries.

This conclusion lets the oddly-located chapter 28, the hymn to wisdom, at least belong in spirit to the book as a whole:

> But where shall wisdom be found?
>   And where is the place of understanding?
> Man does not know the way to it,
>   and it is not found in the land of the living.
>
> (28:12–13)

173

If *wisdom* or *understanding* in this passage (not later, in 28:28) refers to a deep grasp of the structure of God's creation, then the agnosticism expressed here is consonant with that demanded by the Lord's first speech and confessed by Job in his responses. There are mysteries whereof one cannot speak, and thereof one should be silent.

I noted that the Lord's speeches are startling, that their relevance is sometimes hard to uncover; but it is clear that the theme of man's ignorance *is* relevant to the central problems of the book. One of those problems is, of course, the problem of evil in human life. Job and the comforters present different views of how God orders things. The friends believe in the orthodox doctrine; Job denies it, and even mouths the conviction that God hates his creatures, mocks the innocent, and "beams on" the wicked. But the theophany lets us see that Job does not understand the structure, or even many of the details, of God's natural order; we can conclude that he does not deeply understand what is involved in God's dealings with human life. These things must remain, in significant ways, mysteries to Job; they will require of him much silence. But Job's ignorance is not peculiar to Job; no man could answer the Lord's questions from the whirlwind. As I argued early in this essay, I conclude that the prologue also speaks of matters too wonderful; its author cannot understand God's ways deeply enough to know why Job suffered his famous torments. If we take the prologue as descriptive, it is accurate: Job did suffer and in his suffering he was sorely tried. But if we take the prologue as explanatory—"Job suffered because God and a Satan figure wanted to test him"—then the prologue's author, like Job and his friends, speaks of mysteries beyond human grasp, and he too should repent. The theophany undermines the prologue, if we interpret the prologue in that spirit. Or we might just say that the theophany undermines that interpretation of the prologue.

Herbert Speigelberg, the distinguished historian of the phenomenological movement, tells a relevant story of a conversation with Albert Schweitzer. Schweitzer, after his return to Strasburg from his first sojourn in Lamberene toward the end of the First World War, had resumed temporarily his position as vicar at the St. Nicholas Church. At that time Spiegelberg, then a young candidate for Confirmation, had expressed hesitation about taking the required vows because of his belief that evils such as war were irreconcilable with

God's moral perfection. Schweitzer's reply was simply: the problem of evil is insoluble.[1] This view is close to that of the Book of Job. The problem of evil is beyond human solution; we do not see deeply enough to know how or why God deals as He does with the innocent, the upright, or the wicked. These things are beyond our ken.

Besides the problem of evil, the other main issue in the book is the nature of a high worship of God, of high religion, of what it is to "fear" God or to be His "servant" in the most profound way. In the prologue Job is portrayed as a supremely moral man—"on earth there is no one like him" in his moral excellence—and yet the Satan and God agree that he may nevertheless not be all that God requires of His servants. The Satan says that Job, though God-fearing, would be a blasphemer, would curse God to His face, in times of deep trouble. I have argued—treading a path few scholars have even considered[2] — that the Satan was right, that Job was the kind of man who would curse God in adversity. Job's moral bitterness did express itself in blasphemous accusations against God. I have also argued that a pre-supposition of such blasphemy was a certain kind of theology, or a certain conception of how God ought to deal with His creation. It is, in a sense, the theology of Job that produces the blasphemy. But the voice from the whirlwind undermines that theology, by letting Job see that man does not understand the cosmos or God's relations to it. Job needs to give up his presumption. But this means that the theme of man's ignorance is relevant also to the second main issue of the book, the question of how a man should be related to his God. Job begins with a perfect or near-perfect moral character, but also with a sense that God should enforce the Moral World Order; he ends with intellectual humility. Job, like his friends, thought he knew what the world order should be, and that means how God should be dealing with His creatures; when Job saw that the world was not as it "should be," he cursed the God Who, he thought, neglected or persecuted His creatures so "unjustly." Job needed to give up the arrogance, the intellectual pretension, that led to such curses. There is nothing in the Book of Job to suggest that the Lord does not require of men the kind of uprightness, of moral responsibility, Job displays; there is no question here whether a high religion involves morality. But it also involves intellectual humility, and hence silence, about some deep mysteries concerning God and His relation to His creations.

Many people, from before the time of this book until now, believe that God requires upright conduct of us, and that God Himself is required to—and does—deal "uprightly" with us: and that means, to many people, that God must uphold the Moral World Order, in which the innocent and righteous are protected and the wicked are punished—always. The Book of Job denies that such a belief belongs in a high religion, in proper "fear of God," in the right way of being God's "servant." It rejects the claim that God preserves, or has obligations to preserve, the Moral World Order. In that sense, Robert Frost was right in his sequel to the book, when he had God say to Job:

> My thanks are to you for releasing me
> From moral bondage to the human race.
> The only free will at first was man's,
> Who could do good or evil as he chose.
> I had no choice but I must follow him
> With forfeits and rewards he understood—
> Unless I liked to suffer loss of worship.
> I had to prosper good and punish evil.
> You changed all that. You set me free to reign.
> You are the Emancipator of your God. . . .[3]

Frost goes farther than the Book of Job, and probably contradicts it, if he suggests here that what God chooses to do is in fact "evil"; but the basic point is indeed Joban: a high religion does not believe in the Moral World Order, with God as its guarantor. That conception belongs to a religion of people with a hedge about them, fortunate people, whose prosperity blinds them to the truth. In times of adversity such people curse God to His face; they judge Him and find Him wanting. The Book of Job holds that no man understands the structure of the world or God's relationship to it well enough to render such a judgment.

In our own day the Holocaust, Hitler's effort to exterminate the Jews, has been to many people the outstanding refutation of claims that the Moral World Order still stands. It is surprising that a new refutation was needed; honest and compassionate men have always known that such an Order was a lie, and we have even had genocidal campaigns before. But the "belief in a just world" dies hard. So the

efficiency and monumental character of Hitler's atrocities have created a theological crisis for some people. Some have adopted a stance
rather like that of Job before his humbling; they have cursed God, in
the sense in which I use the expression here. They have put God on
the stand, read the charges of injustice, and found him accountable
and guilty.[4] And many individuals in every age, suffering from clear
"injustice" in their own case or in that of their near and dear, rise up
to condemn the God Who, they think, should have ordered the world
differently. The Book of Job rejects the presupposition of such curses.
We do not understand enough to know what God should have done
about our illnesses, our accidents, or small- or large-scale criminality.
"Surely God could have, and should have, killed Hitler as an infant."
Surely? Do we really know what alterations in the structure of things
would have been required? And do we really know that the altered
structure would not be worse? Do we really understand what the
philosopher John Rawls calls "the ethics of creation," defined as "the
reflections an omniscient deity might entertain in determining which
is the best of all possible worlds"? Of course not. And that is a major
message of the theophany. "Certainly we have a natural religious
interest in the ethics of creation," Rawls admits; but then he adds, in
his modest way, "But it would appear to outrun human comprehension."[5] Of course. Much of Judaism has long adopted a Joban view of
such issues, and much of Christianity has, too. Jesus saw the rain
falling on the just and on the unjust, and believed that the Father sent
the sun to shine on both. *Why* does God do this? That would seem to
outrun human comprehension.

Nevertheless, there is a tension between the theophany and the
opening of the epilogue. As I have emphasized, a central message of
the Lord's speeches is that Job is ignorant; and that means that man is
ignorant. But Job is not totally ignorant; and the epilogue makes a
distinction—in Job's favor—between what he has said and what the
friends have said. The Lord says twice to the comforters, ". . . you
have not spoken of me what is right, as my servant Job has" (42:7;
42:8). This praise of Job's words comes as such a shock to some
interpreters that they suggest that the epilogue may have once be-
longed to an earlier story in which the friends, rather than Job, spoke
against God's reign, while Job remained modest and accepting, as he
had been in the prologue. Perhaps there was such a story; much

about this book is obscure. But we do not need that supposition to make sense of the apparent reversal between the theophany and Job's response, on the one hand, and the epilogue, on the other hand. As the book stands now, the Lord both humbles Job (in the theophany) and praises him (in the epilogue), both rejects and accepts what Job has said of Him. All we really need here, to make the book as it stands consistent, is a plausible *distinction*, so that we can argue that God rejects some and accepts some of what Job has said. What God rejects of Job's words must be connected with Job's inescapably human "smallness," since that is what is emphasized in the theophany; what God accepts must have to do with the contrast between Job's words and the friends', since the epilogue draws a distinction there.

Given these constraints, it is clear in the main, I think, how we must distinguish between what the Lord accepts of Job's words and what He rejects. God directs Job's attention to natural forces, and to His own activity in such forces, which man cannot understand. The point must be that the same or analogous forces are at work in the human sphere, too, the sphere about which Job and the friends debated, and so man cannot understand the deep workings of things there, either. In that sense Job and the friends may have been equally wrong; if they all attempted to delineate the fundamental ways of God with man, then they all needed to repent. Job did not know that God mocked the innocent or beamed on the wicked; this sort of talk, "tasteless" and blasphemous, arises out of a presumption that we can advance beyond what we see of life into its deep structures and its Creator's intent. But these things are beyond us. Job needed to be humbled; but so did the friends, if they thought *they* understood how God worked with such fundamental forces.

To give the friends their due, they may not have thought their knowledge extended so far. Throughout their speeches, their emphasis, at least, is not on "deep" claims, or speculations about God's motives; what they stress is their "empirical" claims that the wicked fall, and the upright and innocent are protected. They say that they and their fathers have seen this to be so. They do not attempt deep insight nearly as much as Job does; they remain on (what they take to be) the surface of life, reporting (what they take to be) the different fates of different kinds of men. Eliphaz may attempt something deeper, something more "theological," when he asks, "Can a man be

profitable to God? . . . Is it any pleasure to the Almighty if you are
righteous . . . ?" (22:2–3) Perhaps there are a few overtones elsewhere which could suggest an effort to penetrate deep mysteries; but
mostly the friends remain on the surface, and I believe that Zophar
speaks in the spirit of all of them when he asks Job:

> Can you find out the deep things of God?
>   Can you find out the limit of the Almighty?
> It is higher than heaven—what can you do?
>   Deeper than Sheol—what can you know?
>
> (11:7–8)

And Eliphaz asks Job:

> . . . were you brought forth before the hills?
> Have you listened in the council of God?
>
> (15:7–8)

Granted, in the contexts, the point may be that Job knows less than
the friends, who speak with the authority of tradition; still, there
seem overtones of the fundamental humility required later by the
theophany. The friends really do not push below the surface of life as
much as Job tries to do. In this sense, Job needs the humbling of the
theophany more than the friends do.

The problem with the friends is not so much that they try to
uncover what lies beneath the surface of life; their problem is that
they get the surface wrong. This seems to me the most plausible
reading of God's rebuke of them. They "have not spoken of me what
is right, as my servant Job has." What they say of the safety of the
innocent and the wretchedness of the wicked is not true; the world is
not so neatly, so "justly," arranged. Job is right, against the friends;
his own case, and other cases he cites, show that the orthodox doctrine is false. True, the Lord says that the friends have not spoken "*of
me*" what is right; He does not say that they have not spoken "of the
innocent, of the righteous, and of the wicked" what is right. But we
remember that after the theophany, from which Job sees God's
creatures—His seas, His birds and beasts—Job says "my eye sees
thee" (42:5). As we have noticed, there is no sharp line, in this book,

between God and the world; the epistemological distinction to draw is not between knowledge of the world and knowledge of God, but between surface knowledge and deep knowledge. The orthodox doctrine is patently false; it belies what is open on the surface of life. Job speaks truly of this surface; the friends do not.

There are points, as we have seen, at which Job seems to reverse the orthodox doctrine, to say that the opposite of it is true—that the wicked uniformly prosper, and the innocent uniformly are cut off. I do not think that the author means us to think that God endorses that extreme view. The most plausible reading here, I think, is a negative one: the friends' doctrine is not true; Job speaks truly in rejecting that falsification of experience.

However, the fact that Job has spoken truly here, even in this limited sense, is important. The theophany and Job's response are so heavily weighted toward intellectual humility that one might be tempted to conclude that the author thought we knew nothing. This would be a major misinterpretation. The book regularly presupposes important human knowledge.

From God's rebuke of the friends it is clear that Job did speak truly of something; he did know much of what the human scene is like. This presupposes at least two kinds of knowledge. The debate between Job and the friends concerns the fates of the weak, the upright, and the wicked. To speak truly about some of these cases, as he does, Job must be able to see, to know, who the weak, the upright, and the wicked are; and he must be able to see whether they are prospering or suffering. He does not, of course, have to know everything about everyone on earth; but the book is not fundamentally agnostic about what constitutes righteousness or wickedness or innocence or about what constitutes happy or unhappy circumstances in life. The friends lie about how those things are connected; or they fail to see what Job sees; but these things are there to be seen by men of intellectual integrity. Job himself may suggest at one point that much of this is so obvious that even the beasts, the birds, the plants, and the fish know these things (12:7–8); *that* of course would be another of Job's exaggerations; but it would be an exaggeration of what the author regards as the truth. Our author does not have such a subtle view of righteousness (as Kant did) that no one can know for sure who men of good will are; it assumes throughout that we know what the moral demands upon us are and that we can know, within reason of course, who are living up to those demands. Nor does it have such a subtle view of prosperity (as the Stoics did) that it is difficult to be sure who is leading a happy life and who an unhappy one; the criteria of happiness in this work are commonsensical and easy to apply. And so we can know, in principle and largely in practice, who about us are suffering or prospering in ways they do not deserve. Indeed, some of our moral obligations presuppose such knowledge; for we have duties to the undeservedly weak, and some of us have duties to prevent or remedy undeserved prosperity. The book never suggests any agnosticism about any of this.

On the basis of confidence in our knowledge of these things, the Book of Job rejects the friends' belief in the Moral World Order. We *can* know that the orthodox doctrine is false. Intellectual humility need not extend to toleration of that known falsification. Its defenders must repent, and God forgives them only when Job—who had spoken truly of its falsity—prays for them. As we discussed that doctrine above, we saw many difficulties in it; and it is quite clear that the author of the dialogues was aware of at least many of those difficulties. The most plausible reading, then, of the rebuke of the friends, is that it is a rejection of the orthodox doctrine of the Moral World Order. The world is more complex than that doctrine holds, and we can see that it is. A part of Job's greatness is his intellectual integrity in this matter; he sees what they all should see, and, having seen, he affirms what he sees in the face of the pressures of friends and tradition. The romantics' admiration for the rebellious Job is not misplaced in this respect.

It may be worth noting that the discussion of the problem of evil in the book is conducted in terms of what might be called extreme alternatives. The orthodox doctrine, even with the subtleties we noted, involving variations and delays of God's action, remains an extreme doctrine. It really implies that in the long run wickedness never pays, righteousness is always rewarded, and innocence is always protected. The view Job was tempted to express is equally extreme: that wickedness always pays, that righteousness is never rewarded, and that innocence always founders. It appears to me that the book rejects both of these extremes; and the major motif of man's ignorance may suggest that it is beyond human ability to construct any *other* view we can know to be true. But, as we have seen, the book presupposes that we can know a good deal about the moral character of human beings and about how they fare in the world—on a case-by-case basis, so to speak. That is how Job can reject his friends' orthodoxy. So even though the book chastizes Job and his friends, and never suggests alternatives to their views, one could argue that what the author presupposes about our knowledge of these matters provides bases for more moderate claims made with less dogmatic self-confidence. Though the righteous do not always prosper, nevertheless there may be characteristic rewards of righteousness, and it may be that what we can know of life suffices to let us discover some of the principles involved. We can see, this book assumes, who is unjust and who is suffering; maybe we can see enough of such matters to begin to explore how injustice hurts the unjust—and how it does not. The book would seem to reject views comparable in their sweeping character to orthodoxy and its extreme reversal; but we do know some things about human life, and maybe what we know is sufficient to lay the ground for less pretentious, more piecemeal investigations of the issues involved in the debate between Job and his friends. The book does not explicitly make such a suggestion. But, by attributing to Job both a grand ignorance and a modest knowledge, it opens the door to an approach to its issues that would duly acknowledge both sides of its characterization of the power of our minds. I believe, then, that there could be explanations of the role of morality in human life that would not incur the censure of the voice from the whirlwind.

As we have seen, Job has a genuine knowledge of morality and of happiness which the book never challenges. The book also never challenges man's remarkable technological knowledge, which is praised at such length in the hymn to wisdom:

> Surely there is a mine for silver,
>   and a place for gold which they refine.
> Iron is taken out of the earth,
>   and copper is smelted from the ore.
> Men put an end to darkness,
>   and search out to the farthest bound
>   the ore in gloom and deep darkness.
> They open shafts in a valley away from where men live;

they are forgotten by travelers,
they hang afar from men, they swing to and fro.
As for the earth, out of it comes bread;
  but underneath it is turned up as by fire.
Its stones are the place of sapphires,
  and it has dust of gold.
That path no bird of prey knows,
  and the falcon's eye has not seen it.
The proud beasts have not trodden it;
  the lion has not passed over it.
Man puts his hand to the flinty rock,
  and overturns mountains by the roots.
He cuts out channels in the rocks,
  and his eye sees every precious thing.
He binds up the streams so that they do not trickle,
  and the thing that is hid he brings forth to light.

(28:1–11)

Now this praise of man's technology is a preamble to a humbling of man:

But where shall wisdom be found?
  And where is the place of understanding?

(28:12)

And the way this wisdom is described makes it seem a grasp of fundamental principles of the cosmos, like those referred to in the theophany:

God understands the way to it,
  and he knows its place.
For he looks to the ends of the earth,
  and sees everything under the heavens.
When he gave to the wind its weight,
  and meted out the waters by measure;
when he made a decree for the rain,
  and a way for the lightning of the thunder;
then he saw it and declared it. . . .

(28:23–27)

So the point of view here is probably the same as that in the theophany. But this makes clear that the intellectual humility required by the theophany does not extend to technological issues; though man does not understand the deep mysteries of God's cosmos, man *does* have the knowledge to dam up rivers, "overturn mountains," mine the earth, and smelt and refine the ore he digs. The hymn to wisdom contains and emphasizes a sharp contrast between a kind of knowledge man has—technological, I think it right to call it—and a deep wisdom that we do not have. Though this hymn hardly fits its position in the book, the scholars can believe that the main poet wrote it; and I see nothing in the book that throws into doubt the sharp contrast it presents. So I think we should interpret the agnosticism of the book as restricted in this second way. Our ignorance does not extend to technology, any more than it extends to moral demands or the elements of happiness. Human beings understand *these* things.

So the book takes its place in a long line of works in religion and philosophy that have developed an appreciation for man's reason alongside doubts about his capacity for very deep or ultimate truths, adopting a partial but not total scepticism. The ancient, medieval, and modern worlds all produced such works, and the contemporary scene still includes articulations of this view. The Book of Job clearly belongs in the company of the most distinguished of such works and shares family resemblances with many of them. I will not attempt a comparison of its version of partial scepticism with all the other versions; that project would take us too far afield. But we need to ask at least how science fits into the Joban scheme of things. Does the Joban scepticism exclude the possibility of science?

Of course the ancient world did not have much of what the modern world calls science, and there is no word in this book corresponding to our word. But we get clues of two sorts, which perhaps point in opposing directions.

As we have seen, the book regards man's technology as awesome; but for the modern mind, technology and science are intimately related. So the book might be interpreted as admitting and admiring whatever of science is presupposed in man's impressive technology. The book would then assume a distinction between the secrets science can unlock and deeper secrets of nature and of God which man's reason can never penetrate. The Joban agnosticism would extend to the latter but not the former. I think that this would be a reasonable interpretation of the spirit of the book.

On the other hand, one might note other clues in the theophany; for these suggest that much of what we call science is impossible. In His first speech from the whirlwind, God asks Job about many features of the natural order, and He suggests that Job cannot know such things. But a modern man might well retort that some of these are things we do know, today; and that others are things we can know, in principle—relying upon the methods and results of modern science. Naturally, the author drew the line as we would not, excluding from human grasp some of what we now know to be scientifically ascertainable (even if not directly *observable*, which we understand to be too restrictive a criterion).

Consider God's question for Job:

Do you know when the mountain goats bring forth?

(39:1a)

Now I confess that I am as ignorant as Job about this; but I have no doubt that many people, including, I hope, some of my readers, know quite well (what kinds of mountain goats there are and) when they bring forth their young. I do not doubt at all that some naturalists even "*observe* the calving of the hinds" (39:1b). God asks Job:

Where is the way to the dwelling of light,
    and where is the place of darkness . . . [?]

(38:19)

A contemporary Job might well reply that he knows a great deal (not all!) about light and darkness, including the fact they do not literally have "dwellings." Similarly:

Have you entered the storehouses of the snow,
    or have you seen the storehouses of the hail . . . [?]

(38:22)

Many a schoolchild today can explain a good deal about the formation (not literally the "storehouses") of snow and hail. In sum:

There is much about nature actually known today that must have seemed impenetrable mysteries at the time of the Book of Job. Perhaps much else, not known today, will be known in the future. So our author probably did not rightly guess quite how much human reason would uncover of the surface of nature and of her fairly deep structure. Science can do more than this book suggests; in this sense, the Joban scepticism is exaggerated, and a contemporary revision of our book would have to grant a larger role to what we today call science.

Nevertheless, it seems clear that a revision of the Joban view could be formulated in terms the late twentieth century would find plausible. Though we know far more than was known when that book was composed, we still deal with great mysteries; and many minds are still convinced that some of the most fundamental truths will forever remain dark for human reason. Perhaps we will never know the most basic principles governing the cosmos; or perhaps if we learn what they are, we will never understand why those are the principles, and not others that seem equally possible, or why they are displayed in *this* world, rather than in some other, equally possible world; or perhaps we will never understand quite how the cosmos is related to its Creator, what His role is in its origin, structure, operation, and destiny—if any of these concepts really apply to God-and-His-World. I will not attempt here to work out in detail or to argue for the version of a Joban vision I consider most defensible today; such a project would be out of place here. (Indeed, the author of the Book of Job did not work out or argue for his version very elaborately!) All I want to say here is that the general structure of the Joban vision, with its dichotomy between what we can know and what we cannot know, is certainly still available for use in our contemporary setting, and plausible variants readily suggest themselves; the mere fact that some of the theophany's *details* seem out of date does not really do heavy damage to the basic Joban vision. That vision, to summarize, does not question human knowledge of morality, of happiness, of technology, or of science, but does deny that we can know the deepest truths of nature or of God—and on this double foundation it affirms the reality of genuine evil, of "injustice," in the world, and denies that we can explain why God allows such evil.

All of this presupposes that the Joban ignorance has another limit: it does not extend to ignorance about these truths themselves. Job, at the end, is not ignorant of his own ignorance; nor is he ignorant of God's reality, or of God's creation and rule of the cosmos, or of the fact that God has spoken to him from the whirlwind. For our purposes here, the most important point is that though the Book of Job stresses our ignorance about the intimacies of God's rule, it never questions a great deal of theology; presumably, it never questions what it regards as essential in the theology of a high religion. The theophany takes for granted that God is real and rules—indeed, so does the whole book, the prologue, the dialogues, the epilogue. If we distinguish between God's creating and His ruling—and it is not clear that we should—then perhaps the prologue and epilogue mention only His ruling, whereas Job mentions, and the voice from the whirlwind stresses, also His creating. But throughout the book, including the normative theophany, no one doubts the reality of God or of His rule. Job's final silence, then, does not extend to these fundamentals of religion. Nor does it extend, apparently, so far as to eliminate his awareness that God has spoken to him from the whirlwind, that God is the source of his new sense of his place in the universe. The author must intend—or presuppose—a distinction between these theological grasps of reality, and the deeper kinds that the theophany excludes. So there is a humanly appropriate theology, and there are presumptuous theologies. Only a presumptuous one would try to explain the role of evil in God's rule. The next two chapters will explore two more elements in the kind of theology the book permits.

Much of the permitted, appropriate theology seems to be simply assumed in the book, not argued for or revealed in an act of grace. From the start of the book to the end, the reality of God and of His rule are taken for granted, by the narrator and by all of the characters. There is never any occasion to *introduce* such fundamental considerations, or to ask why one might believe in them. So I see no way of knowing how the author would have answered anyone who doubted them. Are these articles of faith? Revealed truths? Truths of reason? Reports of experience? This sort of issue is simply not addressed in this book. (No book addresses every issue.)

On the other hand, Job's awareness of his deep ignorance is something he comes to as a result of the theophany; so the status of that awareness is easier to investigate. His final insights come from

God's Own activity, so we might understand them as gifts, products of Grace, not as the discoveries of his unaided reason. However, Job's ignorance is revealed to him slowly, cumulatively, *argumentatively*, we might even say; God presents piece after piece of evidence; bit by bit He builds up the case for Job's "smallness" of mind. And God's "argument" operates mainly with questions; it is almost as if Job were being taught Socratically, by being "reminded" of something he already, in some sense, had known and forgotten. So though there is an activity of God in the revelation, God seems to make an appeal to Job's mind. The whole book might have been called *The Education of Job*; here we have something like a teaching situation, in which the pupil really sees for himself what the evidence implies, though he would not have seen it had it not been for the questions, and the riveting sarcasm, of the Teacher.

Job's response may be relevant: "I had heard of thee by the hearing of the ear, but now my eye sees thee." One balks at the letter of this reponse: after all, Job did not literally see God, he heard His voice from the whirlwind. But the hearing/seeing metaphor surely implies a vital contrast between an abstract, perhaps unreliable, report, and a concrete, fully appreciated, veridical grasp—and the book does involve such a contrast. After all, if we state Job's insight abstractly, he learns nothing new from the theophany. He always knew that he was small, of little account; very early in the dialogues he complained of the unseemliness of God's persecution of so trivial a creature as Job. But he had not fully seen, not fully appreciated, that smallness; and so he had not appreciated its implications for the presumption behind his bitterness and blasphemy. From the theophany he fully grasps his smallness and he understands what it implies. In this chapter we have looked at one implication—Job's ignorance; in the next we will explore his weakness.

Chapter 11

Job's Weakness

Job's ignorance, as we have seen, is a major theme of the theophany, and hence of the whole book. His weakness is another emphasis.

In the first speech from the whirlwind, God repeatedly asks Job about his power. Sometimes, the point seems to be that Job does not have the primordial, structural power that God Himself has over the cosmos:

> Can you bind the chains of the Pleiades,
>   or loose the cords of Orion?
> Can you lead forth the Mazzaroth in their season,
>   or can you guide the Bear with its children?
>
> (38:31–32)
>
> Can you lift up your voice to the clouds,
>   that a flood of waters may cover you?
> Can you send forth lightnings . . . ?
>
> (38:34–35)

Such passages, which ask what Job can do, are not sharply contrasted with surrounding passages, which ask what Job *does* or *did*. So asking whether Job *can* bind the Pleiades is probably not very different from asking whether he did or does bind the Pleiades. The intended answer, of course, is that God, not Job, did this/does this/can do this.

God, not Job, structures and rules and can structure and rule the elements of nature.

One set of God's questions, however, seems different:

> Is the wild ox willing to serve you?
>   Will he spend the night at your crib?
> Can you bind him in the furrow with ropes,
>   or will he harrow the valleys after you?
>
> (39:9–10)

We have no notion of how to even attempt command of the stars or the weather; but we do tame some animals and get them to do our bidding. What God implies here is that even in a domain where we have some power over His creatures, that power is limited. Many of the creatures resist our will.

In the second speech, God focuses almost exclusively on that sort of weakness—the limits of our power over the other animate creatures. As we have seen, the opening of that speech sounds a thunder theme (40:9), matching the lightning theme in the first speech (38:35); and there is a brief, puzzling reference to the proud and wicked (40:11–13); but most of the speech is given over to praise of Leviathan and Behemoth. Almost all of the long Leviathan section and much of the Behemoth section are clearly concerned with man's weakness in dealing with such creatures. They are untamable, as the wild ox was; and it is actually dangerous for a man to attempt to capture them. Man lives in a corner of a cosmos of natural forces, populated by living beings other than himself, and his power over those beings and forces is extremely limited. It is not just that man is weak—impotent, really—as compared to God, though that is stressed in the first speech; it is also that he is weak in dealing with the other creatures. This double weakness is a dominant message of the Lord's speeches. God implies that Job is ignorant, but not so ignorant that he cannot see his own weakness.

As we have seen, Job's recognition of his ignorance is quite explicit in both of his brief responses to the Lord's speeches. His acknowledgment of his weakness is not quite so clear. After the first speech, he replies, "Behold, I am of small account . . ." (40:4); I am arguing that this "smallness" is, in part, weakness, but without the context of the theophany we would not know that. After the second speech, Job does briefly address the power theme but, curiously, he does not speak directly of his weakness; he speaks instead of God's power:

> I know that thou canst do all things,
>   and that no purpose of thine can be thwarted.
>
> (42:2)

To make this verse fit the context, I propose that we read it as meaning,

> I know that thou, *not I*, can do all things,
>   and that no purpose of thine, *not mine*, can be thwarted.

Indeed, if I had written the Book of Job, I would have had Job say here:

> I know that I cannot do all things,
>   that there are purposes of mine that can be thwarted.
>   I am not God.

The point, I believe, is that Job confesses his weakness, just as he clearly confesses his ignorance. He confesses his distance from God, in both respects.

My conclusion here needs some defense, because on its face this verse is simply an acknowledgment of God's omnipotence, and many commentators accept it at face value. What is wrong with leaving it simple, and neglecting what I see as its implicit contrast point? Several things.

In the first place, a simple acknowledgment of God's omnipotence would be out of place just after the second speech. That speech emphasizes Leviathan's power; to a somewhat lesser extent it emphasizes Behemoth's power; throughout both sections the main point has to do with their power with respect to human beings—how weak men are when dealing with such monsters. Man's weakness is contrasted with the power of two of God's supercreatures. Now one could, in thought, move from Behemoth and Leviathan to their

Maker (40:15); and so one could think that if they are mighty, God must be even mightier—and one obscure verse (40:19) may indeed suggest that Behemoth is not as mighty as his Maker. Finally, we remember that the second speech opens with a brief contrast (40:9–10) between God's power and Job's. So, by a series of inferences, we could reach the conclusion that Job's response should deal (as it does) with God's power, rather than the power of His nonhuman creatures; but why did we omit the contrast that ran throughout the speech? At every step, except perhaps in some of the Behemoth passage, there is an explicit contrast between men and these creatures; and even in the Behemoth passage, the discussion of that creature's power may imply a contrast with human power. Human weakness is stressed throughout the speech. Job's confession after the speech, then, should deal with his weakness, not with God's power—or not *just* with God's power.

Another reason for this conclusion is that a simple confession of God's power does not fit the first speech, either. To some extent, that speech is like the second, reminding Job of his weakness vis-à-vis animals he might like to domesticate; mostly, however, in that speech God emphasizes the contrast between His own power over nature, His own structuring creativity, and Job's impotence in these respects. So a response to *that* speech should at least imply a recognition of Job's weakness. Praise of God's power would not be out of place after either speech; but the contrast point, recognition of man's weakness, seems required.

In the third place, Job's responses to the theophany occur at the hinge of the book, the point of change; but it is quite odd to locate there a simple acknowledgment of God's power. The whole book, as we have seen, is full of declarations of God's power. All of the characters believe in God's omnipotence. Indeed, His omnipotence is one of the assumptions that generate the problem of evil debated in the central dialogues. Why does an omnipotent God allow a righteous man like Job to suffer such disasters? It would be quite strange, then, to have Job "discover" God's power only in the revelation from the whirlwind!

However, I would grant that something of God's power *is* learned from the theophany, something Job and his friends had overlooked. They all thought of God's power as manifesting itself totally or primarily in human life. When the Lord speaks, He broadens the canvas enormously. The whole of His Creation, extending far beyond man, is revealed. So it might make sense for Job to reply, "I know that thou canst do *all* things—not just rule over the tiny bit of reality that is man's life." In this sense, an emphasis of the theophany *is* on God's power: God's power to create a cosmos older, more multifarious, more powerful, wider, and more glorious than either Job or his friends had taken into cognizance. One of the *implications* of that revelation—viz., Job's ignorance—was considered in the preceding chapter. But another implication is his relative weakness. If this is not acknowledged in his response to the speeches, it *should* be; for it is clearly part of the burden of those speeches.

Interestingly, some commentators think that the theophany implicitly *denies* the omnipotence Job confesses in his response. Job says (to repeat),

> I know that thou canst do all things,
>   and that no purpose of thine can be thwarted.
>
> (42:2)

But, as we have seen, in the opening of the second speech, God says that if Job would "tread down the wicked" (40:12; see 40:11–13), then He Himself would praise Job, or render homage to him. This might imply (and some think it does imply) that there are things even God cannot do, and that always punishing the wicked is such a thing. So God would have spoken here to a central issue of the book, the problem of evil; and His message would have been that His power is limited. In that case, Job's response, instead of acknowledging the message, would seem to contradict it.

Of course, we could soften the contradiction by distinguishing different senses of "canst do all things"; and the history of speculative theology is full of proposals for different ways to understand the concept of omnipotence. But I see no such speculative subtlety in the Book of Job; if we introduce such a distinction, we really have to import it from outside. And, since the spirit of the book is so deeply agnostic, intellectually humble, I have doubts about whether the author would have had much confidence in the required theological complexity. True, the focus of the *Joban* agnosticism is on the deep mysteries of nature and their relation to God, not on the possibilities of rather abstract analyses of theological concepts; so even if human beings are cut off from knowledge of the former, perhaps we can successfully deal with the latter. But again this is a possibility not even mentioned in the book itself. So this proposal, too, comes from outside the book; and it would appear to offer what it takes to be a corrective to the book's emphases. So the book as it stands is subject to a tension, or maybe even a contradiction, between Job's acknowledgment of God's omnipotence, if that is what is meant in 42:2, and God's confession of His own "weakness," if that really occurs in 40:11–14.

However, as may already be clear, I have no faith in either of the readings of these passages that generate the conflict. The emphasis— and so, I believe, the point—of the introduction to the Lord's speech is *Job's* weakness—not God's! And I believe that the point of Job's acknowledgment is that same weakness, in contrast to God's power, *not* any technical sense of omnipotence. (Does the author even believe in technical theology?) We need to interpret brief and obscure lines in the light of long and clear passages; the opposite procedure smacks of the worst of proof-texting. All the "debaters" in the dialogues have agreed on God's omnipotence; then the overwhelming burdens of the theophany's reflections on power are that Job is impotent in comparison with God, and that Job is weak even in confrontation with some of the other creatures.

In such a context, if we want to find a major revision or warning that God too is limited, we need clear and convincing evidence that the poet intended such a radical caveat; but we find no such thing there. All we find is a barely possible implication of one line in a passage that shows less than the highest authorial power. We cannot hang a major interpretive point on such a slender thread. I believe that the interpreters who see such a point there, on such weak textual evidence, are really reading into the book what *they* believe, and so what they *wish* the great poet had said. But it is easy and natural, given the context, to read the two troubling passages as I do; and then they are consistent with each other as well.

However, given the modern interest in "finite" or "limited" theism, theism in which notions of God's power are moderated, it might be worthwhile to ask whether the accounts of God's power in the theopany could be read as tolerating such interpretations. The question then would not be whether the poet intended to moderate a concept of omnipotence; I see no evidence that he did. His reflections on power have other purposes—stressing Job's weakness, and the breadth of God's Creation; and his doubts about human reason make it unlikely, I think, that he would have been sympathetic with efforts to think through carefully the implications of various conceptions of divine power. Probably he would have thought that such matters were "too wonderful" for us. Nevertheless, it may be that a study of his language shows implicit concepts that later theological thought could employ for its own purposes, one of which would be speculation about the significance of evil in the divine life. Did the poet unwittingly give aid and comfort to theologians who would later argue that God's Own power is limited, and so to thinkers who would try in this way to solve the problem of evil, which he thought could not be solved?

One relevant question would be whether the poet wrote of God as having to deal with anything coeternal with Himself: does God speak of Himself as dealing with any primordial matter, or any rival deities, or any other preexisting principles that could be argued to limit His power? Or does God create *ex nihilo* and without all opposition or otherness? In the theophany God does speak of the sea as bursting forth in birth from a "womb" (38:8); the Qumran Targum took that to be "the womb of the deep," "the cosmic abyss," Pope says.[1] Gordis says that the womb is "the primordial abyss of water (Gen. 7:11; Ps. 36:7) 'lying beneath the earth' (Gen. 48:25; Deut. 33:13) from which the sea issued at creation (Isa. 51:10)."[2] Clearly there was a Hebrew tradition—which echoed other Near Eastern traditions—that the sea had a source on which God acted, perhaps a "material cause," so to speak. But this brief reference may be just literary adornment; and it is not said that the sea's "womb" presents limits to God's activity, or even that such a womb is itself "primordial."

The Lord speaks of the morning stars as singing together when He laid the foundation of the earth (38:7a), and those stars were *gods* in the pagan cults; the next line (7b) speaks of "the sons of God" (literally, "the sons of the gods") shouting for joy; probably the poet has made the pagan deities into sons of the one deity, as Isaiah made them into something like members of God's army (Isa. 40:26). These "sons of God," with the Satan, had already presented themselves before the Lord in the prologue (1:6, 2:1). But though these "sons" are present at the laying of the earth's foundation, it is not said that they are not *also* creations of God; there is no clear modification of a strict monotheism here.

Yahweh praises the dawn in 38:12–15; now the dawn was a god in at least one Ugaritic poem, and the name here (*sāhar*) is the same as in that poem.[3] But an emphasis here seems to be on God's *command* over the dawn, so it would be odd to treat it as a force limiting God's power. To conclude: I see no reason to suppose that the poet's language commits him to any eternal or primordial limit to God's creative power. That route to a restriction on omnipotence is not seriously implicit in our book.

The other main route theorists take is via an analysis of the notion of power itself. In the theophany God stresses His power,[4] not the limits of His power; in contrast to Job, God controls the sea, the dawn, the forces of the weather, and the stars, and He makes provision for His animate creatures. But some theorists argue that all language of power, control, provision, and so on, assumes obstacles to be overcome, and presupposes that the subjects or objects acted on have their own natures and powers, and so that "all-powerful" really makes no literal sense. When I "control" an employee or an underling in a heirarchy, I issue orders that he carries out in his own style. When I "control" an animal or a plant, I use energy to make it do one of the things its nature permits, not something that only other creatures can do. And even when I "control" a mere puppet, with no activity or mode of growth of its own, I must act against the inertia of the thing, and it will only do what such puppets can do. We have no experience whatsoever with sheer control, sheer magical power, where we think or say the thing and it is done. For us, control is always control over a reality with powers of its own. So perhaps we have not even a notion of a divine "omnipotence" that would render null the power of the creatures. This is what some modern theorists argue.[5]

Now this argument may be sound; it certainly has at least the appearance of great penetration. If we accept at all the possibility of rational theology, disciplined theological reflection, then this argument needs to be addressed by defenders of "absolute" omnipotence;

they cannot reasonably ignore such considerations. And if, in the final analysis, the argument turns out to be sound, then even the account of the Lord's power in the Joban theophany, regardless of the poet's intentions, does presuppose some contextual (not primordial) limits to God's power. We will have to consider the implications *for God* of the creature's power, just as we have to consider the implications *for Job*. And the implications might provide the bases for a sophisticated solution, or aspects[6] of a solution, to the problem of evil— even if the Joban poet did not believe we were capable of constructing a solution.

I will not here enter into the complex debate over the force of these ideas. But whatever the outcome of that debate, I see no sign in the Book of Job that the author himself was aware of such issues. It seems quite clear that he saw the power of the creatures—especially of Leviathan and Behemoth—and knew that this implied limits to *Job's* power; but I see no evidence that he thought a related logic implied limits to *God's* power. It seems that he accepted without question the idea that God was *all*-powerful; and that he saw no way for human minds to solve the problem of evil God's omnipotence generates. So I conclude that the proposal to see in the theophany confessions of limitations, though on its surface and from Job's response it seems to proclaim omnipotence—this proposal represents a criticism of the Book of Job, not an interpretation of its point of view.

Let us return, then, to our main issues. An emphasis in the theophany, and hence in the book as a whole, is on Job's weakness. Job is impotent when compared with God, and he is weak in conflict with many of God's creatures. These points are clear in the Lord's speeches. But *why* are these points emphasized? How do they bear on the issues of the book? That is not so clear.

Now as we have seen, throughout this book there is a very close connection between knowledge and power; to know, regularly, is to know how to do, and to know how to do is to be able to do. We might then argue that the emphasis on Job's weakness is just another version of the emphasis on his ignorance, and we have already explored at length the implications of that. We might conclude that we have already explained the point of the weakness theme.

There are two difficulties, however. One is that we would have to explain why the ignorance motif swallows up the weakness theme, why the weakness theme loses its independence, rather than the other way around. The other problem is that it is most implausible to argue that *all* of the weakness claims are really ignorance claims; the texts do not lend themselves readily to such a reduction. The power of Behemoth is displayed not only against men (40:24), but also against rivers (40:23); but it would be odd to take that as showing the *ignorance* of rivers in respect to him. The power of Leviathan is displayed in his resistance to hooks, harpoons, swords, spears, darts, the javelin, arrows, slingstones, clubs; surely we are thinking of power and weakness, not of knowledge and ignorance. It is not just that man does not know the way to pierce Leviathan's armor; there is no way, given human implements. One might *argue* that somehow all these kinds of human weakness could be remedied if we only knew enough, and so that, in a sense, all weakness stems from ignorance; but that would not show that weakness just *is* ignorance, and there is no sign that the poet himself had in mind such an argument. As we have seen already, the association in this book between power and knowledge is close but not complete. So I think we must come to terms with man's weakness itself, and see what it implies for the book's issues.

Some readers have concluded that the point of the book is that man is weak and consequently has no rights. Job has complained that he and others are treated unjustly by God (or life). God replies that Job is weaker than He, and even weaker than some other creatures. The point must be, some readers say, that the weak have no rights. It is not unjust for the powerful to treat the weak as they please. Might makes right. The weak, simply because they are weak, have no right to complain of injustice. So Job acknowledges God's power and shuts up. On this reading, regardless of the theme of ignorance, we *do* know enough to solve the problem of evil. The solution is that there *is* no evil, if that means injustice or the violation of rights. For human beings have no rights against God, and so nothing God does to them can be unjust.

This was the way Thomas Hobbes read the book,[7] and he liked what he read, because he wanted to argue that citizens could not be treated unjustly by the sovereign of a commonwealth (which he called a Leviathan, a "mortal god," in relation to the citizens). Hobbes believed that might *could* make right. And many readers have seen this message in the book and disliked the book on those grounds, or disliked the theophany and the ending, even if (especially if) they liked the "rebellious" Job of the dialogues. It is, after all, a firm belief of most of us that might does *not* make right. Many of what we call horrors are committed by the mighty of the earth; and any evil requires some might for its execution. Does the Book of Job really intend Job's weakness to imply that God can do him no injustice? Leviathan and Behemoth are beyond good and evil—beyond morality, that is—because they are animals; is God beyond good and evil because He is omnipotent? Is that really the import of the weakness theme?

There is one passage in the theophany that some have read as implying this. Just after God has said of Leviathan that "No one is so fierce that he dares to stir him up" (41:10a), there are three lines quite difficult to interpret. The RSV translates:

> Who then is he that can stand before me?
> Who has given to me, that I should repay him?
> Whatever is under the whole heaven is mine.

> (41:10b–11)

This is the language I did not discuss above, in my survey of the second speech; it seems to introduce ideas not found elsewhere in the theophany. It suggests that, as no one can stand before Leviathan, even less is anyone able to stand before God. Then, perhaps as a consequence of this power relation, no one has given anything to God; so God has no debts—and no obligations?—to anyone. Everything is "mine," He says; so is He the absolute Owner? And so has He a right to do whatever He pleases? And does His might create His right?[8]

Such ideas are not expressed in the rest of the Lord's speeches, and they seem an intrusion here. The ancient texts vary; and some of the modern versions seem literally meaningless; so some interpretation and conjecture are necessary here. But for various reasons, mainly reasons of context, "most scholars"[9] now reject the RSV-type reading of this passage. Gordis translates, after "No one is foolhardy enough to stir him [Leviathan] up":

for who can stand up to him in battle?
Who has confronted him and emerged unscathed?
Under all the heavens—no one!

Pope's reading is similar:

Who could stand before him?
Who could confront him unscathed,
Under the whole heaven, who?

Gordis and Pope, like most others, are convinced that this passage tells more of Leviathan's power, not something of God's power, much less of God's rights.[10] If the majority are correct, then, there is no clear statement in the theophany of the idea that God's might implies that He can do no wrong.

Moreover, this idea is in conflict with the clear import of the ignorance theme, which entailed that we could not solve the problem of the "injustice" in human life; for this interpretation offers a solution—it denies that there *is* any injustice in human life. God has a perfect right to do with us as He pleases, just because He is more powerful than we are. Now that solves the problem (in a way that is unpalatable to many of us). But the book makes clear that we cannot solve the problem. So this interpretation must be rejected, if the book is consistent.

Moreover, the general idea that might makes right, or that a powerful being may rightly do as he pleases with the weak, is incompatible with the conception of morality worked out so elaborately in the central dialogues. Job and his friends agree about the demands of righteousness, as we have seen; and those demands focus fairly prominently on the obligations on the strong to care for the weak— the poor, the sick, the injured, the widows, the orphans. The weak are vulnerable to exploitation by the strong; such exploitation is a major form of wickedness; and major forms of righteousness consist in helping the weak and in resisting their abuse. Nothing could be clearer than that the weak *do* have rights, and that their weakness lays them open to real injustice. The Book of Job is firmly in the prophetic tradition of concern for the unfortunate. The problem of the book is why God allows the weak, the righteous, and the wicked—construed in this social-conscience way—to suffer or enjoy the fates they do undergo in the world. It would be strange indeed if the conclusion of the book rejected the understanding of morality that informs the problem it addresses. So the theme of human weakness and God's power could not imply, pace Hobbes, that strong men may rightly do with weak men whatever they please; at the very most, it could imply that an analogous principle holds at the religious level—that God may rightly do with men whatever He pleases, just because He is mightier than they. But then we would need to explain why this principle applies at that level but not at the human level; and the book offers no discussion of this. And we would have to explain why man's weakness vis-à-vis the other creatures is stressed in the theophany, and not just our weakness vis-à-vis God. (Of course the animals do us no injustice, but the reason is that they are animals; their power is not the reason.) Apparently, then, there is a hornets' nest of problems facing the might-makes-right interpretation. But if we reject that, why then *does* the theophany stress Job's weakness, in comparison with God and even with some of the other creatures? What *is* the point?

The point, I believe, has to do with the motivation behind the idea of the Moral World Order, the orthodox doctrine the friends accept and Job wishes were true. As we have seen, the Book of Job involves a sophisticated sense of man's obligations to his fellow men, a sophisticated "morality," we have called it; but Job and his friends also wish to believe in a Super-Morality, a sense of *God's* obligations to human beings. That Super-Morality is analogous to human morality. As we have obligations to protect the weak, so does God; as we have obligations to resist and punish the wicked, so does God; and, in addition, God has obligations to reward the righteous. The friends believe, wrongly, that God fulfills such obligations; Job sees that God does not, but he believes God *should*, and so he curses God. The wish for God to be Moral—"With forfeits and rewards he [man] understood," in Frost's words—creates Job's bitterness and blasphemy.

Now we have already seen one aspect of the theophany's assault on the Joban presumption. Job, like his friends, believes he understands how God should order the cosmos, that he understands the oligations on the Creator. The theophany rejects that assumption. No man understands the deep principles of God's rule, and so no man understands enough to know how God should order our lives. We understand how *we* should live; we know what *our* obligations are. But we do not understand how God should manage the world.

Now we see a second aspect to the theophany's assault. If God's speeches do anything, they get Job to reflect on the insignificance of his power in the cosmos; they lead him to remember that the structure of the world antedates him and cannot be altered by him, and that in it live creatures who will not bend to his will. Why is it necessary for him to reflect on his weakness? The reason, I suggest, is that behind the idea of the Moral World Order, behind orthodoxy, lies a perversion of what Nietzsche called the will to power: the will to dominate. The reason Job and his friends wish there to be a Moral World Order is that they wish to perfectly control their destinies, to be ultimately secure, to be complete masters of their fates. The theophany lets Job see, lets us see, that this wish is unrealistic, is irrational. It is not just God's message that Job must give up his notion of the Moral World Order; Job must give up the will to dominion lying behind that notion. God rules; we do not; in some sense, *He* "can do all things"; but we cannot.

There is no doubt that Job *had* the will to dominate life; in the prologue we hear that he hoped to control even his sons' destiny. We hear that he offered burnt offerings for them, thinking, "It may be that my sons have sinned, and cursed God in their hearts" (1:5). So the ritual in his religion rested on the will to be master of life. But what of his religion of morality that is mainly at issue in the book? What motives, what states of heart, underlay it?

If the friends are to be trusted, the great advantage of righteousness is that it makes one safe, secure; it seems fairly clear that *they* do not wish to face their creaturely insecurity. They believe that by being upright they can get the Lord Himself to protect them against the consequences of human frailty. Eliphaz says that God can make one laugh at destruction and famine (5:22) and know that one's tent is safe (5:24). Those who delight in the Almighty will not be subject to hostile forces: "You will decide on a matter, and it will be established for you" (22:28). Zophar says to Job that if he reforms, "you will be secure, and will not fear. . . . And you will have confidence . . . you will be protected. . . . You will lie down, and none will make you afraid . . ." (11:15, 18, 19). Throughout the friends' speeches they detail the contrasting *insecurity* of the wicked. (Job, of course, reverses that theme, and waxes eloquent on the security of the wicked. See especially chap. 21.)

Henri Bergson argued that there were basically two sources of morality and religion.[11] One was mystical; but the more common one was the will to control what could not be controlled. The savage aimed his arrow as well as he could; but after it left his bow it was beyond his dominion. Yet not quite, he hoped; and so he developed magical practices, and then moral and religious ones, to extend his power into the gap. I suspect that this is close to the view of the author of the Book of Job. Now man does have real power in his measure; morality presupposes his power to carry out his obligations; and the hymn to wisdom glories in man's technological might. Total impotence, like total ignorance, is foreign to this book. But however great our power becomes, the ultimate status of man involves weakness and insecurity; the cosmos and its creatures retain their own intransigence and resistance to man's will. The appeal of the orthodox doctrine is that it seems to offer an escape from the human predicament, an escape into ultimate security. True, it says, we cannot master our fates by ourselves; but God is all-powerful; and if we will obey Him, and be faithful to Him, He will be Master of our fates, and so we can escape our creaturely weakness after all. Wars will come, and floods, and plagues, but we will not fear: we will rest in the hand of God. The message of the theophany is that this is a lie, and an attempt to escape from man's essential condition. "The illusion of control," as many psychologists call it, *is* an illusion.[12]

Another way to see this is to look at the absence of morality from the theophany. The Lord's speeches present a vision of the *natural* world, the nonhuman cosmos, and of man's weakness in it. There is virtually no mention of human beings in the whole theophany (and if I am right, there *should* be no mention at all), except as it indicates how weak we are in mastering that world. But the rains, the seas, the eagles, the oxen, the superbeasts Leviathan and Behemoth, all of which are beyond man's dominion, are *amoral*, are neither righteous nor wicked, are neither just nor unjust. Man then exists in an amoral cosmos, subject to amoral forces—powerful in their own right. This is what Job is forced to remember and to reflect on. Is it really reasonable to believe that this whole natural, amoral, powerful order, which he cannot control, somehow *is* controlled for his benefit, once he becomes moral? Is our fundamental status in the natural order over-turned by our righteousness? Job may be upright; there may even be, I think the poet could grant, fundamental rewards for righteousness. But is it plausible that the lightning, the seas, or the wild oxen—or microbes, or radiation, or genetic codes—will serve Job simply be-cause he is righteous? Isn't it clear that nature has its *own* principles and powers, and that these are not subject to moral rule? And isn't it clear that a man cannot escape nature, even by being moral?

I think that this is the second message of the theophany: man's fundamental weakness is not overturned by his righteousness. A man may live in the kingdom of right, but he remains in the kingdom of natural might. Man is ignorant, but not so ignorant that he cannot see that. He *is* too ignorant, however, to understand *why* he lives in such a natural world, or why that nature is the kind of nature that it is. These things "would appear to outrun human comprehension" (Rawls). That was the first message of the theophany.

The effort of orthodoxy to escape human frailty, the effort Job shares before he is humbled by God's voice, might be seen—and some interpreters do see it—as an attempt to be God, or to be the equal of God. In a sense, this is misleading, as I have already noted; for Job and his friends never suppose that they, *by themselves*, could control their destinies. They only suppose that if they are upright and faithful to God then *He* will control their destinies for their ultimate benefit. Job knows that he cannot save himself, that his own right hand cannot give him victory (40:14). He never thinks that he is God or has God's power. Moreover, his protest, as we have seen, is often made on behalf of others, not just of himself; so we do not quite have a contrast between "egoism" and "theocentrism" in this book.

Nevertheless, the security that Job seeks, and the enforcement of his ideas of how the world should be ordered, do indeed approach what this book regards as the prerogatives of God alone. And so the interpreters who speak of Job's efforts to deify himself, or of his "inflation," are not really wrong, for Job does imagine himself a kind of equal of God. (That is why so many romantics admire him.) "[L]ike a prince I would approach him," Job says (31:37). Indeed, the cele-brated and obscure passages about a redeemer, an umpire, or God Himself between Job and God show Job's assumption that he and

God are somehow equals. "There is no umpire between us, who might lay his hand upon us both" (9:33), Job complains; but why should there be an umpire between Job and God, and why should they "come to trial together" (9:32), unless they are in some way equals? "Then call, and I will answer; or let me speak, and do thou reply to me" (13:22), Job asks; surely this is the voice of one who imagines himself an equal of God, somehow, however much he compares himself to "a driven leaf" or "dry chaff" (13:25). Job wishes God "to maintain the right of a man with God, like that of a man with his neighbor" (16:21); is *that* how a man is related to God, the way he is related to his neighbor? And even the famous Redeemer passage may belong here: "For I know that my Redeemer/Vindicator/Kinsman/Avenger lives" (19:25). Much is obscure here; but what is fairly clear is that Job imagines himself related to God as a wronged man is related to another man who does him wrong, and so he asks for—or says he knows he has—a kinsman who will act on his behalf against God. Whether this "kinsman" is or is not, somehow, God Himself, we seem to have the presumption again that Job and God are fundamentally equals. So I would think that this celebrated passage must be another the theophany rejects.

Some interpreters wish to see Job as a kind of Jacob, wrestling with God and prevailing. Job does wrestle—with orthodoxy, with suffering, with injustice; and he does win a confrontation with God. But in his encounter, he does not prevail; God thoroughly humbles him. Of course, Jacob came away from his celebrated "victory" with a limp! It is hard to see what *he* won, except a new name; but he did manage to save his life. As he said, "I have seen God face to face, and yet my life is preserved." (See Gen. 32:22-32.) These heroes of confrontation are not, in any obvious sense, victors over God; they "see" God and live; but unlike Prometheus, they do not take away any divine prerogatives. What Job receives is insight into his own "littleness." All assumption of equality before God is to be abandoned.

The reasons, to repeat, are two. First, man is profoundly ignorant; he is not able to understand God's management of the cosmos. Second, man is profoundly weak; a man's relation to God cannot be understood as analogous to his relation to his neighbor. The book *never* suggests that weakness among men is a basis for lesser rights, among men; the weak are a primary focus of the obligations of the strong. Might does not make right. But a man's weakness vis-à-vis God and His creation is so profound that he cannot hope that his righteousness—or anything else—will render him able to overcome his creaturely fragility. It may be that there is *some* power in righteousness; the book does not really explore the options here. But the kind of ultimate power the friends believe in, and that Job desires, is an illusion—and shows presumption, a will to omnipotence.

Job's fundamental weakness is relevant to the interpretation of the epilogue. As we remember, in the final scenes of the story all of Job's former prosperity is restored: he regains the comfort and aid of his brothers and sisters, doubles his former wealth, and has new sons and daughters, most beautiful daughters; and he lives to see "his sons' sons, four generations." All of this occurs after Job repents of his presumption and prays for his friends. But what does this restoration of happiness mean for the issues of the book?

The worst interpretation is that it shows that the friends were right, after all—that righteousness like Job's does pay off in the end, and does make a man secure against all of life's forces. That interpretation makes nonsense of the whole book. That would mean that *the friends* spoke of God what is right, contrary to 42:7, 8; and that they should have prayed for Job, rather than the other way around. It renders the theophany superfluous and irrelevant. It renders Job's response pointless. And it makes quite odd the sense most readers have, and that Elihu had, that the friends had "no answer" (32:5) to Job.

Few readers know the real contents of the Book of Job—for good reasons. First, the book is difficult; and second, it fiercely rejects a central belief of much of the rest of the biblical writings. In the New Testament, despite its preoccupation with suffering, we find Job mentioned only once, in the letter of James:

> Be patient, brethren. . . . Behold, the farmer waits for the precious fruit of the earth, being patient over it until it receives the early and late rain. . . . As an example of suffering and patience, brethren, take the prophets who spoke in the name of the Lord. Behold, we call those happy who were steadfast. You have heard of the steadfastness of Job, and you have seen the purpose of the Lord, how the Lord is compassionate and merciful.
>
> (Jas. 5:7–11)

But the message of the book is *not* that if we are faithful and patient, God will eventually protect us. The book rejects that view.

The second worst interpretation of the epilogue is that if we are righteous *and humble*, then God will ultimately protect us. Job was righteous at the beginning, and he was not protected. Later, after the theophany, he was also humble, and then he prospered. Is *that* the message of the ending? Job began with a religion essentially moral; he was upright, morally. That did not work. After the theophany, he found a religion that transcended morality—it was humble, as a merely moral religion need not be; and he no longer sought to impose upon God any human, all-too-human notions of how the cosmos should be ruled. Is the book's message that *this* kind of religion does work, does bring our brothers and sisters back, does save our children, our fortunes, and our health? Such a reading is absurd. It makes mincemeat of the theophany that produces the humility this reading claims to celebrate. The theophany reveals man's condition in the cosmos, a condition of weakness and ignorance; but this interpretation announces that we are *not* ultimately weak, that there *is* a protection against all hostile forces, and so that we *do* understand how God manages the world. This interpretation, as it stands, is hardly better than the interpretation of the friends.

Nevertheless, we must make something of Job's final prosperity and happiness, unless we just throw up our hands and say that the book as we have it is incoherent. That is the view of some interpreters, though they rarely say that outright. Instead, they remind us here that the story of Job already existed in prose form before our poet added the speeches, the theophany, and Job's repentance; and they say that we have in the epilogue the *old* view, not the poet's view, but the old view that eventually God protects the righteous—roughly, the view in the letter of James in the New Testament. Perhaps a prose epilogue did antedate our book, and perhaps it did have a Jamesian meaning; but what is the meaning of the epilogue we have, in its context? What does it mean here?

In the next chapter I will say a little more about this subject, but a part of the meaning should be clear already. It is obvious, I think: there is a blessing to be found in a recognition of man's finitude, in a surrender of the presumption that motivates both sides of the debate in the central dialogues. We have already explored the psychological costs of the Joban bitterness; surely one is better off without the illusions that inform it. This is what the epilogue means, in the book as we have it. Job's repentance, with his prayer for those still in thrall to the Moral World Order, leads to a new happiness. We must not exaggerate here: the point is not that it leads to an escape from the human condition. *This* is not possible. But it does provide a kind of peace. Other things being equal, a man is happiest when he knows that he is only a man, and can reconcile himself to the limits of his knowledge and his power. The epilogue is so hyperbolic (and perhaps so traditional) that it threatens to undermine the truth that it symbolizes—or, to speak candidly, to undermine the interpretation of the book that I argue for here. There is a severe tension between the letter of the epilogue and the fairly clear meaning of the dialogues and the theophany. The way to deal with the tension, I believe, is to interpret the epilogue as a symbol. If we do, then the book coheres.

Marianne Moore asked, in a Joban spirit:

> What is our innocence,
> What is our guilt? All are
> naked, none is safe. . . .

And she answered, also in kinship with Job,

> He
> sees deep and is glad, who
> accedes to mortality. . . .

Mortality is less than she means; she means human frailty, with mortality as its symbol and ultimate expression. The message of the epilogue is that an acceptance of our frailty brings a reconciliation and a peace. Still, this is not the full story; for peace is not yet "joy."[13] And Job's latter years are not merely peaceful; they are "glad." An element in the theophany is still missing. The final chapter of this book will attempt to recover it.

Chapter 12

"The Morning Stars Sang Together"

> And in all the land there were no women as fair as Job's daughters; and their father gave them inheritance among their brothers.
>
> —(42:15)

The Book of Job, as we have seen, is in large measure a negative work. It rejects the overly optimistic picture of life painted by "orthodoxy"—the picture of the Moral World Order, where righteousness and innocence are always ultimately protected, and where sin is always ultimately punished. This means that the book is historically rebellious; much of religious thought, inside and outside of Judaism, is rejected. But Job, the rebel, is also criticized; and the book concludes with a revelation of man as deeply ignorant and weak. This book, which does not blink at the injustice in life, presents a critique of religious tradition and of human pretensions to knowledge and power.

Yet the ending is decidedly upbeat; the epilogue presents a picture of Job's reconciliation with friends and family, restored prosperity and health, new sons and daughters—beautiful daughters—and grandchildren and great-grandchildren to round out a happy and ripe old age. I have argued that all this is symbolic of a blessing, one that comes in part from acceptance of the human condition.

The blessing is also communal and practical. The doctrine of the Moral World Order is divisive and uncharitable: it represents the oldest psychology on earth, "blame the victim." It allows the fortunate to deny solidarity with their fellow men and to neglect their duties to the weak—duties seen throughout the book as central to religious morality. After the Moral World Order was overthrown:

> Then came to [Job] all his brothers and sisters and all who had known him before, and ate bread with him in his house; and they showed him sympathy and comforted him for all the evil that the Lord had brought upon him; and each of them gave him a piece of money and a ring of gold. (42:11)

To repeat part of the message of the theophany: the world is in large measure a *natural* world. This means that the cures for its ills—to the extent that there *are* cures—are largely natural, not moral. Job did not need to be more righteous. He needed comfort and companionship; he needed friends and family to side with him—against God, if necessary; he needed useful and ornamental gifts. The old claim that Job suffered from neglect of his duties served nicely to prevent his fellow men from carrying out *their* duties to *him*. Indeed, if I had written this book, I believe I would have placed this message in the theophany, as well as in the dialogues and in the epilogue. As the theophany suggests, a source of belief in the Moral World Order is a misguided will to power; but another source, even more important in my opinion, is the will to escape responsibility and to feel oneself morally superior to the victims of the world's forces. I only quibble. Both messages are in the book. And the book ends with the restoration of human comfort and practical aid, and perhaps with a dramatization—hyperbolic—of their helpful consequences in the life of the sufferer.

But there is another, more subtle but more profound, meaning of the blessing which rounds out the story of Job. It connects the epilogue *directly* with the message of the theophany—or with a side of that message we have not yet fully appreciated. In the two preceding chapters I have emphasized the negative import of the theophany, but there is an affirmative implication there too.

Many interpreters have seen that the theophany has a positive side, but some of them have suggested interpretations of this I do not think can be defended. It has been said, for example, that God's speeches show that God exists, is real; and of course they do; unless God were real He could not speak to Job.

Some modern thinkers who worry about the problem of evil wind up accepting atheism. The theophany implicitly rejects that resolution of the problem. But the modern temptation to atheism is not present in the Book of Job. As we have seen, no one in the book wonders whether God exists or not. God, throughout the book, is manifestly real—too real, Job sometimes suggests. So this interpretation is not relevant to the understanding of the problems in the book itself.

Another interpretation sometimes advanced, especially by evangelicals, is that what God's speeches offer Job is not so much a message as God Himself—that Job encounters, meets, confronts, the Lord Himself. In Job's second response he says,

> I had heard of thee by the hearing of the ear,
>   but now my eye sees thee. . . .

(42:5)

These interpreters take very seriously this hearing/seeing contrast; and they conclude that Job did not just receive ("hear") a message from God, but instead "saw God"—confronted Him, was confronted by Him. They say that learning about a person is different from meeting him; they believe Job *met* God, Who gave Himself in communion with Job. They see the blessing of God's presence, of meeting Him, as in itself healing to the stricken Job. Some of these interpreters borrow Martin Buber's notions of the I-it relation and the I-Thou encounter, and they say God became to Job a Thou in the theophany, so that articulable messages, relevant only to objects or "its," all fall away.[1]

The great problem with this idea is that the theophany clearly *does* convey a message (or messages); Job says "my eye sees thee," but he actually hears a voice; and what that voice lets him "see" is a picture of himself, man, in relation to the natural world and to God. The messages do *not* defy articulation; they *are articulated* at great length in the Book of Job, in four whole chapters. And in the preceding four chapters of the present work I have been attempting to explicate them. There is no doubt, really, that there are themes, contents, in the speeches from the whirlwind—that God says something there. But if the sheer-encounter interpretations were correct, God might as well have been silent, and the poet could have said simply that God visited Job and met with him face to face. God does visit Job; but when He visits He speaks, and that speaking is informative.

God's speeches let Job see that he—that is, man—is small in knowledge and in power; but Job also sees the goodness, or beauty, or awesomeness of the created world of nature. God says that when He laid the "foundation" of the earth:

> . . . the morning stars sang together,
>   and all the sons of God shouted for joy.
>
> (38:7)

Man may be "of small account" (40:4); but the created natural world is not. It is awesome. As we have seen, the language throughout the theophany is the language of praise. The seas, the storms, the stars, the wild birds and animals, even the monsters, Behemoth and Leviathan, are revealed as worthy creations and subjects of the good Lord of nature. God Himself sings the praises of the spectacle of nature. The spirit here is that of the opening of Genesis: "And the Lord saw that it was good." This is the positive, upbeat, affirmative side of the humbling theophany.

It must be emphasized that what the theophany praises is *nature*, in the sense in which we distinguish between man and nature: it is the world without man, before man, beyond man, even dangerous to man. Job and his friends had debated the fates of righteous, wicked, and innocent human beings; God changes the subject, and discusses the parts of the Creation in which man's affairs are absent, or virtually absent. Those realms of Creation are also, therefore, realms in which the very ideas of the Moral World Order are inapplicable: there are no righteous or wicked storms or seas. If the needs of some of God's natural creatures are met—and the theophany suggests that they are—it is not because those creatures are righteous. God moves the discussion to the natural world, which is beyond moral good and evil, and so beyond any question of whether the righteous prosper or suffer.

This means that the vindication of nature, its justification, its glory—the reason it caused the morning stars to sing together, the sons of God to shout for joy—the reason cannot be *moral*. Nature is good, as God saw in Genesis; but it is not good in the sense of being righteous. Natural powers are not righteous (or wicked). Nor, therefore, is nature good in the sense of displaying the Moral World Order; it is not a scene in which the righteous are protected. The goodness of the natural world is not moral goodness.

Nor is it aesthetic in any frivolous sense, any sense of prettiness. The scenes the Lord paints are not pretty. God does not take Job out to look at sunsets, fields of wildflowers, or birds of lovely colors. The nature He asks Job to remember is mainly strange, distant, and mighty: harsh deserts, unpredictable storms, war-loving animals, monstrous aquatic beasts—the wilder side of Near Eastern nature. If the Book of Job had been written in the United States in our time, God might have reminded Job of places like Death Valley and the Okefenokee wilderness. These kinds of scenes, and their denizens, are mainly what the author had in mind.

There is no doubt that men have long found elements of inspiration in such scenes. Wise men and prophets have retreated into the desert to gain perspective before returning to their missions. Ordinary men and women find some kind of restoration in visits and vacations in such extraordinary places. People experience some kind of goodness there.

As I say, *prettiness* is the wrong word for this, but we might say *beauty*, as some commentators do, if we mean this in a grand sense that preserves the character of nature as considerably alien to human control and even insight, and that includes an element of natural provision for many of the creatures' needs.[2] Charles Darwin, for all his grasp of the struggle for survival, called the web of life beautiful. Naturalists often speak of beauty in the nature they study and portray for the rest of us to appreciate. Throughout the last four chapters I have spoken of God's revelation of the *cosmos*; the connections of this word with concepts of beauty do not seem to me inappropriate in this context, so long as we are cautious. Whatever words we use here, we must remember that Job's vision of nature is not only daunting; the nature revealed in the theophany is also glorious, grand, somehow "good"—and this is the positive, affirmative side of the message from the whirlwind. We sense this goodness of nature in the poet's descriptions of the world, in God's pride in His creative activity, and in the singing and shouting of the heavenly witnesses (38:7).

In the twentieth century we have become aware that the natural world needs the protection of human beings (protection, largely, against ourselves). The wonders of nature can be destroyed—some have been destroyed—and most of us believe that man has an obligation to protect the beauties around us. We owe it to our children; perhaps we owe it to the other creatures themselves. In the theophany, God seems to imply that He has providential concern for *them*, and not just for us. So the author of our book would not find strange the moral concerns behind modern ecological and environmental movements. St. Paul asked ironically whether God cared about oxen;[3] it seems fairly clear that the Joban writer thought He did.

Nevertheless, it would be wrongheaded entirely to see in the theophany a new duty of man, a new requirement of righteousness. The nature portrayed in the Book of Job can get along nicely without man. And the point of God's praise of nature is not to lay upon poor Job a new obligation. The point is to remind Job of the great domains of life lying beyond the moral order, and, in part, of the goodness or beauty of those domains.

We remember that one of the central issues of the book is the problem of evil in human life—the failure of the human world to display the moral order. Now the theophany suggests a goodness not moral but displayed in the natural world. Is this suggestion somehow directly relevant to the debate between Job and his friends? They were not debating that; they focused on the world of men, not nature; and they looked for a moral order there, not an amoral beauty. Still, is there a connection? It is hard to resist the sense that there is a relevance here; but it is not easy to say what the relevance is.

Perhaps the most common interpretation is that the goodness of nature is evidence somehow for a deep justice in the world, too. This interpretation is worked out most carefully perhaps by Robert Gordis, who believes that the theophany implicitly presents an argument by analogy. He holds, as I do, that the nature God describes "is not merely a mystery, but is also a miracle, a cosmos, a thing of beauty."[4] Or, as he puts it elsewhere, nature displays "beauty and harmony,"[5] "beauty and order."[6] He believes that "This suggests that there is a similar order and meaning in the moral universe, even though man cannot always grasp it"[7]—that we have grounds, therefore, for a faith "in the essential rightness of things."[8] Though he repeats his warning that the "essential rightness" cannot always be grasped by man,[9]

Gordis seems to believe that this "rightness" is located "in the *moral universe*"[10]—that it is, in some way, a *moral* rightness. The beauty in nature implies that *"there is order and meaning in the moral sphere,"*[11] that "there are rationality and justice" "in the moral order."[12] For Gordis, then, the theophany, though it speaks directly of the amoral (mainly), has implications for the moral; and so—though Gordis does not say this—*in spirit* the friends were right: the world *is* a moral world, a world of justice; though they were mistaken in thinking we could always grasp that justice. In this way Gordis hopes to hold fast to the intellectual humility of the book, while still maintaining the spirit (not the letter) of the Moral World Order. There is a deep justice, though its details are often obscure to us. For Gordis, then, nature is introduced in the theophany as an argumentative device, so to speak; its point, and the focus of the book, remains moral.

I think that this is a possible interpretation, in that I know of nothing that directly contradicts it; but I do not think it is correct. To my mind, there are two difficulties in it. One is that it is not at all clear what "an essential rightness" "in the moral sphere" is, what "justice" is, if it is not what the friends and orthodoxy claimed: the protection of the innocent and righteous and the punishment of the wicked. But Gordis sees as clearly as anyone that the Book of Job denies that there is that kind of "perfect justice" in the universe. So what kind of justice is hinted at by the beauty of nature?

In the prologue of the book, the patient Job suggested a different kind of "justice":

> Naked I came from my mother's womb, and naked shall I return; the Lord gave, and the Lord has taken away. . . . (1:21)

and

> Shall we receive good at the hand of God, and shall we not receive evil? (2:10)

This conception of what we might call justice is that we have no rights at all against the universe, and so whatever it (or God) gives us is an unmerited loan, and the Giver has a perfect right to take it away at any time. And if we remain in life and accept good from the universe (or God), we are bound by right to accept evil as well. This is a kind of justice, too; but is it what the theophany intimates? The problem is that the theophany does not fit that. This conception holds that, whatever God sends us, His sending it was just. But in that case the theophany need not have stressed Job's ignorance, for there is nothing mysterious here; we can see what God sends us (and we know, on this conception, that it is just). And the theophany need not have presented a *beautiful* world; for whether the world is beautiful or ugly, we have no right to complain. So this conception of justice, Job's prologue conception, does not match either of these clear themes in the theophany. It might match the weakness theme, if we interpret that as the RSV interpreted 41:10–11; but as we have seen, most scholars reject that reading, and we have found good sense in the weakness motif *without* that conception of justice.

So neither of the book's conceptions of justice is tenable as a rendering of divine justice. What, then, *is* an appropriate conception of God's justice? I think it clear that the book leaves us with none. Now Gordis might not be daunted by these arguments. He might reply, I believe, that he has insisted we cannot fully understand God's justice. And of course I agree with his stress on our ignorance. But if this justice of God's does not correspond to either of the conceptions of justice in the book, why call it *justice*? And do we really have a concept here? Are we really talking about justice, once we deny that it is either of the kinds of justice in the book? Are we really talking about anything?

The other problem for Gordis is that the theme of ignorance does not explain why we should speak here of justice at all. Whatever the theophany implies, it must mean that we do not fully understand God's workings in that realm; but why think that it implies an order, something analogous to beauty, *in the moral sphere*? Why doesn't it imply something *else* we do not fully understand? It is clear that the theophany is a celebration; but why think that it is by implication a moral celebration, a celebration of (admittedly obscure) justice? Its overwhelming themes are not moral at all. Why not leave it as an amoral celebration, a celebration beyond questions of moral good and evil? The book has repeatedly attacked the Moral World Order, the over-"moralizing" of life that leads to bitterness and blasphemy in

Job, and to a neglect of the moral obligation for compassion in the witnesses of Job's suffering. Why resurrect the spirit of the Moral World Order at this point? Isn't that counter to the overwhelming thrust of the theophany, and of the book as a whole? I think it is. I think the book is more revolutionary than that—or, as I will suggest below, more counterrevolutionary than that.

The question is, what shall we make of the theophany's praise of the natural order? Nature is seen there as good, as *beautiful* in some amoral and often harsh sense; I suggest we take that to be exactly the point, instead of merely an analogy for some moral point. As the Book of Job makes clear in many ways, the world is *not* perfectly moral; and so the goodness of the world, of life, cannot be in its perfect morality. The reasons "the sons of God" can celebrate Creation, the reason the sons of man can celebrate human life in the world, is not that the scene is (even implicitly) one of perfect morality. The goodness of the world, of life, is its amoral, often harsh, beauty. *That* is what justifies the world. Much of Creation has no relevance to man's life, and hence is totally beyond moral good and evil; and I think the theophany implies that much of *human* life is similarly amoral. The animals God describes die when they have no food; man, too, dies without food—and his righteousness cannot save him from that natural ordering of things. The Moral World Order is an illusion; but then the moral justification of life is an illusion. The world *is* justified, but *as nature*, as Creation, as glorious if frightening beauty. It is for *that* that the morning stars sang together.

Job and his friends are well agreed about how a man should live his human life; they have comparable notions, moral notions, of how God should order the world—or perhaps we should say, Super-Moral notions. Job curses God when he sees that the world is not moral. But all this assumes that a good God, because He is good, *would* be dominantly concerned for the Moral World Order. And that means that a good God would care dominantly about man, and about the side of man's life most bound up with morality. The theophany speaks for a God whose concerns are broader than that, who cares for nature, and who sees that it is good. He cares for the world beyond man; presumably He cares for the natural side of man's life, too. For this God, a justification of life would not be exclusively, or even dominantly, moral. For this God, the world *is* good; but its goodness is a natural goodness, a "beauty."

The other central issue of the book is the nature of high religion, of high "fear of God," of the finest way of being "God's servant." We remember that the Satan suspected that Job "feared God" in some way intimately bound up with his prosperity, and that in adversity Job would curse God. The Satan was right. But a religion that focuses on the Moral World Order produces men like Job—or, more commonly, like his friends. We have seen how elements of the theophany, and of the rest of the book, criticize the pretensions in and behind belief in the Moral World Order. Now what of the affirmative side of God's speeches? What of the amoral goodness of the world? Is that somehow relevant to these issues? Does it say something about what it is to "fear God" in a deeper way than either Job or his friends did?

Clearly the answer is yes. The religion of the Moral World Order is provincial; it sees God only in the moral machinery within the lives of human beings. The religion of the theophany sees God even in the desert, "in which there is no man" (38:26). And it sees a goodness there that transcends the moral. A religion with moral demands is a religion for human action; it tells us what to do, how to behave. But human beings are patients as well as agents; we are spectators; we are acted upon; we live in a world we cannot master. The religion of the theophany is a religion for the passive, responsive, undergoing side of life. Some of this side of life will be suffering; but the theophany presents the powers that sometimes afflict us as good or beautiful in their own right.

The intuitions behind such a religion are not worked out in detail, nor are the many problems that such a vision entails grappled with in this book. The book remains predominantly a critique of the alternative religion, the religion of the Moral World Order; the messages in the theophany, and in the rest of the book, are largely focused on attack. But we do sense the outlines of the author's higher vision, and we sense the role of the goodness of nature in that vision. God would remain a God who requires upright and responsible conduct of human beings; the author attacks the Moral World Order, not morality. But God would be intimately connected also with the goodness of the natural order; and His worship, His service, fear of Him, would be focused at least equally on humble appreciation and celebration of that order.

Curiously, the *name* of God in this higher religion would be JHVH (Yahweh)—or maybe we should say "the Lord," to keep from writing the sacred name.[13] What is striking is that this Hebrew name occurs fully five times in the frame of the theophany (38:1; 40:1, 3, 6; 42:1), though it has been absent from the central dialogues of the book (except for 12:9, which quotes Isaiah 41:20; see also 66:2). The book uses this sacred name in the prologue and epilogue and in the theophany. In the books of the Old Testament, Yahweh is often revealed in a storm, or in association with a storm; at Sinai, Yahweh revealed His will in thunder and lightning; here in the Joban theophany He speaks from a whirlwind. After the virtual absence of this name from the dialogues, its sudden appearance helps to dramatize the shift from the voices of men[14] to the voice of God Himself. But it also dramatizes the shift of subject matter, of focus. In the theophany, the peculiarly Hebrew name for God is detached from the debates over the Moral World Order and associated with the goodness, power, and mystery of the natural order.

Given a dominant understanding of Judaism, this is a remarkable verbal maneuver; but then the Book of Job *is* remarkable. Many of us think of Judaism as a *moral* religion; we think of the God of the Jews as a demanding God, and we think that what He demands is righteousness. Without really denying any of this, the author of our book links the Hebrew name for God with *nature*. Judaism has many elements: some are ethnic, concerned with the history and destiny of the Jewish people; some are universalistic. Judaism incorporates rituals; moral demands, with associated promises and warnings; and appreciation of the natural order. The Book of Job ignores Jewish ethnicity; it virtually ignores rituals. It constructs an elaborate critique of the linking of moral demands to the warnings and hopes of the Moral World Order, and it highlights an appreciation of the natural world.

One might say, almost, that the book is an appeal for a return to a nature religion. The Hebrews were surrounded by nature cults, and their scriptures are full of accounts of their struggles against such religion—against temple prostitution, sun and moon worship, earth and harvest divinities. Their God always demanded that He, and not His creations, be worshiped, but the demand was *needed* by these people, given their roots. Their Abram was represented as originating in Ur of the Chaldeans, and their history is linked from earliest times with that of Egypt, and we find natural forces divinized in both places. Why would nature religions have been such threats to the Hebrews, unless in their own lives something moved that resonated in harmony with those religions? And we *see* elements of nature worship in the Creation story in Genesis, and in many of the psalms. The Lord of the Hebrews was the Creator and Ruler of nature; and He saw, and they saw, that it was good. Even the elaborate food laws, which have been so opaque for centuries, probably have an origin in a respect for nature; nature weirdly conceived, by modern standards, let us admit, but nature, nonetheless.[15] What is striking is that the Book of Job emphasizes *this* side, the nature worship side, of Jewish faith.[16]

We do not know precisely when the Book of Job was composed; but we know that it is late enough to have been influenced by the strongly moral and cosmopolitan motifs of the eighth-century prophets, at least. And we know it was late enough to have kinship with other worries over the rewards of righteousness, worries that we see in Jeremiah, Isaiah 40–55, and Ecclesiastes. But it takes a course radically different from the others. It rejects the Moral World Order entirely. It does not even mention the special form of the problem presented by the calamities suffered by the chosen people; given what it says about man and nature, and given its general cosmopolitanism, I suspect that it regarded notions of a special covenant[17] with Yahweh as provincial and presumptuous. And then, with the use of the sacred name in the theophany, it associates the peculiarly Hebrew with the *natural*! Many of the Old Testament writers, and many modern scholars, think of the historic Hebrew contribution as a movement away from nature toward morality; if the writer of our book agreed, he thought the movement had gone too far. He was in spirit a counterrevolutionary. He wanted to move back toward nature. And by introducing the Hebrew name for God at the point of climax, at the theophany, he said to his Hebrew readers, "*This* is our source, our origin, our ethnic root. Let us return to the God of our ancestors. The debates over the Moral World Order are for 'wise men' of the east; we Hebrews worship the God of nature!"

The theme of appreciation of an unmoralized nature—though

not the daring claim that such worship is the Hebrew genius—is present throughout the book in the manifold allusions to the Baal myths. One of the great achievements—perhaps the greatest achievement—of modern Joban scholarship has been the revelation that the book is saturated with motifs shared by Baalite writings.[18] I have mentioned the connections of Baal worship with Behemoth and Leviathan; Leviathan clearly figures in the Ugaritic myths, and monsters similar to Behemoth are also present. It is clear to the scholars now that the author of our book knew and alluded regularly to the Baalite literature; and that such allusions continue, are not rejected, in the theophany. The conclusion I draw is that the author did not merely *know* that literature; he loved it, and he was deeply impressed by the wisdom of the reverence for nature in it. He saw in it a corrective to the overmoralization of life which his book attacks.

Finally, we should mention the striking focus on Job's three daughters at the end of the epilogue. Curiously, most commentators make nothing of this;[19] and yet the picturesque detail certainly calls for interpretation. One might say, I suppose, that when Job gave his daughters inheritance among their brothers (42:15)—which is "remarkable and *unique* in the OT"[20] —the author heralded some new era of women's liberation; "the author appears to be exceptionally profeminist," Terrien says.[21] But why introduce a new moral obligation here, at the end of the book—at the end of *this* book? Or we might imagine that this detail of elevated status for women is a token of the patriarchal age the book takes as its setting;[22] or we might think that it reflects "the customary norms of the post-Exilic era"[23] in which the book was written. But none of these suggestions connects the detail with the themes of the book, nor with the other details about these women.

"And in all the land there were no women as fair as Job's daughters . . ." (42:15). Why the stress upon their beauty? And let us not overlook their names; the author records these names, though for the sons he merely tells us how many there were. The names (42:14) were Jemimah (or Yemimah); Keziah (or Qeziah); and Keren-happuch (or Qeran-happuk). These names mean, probably, *dove*, often a symbol of the beautiful woman;[24] *cassia*, a variety of cinnamon, used as a perfume, apparently—maybe by the adultress in Proverbs 7:17; and *horn of antimony*, which was used as eyeshadow "from very early times."[25] So what we have emphasized here is *not* a liberation of woman to become an equal of man, but painted, perfumed sexual beauty. Job's old age is blessed with the almost illicit pleasure of sexually attractive daughters. What better way to suggest again the amoral goodness of the natural order?

We should also remember the parallel, right at the end of the book, between our Job and Baal himself in the Ugaritic myths. Baal too had seven sons (or perhaps he had eight, but that is close), and they, like Job's sons, remain nameless; and Baal too had three daughters, whose names are given several times. Those names, like the names of Job's daughters, are suggestive of feminine seductiveness: they meant something like Dewy, Earthy, and Flashy.[26]

What does it mean that Job gave inheritance to such daughters? It means that after Yahweh revealed himself as a God of nature, Job prized the natural goodness of the earth, including the beauty of the sexual. I do not believe that this reading is merely a faddish, late-twentieth-century projection. The Book of Job has many allusions to the sexual, generative process. In the very first verse, after the prologue:

> . . . Job opened his mouth and cursed the day of his birth.
> And Job said,
> > "Let the day perish wherein I was born,
> > and the night that said,
> > 'A man-child is conceived.'"

> > > > > > > > (3:1–3)

Job's very first words of poetry curse the night of his conception and the day of his birth. He continues:

> "Why did I not die at birth,
> > come forth from the womb and expire?
> Why did the knees receive me?
> > Or why the breasts, that I should suck?"

> > > > > > > > (3:11–12)

And Job speaks to God of his formation in the womb:

"Didst thou not pour me out like milk
    and curdle me like cheese?
Thou didst clothe me with skin and flesh,
    and knit me together with bones and sinews."

                                                    (10:10–11)

The scholars are convinced that these metaphors all refer to the processes by which semen somehow initiates the fetal development, and to that development itself. Like Eliphaz (15:14) and Bildad (24:4), Job connects his troubles with his birth from a woman:

Man that is born of a woman
    is of few days, and full of trouble. . . .
Who can bring a clean thing out of an unclean?
    There is not one.

                                                    (14:1, 4)

Job's curse on God, like his curse on his own life, has been bound up throughout with a curse on the generative process, and with the idea that woman is "unclean."[27] It is appropriate, then, that at the end of this book Job not only becomes again a father, but also glories in the sexual beauty of his daughters.

And this reading even makes *some* sense of the sexual theme in the troubled passage about Behemoth. The theophany speaks regularly of parents and offspring in the animal world, and it even refers to the gestation period and the birth process. I do not see that we can defend every detail of the Behemoth section. But surely it is appropriate, given its meaning, for the theophany to praise the sexual power of at least one of God's creatures. This book really calls for a return to nature, and its author knew that sexuality was near the center of the natural world—and involved in its goodness. If one is to "fear" the God of nature, one must learn to love and respect the fundamental processes of that nature; one must be a "yes-sayer" in that sense, too.

The Book of Job is a book full of mysteries, and it deals with some issues with only hints. But many of the hints are comprehensible. The book represents a critique of the human, all-too-human effort to see the world in purely "moral" terms, or to imagine that the world and its God are under obligations analogous to the obligations human beings bear toward each other in this vale of beauty and calamity. That imagination leads to lies about the world and undermines morality itself; or else it ends in bitterness and blasphemy. It tries to avoid the fundamental frailty of human life, and in this respect it represents a kind of idolatry of man, an attempt to make man into an omnipotent deity. It imagines that it understands how an omniscient Creator would best order his ancient and multifarious world. When it yields to Joban blasphemy, it indicts the Creator for neglect or malice against His own creatures. In one way or another, it says no to the real world God has created, and so to God Himself.

The theophany and the epilogue do not fully develop an alternative sense of religious awe, but they strongly suggest that the God of things as they are wants worshipers who appreciate the goodness really present in His world more than worshipers with notions of how He ought to govern, even when those notions mirror the moral notions that God Himself endorses. The obligations of morality are obligations *we* are under; if God Himself is under obligations, we cannot know what they are. But we can see the goodness in the world He creates and rules. That goodness does not enable us to "solve the problem of evil," for we cannot solve that problem—it transcends our powers. But appreciation of that goodness and a recognition of our limitations are elements in the higher worship. God and the Satan agreed from the start that a wonderfully upright Job, wonderfully rewarded, could still fail to "fear God" as he should. By the end of this book we see what they sought—and what Job himself finally found.

Notes

Preface and Acknowledgment

1. Revised Standard Version. See my discussion of biblical quotations at the end of this preface.
2. Gordis 1965, p. v. Gordis placed "Mount Everest" in quotation marks; perhaps he was quoting.
3. Gordis 1965, p. v.
4. William Beardsley, Jack Boozer, and Hebe Rece.
5. Rawls; see pt. III, especially sec. 73–74.
6. Gordis 1965 and 1978.
7. Terrien 1954; also Terrien 1957.
8. Pope 1973.
9. The literature on the Book of Job is awesome in size, and growing. Each of the Job studies mentioned above has a bibliography that might be consulted, if the reader wishes to investigate the riches in this field. Two useful samplers from the literature are Sanders 1968 and Glatzer 1969. *The Journal of the American Oriental Society* (Sasson 1981) was devoted to surveys of the scholarship on ancient Near Eastern wisdom literature. One might also look at the bibliography in Bergant 1984; or p. 100 of Terrien 1987.

Introduction

1. See Weiss.
2. Some discussion of this Satan figure, and an explanation of the article—the Hebrew seems to require that we say *the* Satan—will be found in my chapter 5.

3. Many interpreters handle the problem in chap. 24 by saying that in 24: 18–20 Job is *quoting* the friends. The RSV, for example, inserts "You say" before these three verses. In the Book of Job, as in many other ancient works, it is difficult to know when the author intended a quotation.
4. See e.g., Pope lvi–lxxi.
5. Before the Common Era, or B.C. (Before Christ), as many Christians still say.
6. Much of the material in this chapter is drawn from direct reading of the Book of Job itself; much is from reading in the scholarship. See my Preface and Acknowledgment section.

Chapter 1

1. Lerner. Some of Lerner's experiments are striking; observers see desert no matter how he sets up his scenes for them to observe. (Their conception of desert, however, is not exactly Job's. It is often closer to Benjamin Franklin's.)
2. Once we determine what the view of the friends is, we are in a position to explore two other interesting questions: (1) to what extent is this view present in other Old Testament writings, especially in those we think are earlier than Job? And (2) to what extent is this view present in other Near Eastern literatures? Either of those questions would require another book-length study. Pope (p. 65) apparently thought the second question was easy to answer: "Bildad's assertion that the wisdom of the ancients is in accord with his doctrine and counsel is quite correct, as confirmed by much of Mesopotamian Wisdom Literature; cf. Lambert, BWL [1960], pp. 10–20." Of course we know that views closely related to the friends' were common in and out of the Hebrew tradition. And we still have them.
3. A few scholars speak of the friends' view as that of Deuteronomy. I think it best not to use that terminology, which invites an inquiry into the complex relations between Deuteronomy and "orthodoxy" as presented in the Book of Job. I will note, however, that Deuteronomy has a much larger place for ritual than our book has. See my discussion in chap. 3.
4. The full-blown Augustinian sense of "original sin" is, of course, not present in the book.
5. Literally, "the sons of Resheph," a Phoenician god associated with sparks or flames or pestilence.
6. The *emphasis* on nature in the theophany may be meant as a challenge to this aspect of orthodoxy. I interpret it in this way in the last chapter of this book.

Chapter 2

1. The term is notoriously difficult to translate, but the complexities do not affect my argument here.

2. "It seems somehow natural to start thinking about character when you get ahead of somebody, especially about the character of the one who is behind." Maclean, p. 90.

Chapter 3

1. There is another method used in some scholarship: assume that a term like these has a constant meaning throughout the Hebrew scriptures and try to discover that ("*the* meaning of 'blameless' in the Hebrew Bible," such scholars say), and then claim that what is important about the term in the Book of Job is this common meaning. But books in the Bible criticize each other; and surely Job criticizes other books. I reject this method. The question is, What do these terms imply (not mean) *in the Book of Job*?
2. So I am not only sketching an account of Job's exceptional merit and (eventually) of how even he falls short; I am also preparing for an account of what *sin* and all the rest of these terms imply *in the Book of Job*. But I do not try to work out definitions of such terms, and I am not confident that such definitions would add much understanding.
3. In chaps. 8 through 10 below.
4. See the next chapter.
5. See the opening discussion, at Cephalus's house, between Socrates and his host, in the *Republic* (Plato).
6. Literally *heart*, but as Pope says, p. 8, "It is more the seat of the intellect and the will than of the affections and emotions. . . . Hos vii 11 is a striking illustration of this meaning:

   Ephraim was like a dove,
   Silly, with no sense [literally heart]."

   So many translators say *mind* rather than *heart*. But I think the questions of motivation I raise here are still appropriate: the mind is not unmotivated.
7. Bishop Joseph Butler, in his *Sermons* in the eighteenth century, developed one of the best critiques of the view that all motivation is self-interested. Since Butler most philosophers have rejected the view, but it continues to live among sophomores, in and out of college. See Butler and, for a recent summary and appraisal of his arguments, Penelhum, especially pp. 12–14, 26–57, 79–85.
8. Hunt.

Chapter 4

1. In Conrad, *Nostromo*.
2. In Kleist, *Michael Kohlhaas*.

3. Pope, p. 23.
4. P. 922. Gordis is on Terrien's side on this issue; see Gordis 1978, p. 22.
5. Maimonides, par. 7.
6. Maimonides, par. 8.
7. Maimonides was clearly following the Mishnah, Sanhedrin 7.5. As cited in the Babylonian Talmud, Sanhedrin 55b–56a, it uses the same example, "Let Jose smite Jose," and specifies exactly the court procedure Maimonides describes. I thank Samuel Morell for this information, and for letting me study his translation of this part of the Mishnah.
8. I have heard related euphemisms, however, in "I blessed him out" and "I'll be blessed if I'll do that." *Cursed* and *damned* are meant, respectively.
9. *Eulogesei* is the Septuagint reading for 1:11 and 2:5. For 1:5, it has the sons perhaps thinking evil (*kaka*) against (*pros*) God; in 2:9, it has Job's wife urging him to say some words at (*eis*) the Lord.
10. In 3:1 "Job cursed the day of his birth"; what he did was to *lay a curse on* that day. He said, "Let the day perish wherein I was born . . ." (3:3). In much of the book he curses (says terrible things about) his life.
11. Pope, p. 76; also p. 146.
12. There are almost three persons, a trinity: the satanic persecutor, the unreachable High God, and (almost) an Umpire, Witness, or Redeemer, who meditates. And the resolution of the book involves a mediation: God speaks from the whirlwind (see pp. 187–88).
13. Job says in 19:23, if the RSV can be trusted, "Oh that my words were written! Oh that they were inscribed in a book!" Of course, they *are*. This kind of joke is typical of self-consciously literary artists. However, though *words* is a correct translation of the Hebrew, *book* may not be; see Pope, pp. 143–45.

Chapter 5

1. I have not been able to locate the source of this story.
2. See pt. III of Rawls.
3. See Camus.
4. Some writers say that Job's "faith in God" is tested; I avoid this expression, because of its vagueness. Clearly Job's belief that God is real and active is not shaken! But he does come to doubt God's justice. "W. Germans losing faith in allies," the *Christian Science Monitor* headline of June 15, 1987, said; the meaning was, "We are being sold down the river," as a West German policymaker put it. In *that* sense, Job's "faith in God" was tested.
5. "God-intoxicated" was what Novalis called Spinoza (who had been called an atheist in his own day). Spinoza spoke of "God or nature"—as I do sometimes in this book; the intimacy between God and actuality, in the Book of Job, is what tempts me to this expression. It is a pity that Spinoza never wrote a commentary on Job; many of his views were intimately related to Joban themes.

6. Terrien 1954, p. 899.
7. Scherer, p. 913.
8. Renan, as found in Glatzer, p. 116.
9. Kierkegaard, as found in Glatzer, p. 263.

Chapter 6

1. Or "the people that count" (Gordis) or "the gentry" (Pope)—Job 12:1.
2. Quoted by Hare, p. 189n. It may be obvious that my discussion here was completed before Salman Rushdie was threatened with death for his alleged blasphemy.
3. Terrien 1954, p. 967.
4. Terrien 1954 speaks (p. 982), as I do (in chap. 4), of some of Job's declarations as "the usual build-up for the utterance of blasphemy (cf. 7:11ff.; 13:13ff.; etc.)."
5. Again: Job and the three friends do not seem to be Jews; see my Introduction. But *Elihu* is a Hebrew name.
6. Gordis 1978, p. 396.
7. Terrien 1954, p. 1142.

Chapter 7

1. Nietzsche's language at the opening of pt. I of *Thus Spoke Zarathustra*.
2. Glatzer, p. 15.
3. This is a play on "the wisdom of feeling good," in "5/1/80," Patricia Wilcox 1981.
4. Patricia Wilcox suggests that most contemporary productions of Sophocles' *Antigone* weaken the play's tragic resolution and impact by caricaturing Creon and presenting an Antigone too heroic.
5. I thought this was Shaftesbury, but I have not found the source yet. I am still searching.
6. Perry Miller comments on the story on the first page of his preface to Miller 1963.
7. Perry Miller says, on the same page, "Margaret Fuller comes off from the exchange with honor"—because Miller sees in Carlyle an advocate for "the rule of unmitigated force."
8. This point is qualified in my chap. 10.
9. 1 Sam. 31:3–5 reports the deaths of Saul and his armor-bearer by their own hands; and Judas hanged himself, according to Matt. 27:5.
10. *Ahab* is, indeed, almost *Job* in Hebrew.
11. My interpretation of Nietzsche is drawn from years of study of Nietzsche and of the scholarship on his thought. Two important sources of the ideas expressed here are John T. Wilcox 1974 and 1982; and Kaufmann.

12. *The Autobiography of Bertrand Russell*. Quoted p. vii, Magnus.

13. See, however, chap. 12 below. By the end of his ordeal Job has a deep kinship with those aesthetes—and with much nineteenth- and twentieth-century philosophy, theology, and art, influenced by the Nietzschean themes we discuss here.

14. This truth about *human* caring is one support of those theologies that understand God as vulnerable, too. Must a *loving* God necessarily suffer crucifixion? Was there a truth in the Patripassian heresy?

Transition

1. I have mentioned the relevance of Elihu's views several times above. I do not see any need for a new discussion of them at this point. It may be that Gordis 1978, pp. 546–54, for example, gives a way of looking at the Elihu section that keeps it from detracting from the Book of Job (as many readers still think it does), and that we do not have to assume that a different author wrote it; but I have not been convinced that Elihu *adds* much to the book.

Chapter 8

1. Obviously this assumption is too easy. In chap. 10 we will discuss the theophany's underestimation of human inquiry.

2. Though the poet has no single word to be used as I use *nature* in this chapter, this verse (38:26) shows clearly that he can make the required distinction between man (and man's doings) and the rest of God's creation.

3. The meaning of this term is uncertain. Various interpretations have been proposed, all involving the stars, since surrounding references are astronomical.

4. Gordis 1978, p. 451.

5. See Gordis 1978, pp. 452–53; Terrien 1954, pp. 1178–79.

6. Or should we say that the ostrich's unwisdom—its lack of concern—is something Job, in his overconcern for fruits, could learn from? Might this be like Jesus' "consider the lilies"?

7. Gordis 1978, p. 558. Of course, Gordis may be using *wild* as I myself use *wildest* a few lines later.

8. Pope, p. 157.

9. In chap. 12 below I relax my caution about the word *beauty*. Here I try not to stretch its meaning.

10. Otto. See especially pp. 93–96.

11. Gordis 1978, p. 442.

12. Terrien 1954, p. 1174.

13. Terrien 1954, p. 1176.

14. Quoted in Pope, p. 296.
15. Gordis 1978, p. 448.

Chapter 9

1. This is close to the language in which Job himself was introduced in 1:8 and 2:3. Is *Job* the marvel? Look at Leviathan! (Today one also notes Luther's "A Mighty Fortress" language for Satan: "on earth is not his equal.") Job 41:1–8 is 40:25–32 in the Hebrew Bible; Job 41:9–34 is 41:1–26 in the Hebrew.
2. Gordis 1978, p. 571.
3. Ibid.
4. Ibid.; also Gordis 1965, p. 120.
5. Gordis 1978, pp. 558, 566; Gordis 1965, p. 120.
6. Gordis 1965, pp. 133, 134, 155.
7. See Gordis 1978, p. 569, and Pope, p. 320. Since writing this, I have been informed that there is a recently defended view that Leviathan *is* Behemoth, but I have not had an opportunity to locate the argument in the literature. My informant suggests that the argument is as follows: Often in Hebrew poetry a general term is mentioned first and then the specific is given. So here: Behemoth is the Beast (par excellence). Which beast? Answer: Leviathan. This is an interesting argument. I do not see, however, that it would require much revision of the reading I present here.
8. Pace Gordis 1978, p. 571, point A.
9. Pace Gordis 1978, p. 571, point E.
10. Terrien 1954, p. 1186.
11. Pope, p. 328.
12. Gordis 1978, p. 477.
13. Terrien 1954, p. 1187.
14. Pope, p. 143; Terrien 1954, p. 1050.
15. Pope, p. 143.
16. Pope, p. 321.
17. Pope, p. 325. *ANET* is Pritchard.
18. Gordis 1978, pp. 477–78.
19. Pope, p. 326.
20. Gordis 1978, p. 571.
21. Pope, p. 318.
22. Terrien 1954, p. 1185.
23. Ibid.
24. Ibid.
25. Ibid.
26. Pope, p. 318.
27. Gordis 1978, p. 475; Terrien 1954, p. 1186.
28. Gordis 1978, p. 475.

29. Ibid.
30. Pope, p. 320.
31. Terrien 1954, p. 1186.

Chapter 10

1. I heard Professor Spiegelberg tell this story over twenty years ago. He has been good enough to repeat it, in private correspondence, for my use here.
2. Many scholars say that Job approaches blasphemy, or say in passing that Job blasphemes. I have not seen any other scholarship that takes cursing God as central to the book.
3. "A Masque of Reason," in Frost.
4. The literature showing theological reactions to the Holocaust is vast. Some important works are Berkovitz; Eckardt and Eckardt; Fackenheim 1968, 1970, and 1973; Friedman; Friedlander; Lelyveld; Nora Levin 1973a and 1973b; Rubenstein; Rubenstein and Roth; Troster; Wiesel (all his works). I did not read Rubenstein until after this book was completed; I thank Leon Goldstein for pointing out to me (with much else) how close much of Rubenstein's 1966 view is to the Book of Job's as I interpret it.
5. Rawls, p. 159.

Chapter 11

1. Pope, pp. 293–94.
2. Gordis 1978, p. 444.
3. Pope, p. 295.
4. And Job's weakness, and the power of some of God's other creatures! See above.
5. So I interpret many of Charles Hartshorne's arguments. My reflections here are strongly influenced by my years of association with this great contemporary philosopher. For an introduction, see Hartshorne 1984.
6. I am not certain *how far* Hartshorne thinks he has gone toward a solution. He says that the [Joban] argument that "we are not wise like God and probably not in a position to second-guess divine decisions" "becomes at least far stronger" once we give up absolute omnipotence (p. 24).
7. In his *Leviathan*, chap. 31. Hobbes said that God's right to reign is derived "from his *irresistible power*" (p. 279); and that God decides Job's case "not by arguments derived from Job's sin, but his own power" (p. 280). Hobbes connected John 9:3 with this issue.
8. Terrien 1954, pp. 1188–89, is warm in his appreciation of these lines in this translation, seeing in them the poet's "concept of pure religion," an "indictment of all ritualistic or moralistic attempts to force the hand of the Deity," a song of "*sola*

gratia" ("only grace"). "Man cannot bestow any gift upon God. . . . God does not owe Job anything. . . . " Terrien does not seem to see or to grapple with the Hobbesian twist to all this. Nor does he see the tension with his own idea, stated earlier (p. 967), that "a Deity who would be impassive and insensitive to human conduct . . . is an idol. . . ."

9. Gordis 1978, p. 483.
10. This majority opinion does not seem influenced by what I think is the moral offensiveness of the RSV interpretation. Pope calls the RSV sense of 11a "lofty" and "exalted" (pp. 337–38), and Gordis 1978 says that the idea in the RSV 11b is "[u]nexceptionable" (p. 483). This makes more impressive their rejection of these readings.
11. Bergson.
12. See the seminal essay by Ellen J. Langer 1982, excerpted from her essay 1975.
13. Moore concludes her poem,

> . . . satisfaction is a lowly
> thing, how pure a thing is joy.
>   This is mortality,
>   this is eternity.

The poem is "What Are Years?" It was in a volume with the same title, 1941. I have taken it from Moore 1952.

Chapter 12

1. I had forgotten that Buber himself spoke this way in Buber 1949. Reprinted in Glatzer, pp. 56–65. Buber's most-read work is Buber 1958.
2. See my chaps. 8 and 9.
3. 1 Cor. 9:9–10.
4. Gordis 1965, p. 133.
5. Ibid., p. 155; "harmony and beauty," p. 302.
6. Ibid., p. 156.
7. Ibid., p. 302.
8. Ibid., p. 156.
9. Ibid., pp. 133, 155, 302.
10. Ibid., p. 302, my emphasis.
11. Ibid., p. 133, Gordis's emphasis.
12. Ibid., p. 155.
13. *Jehovah* is now regarded as based on elementary misunderstanding.
14. The men in question, except for Elihu who has now disappeared, may not be Hebrews—see my Introduction. If they are not, then the *simplest* explanation of the sudden reappearance of Yahweh's name is that we have returned to the voice of a Hebrew, namely, the narrator. But my substantial point is untouched: in this

provocative book, when we return to the peculiarly Hebrew name for God, we return from the Moral World Order to an unmoralized natural order.

15. See Douglas 1966 and Soler 1979.

16. A recent essay, slight but provocative, makes a related maneuver: see Gardner. The issue is of much current interest. See, for examples, Schwarzschild, and the heated rejoinder by David Ehrenfeld and Joan C. Ehrenfeld.

17. It is striking that no one in the dialogues suggests that God has any kind of covenant with anyone; the presupposition throughout them that God has obligations (analogous to ours) does not seem to rest on the idea of a covenant. Of course, as I have had to note before, Job and his friends do not *seem* to be Hebrews. But the prose frame never suggests a covenant, either.

18. Accessible accounts of these motifs are prominent in Pope's *Job*.

19. An exception is Mitchell 1987, in the Introduction to his translation, p. xxx. His Introduction was published earlier: Mitchell 1986.

20. Pope, p. 353; my emphasis.

21. Terrien 1954, p. 1196.

22. Pope, p. 353. "For similar examples from the Homeric World," Pope directs us to Gordon.

23. Gordis 1978, p. 499.

24. Pope, p. 352.

25. Pope, p. 353.

26. The point and the details in this paragraph are from Pope, pp. 352–53; but Pope does not argue, as I do here, that these Baalite parallels make sense in terms of an appreciation of nature in the Book of Job. Pope is a wonderful source for the Baalite influence; but shouldn't we ask *what it means* that the Book of Job is so rich in allusions to the Baal myths?

27. I read these traditional formulas about birth from a woman, and suggestions that women are unclean, as significant in their rhetoric, given the other hints in the book about the roles of sex and women in the overall issues, and given the importance of nature in the thought of the book. Sex, women, and nature are often connected in symbolic and mythological thought.

Sources

Biblical or Closely Related

Alter, Robert. "The Voice from the Whirlwind." *Commentary* 77 (1984): 33–41.

Alter, Robert, and Frank Kermode, eds. *The Literary Guide to the Bible*. Cambridge: Belknap–Harvard University Press, 1987.

Bergant, Dianne. *What Are They Saying About Wisdom Literature?* New York: Paulist, 1984.

The Book of Job. A New Translation According to the Traditional Hebrew Text. Introductions by Moshe Greenberg, Jonas C. Greenfield, and Nahum M. Sarna. Philadelphia: Jewish Publication Society of America, 1980.

Buber, Martin. *The Prophetic Faith*. Trans. C. Witton-Davies. New York: Macmillan, 1949.

Cook, Albert Spaulding. *The Root of the Thing: A Study of Job and the Song of Songs*. Bloomington: Indiana University Press, 1968.

Cox, Dermot. *The Triumph of Impotence: Job and the Tradition of the Absurd*. Analecta Gregoriana 212. Rome: Università Gregoriana Editrice, 1978.

Crook, Margaret Blackenbury. *The Cruel God: Job's Search for the Meaning of Suffering*. Boston: Beacon, 1959.

Crossan, John Dominic, ed. *The Book of Job and Ricoeur's Hermeneutics*. *Semeia* 19 (1981).

Damon, Samuel Foster. "The Doctrine of Job." *Illustrations* [by William Blake] *of the Book of Job*. New York: United Book Guild, 1950.

Fingarette, Herbert. "The Meaning of Law in the Book of Job." *Hastings Law Journal* 29 (1978): 1581–1617.

———. "What Did Job Learn?" Evans-Wentz Lecture. Unpublished typescript.

Glatzer, Nahum N. *The Dimensions of Job: A Study and Selected Readings*. New York: Schocken, 1969.

Gordis, Robert. *The Book of God and Man: A Study of Job*. Chicago: University of Chicago Press, 1965.

———. *The Book of Job: Commentary, New Translation, and Special Studies*. Moreshet Series 2. New York: Jewish Theological Seminary of America, 1978.

Gordon, Cyrus H. "Homer and Bible: The Origin and Character of East Mediterranean Literature." *Hebrew Union College Annual* 26 (1955): 43–108.

Greenstein, Edward L. "The Job of Translating Job." Photocopy of two-page article. Source unknown.

Habel, Norman C. *The Book of Job*. London: Cambridge University Press, 1975.

Hengstenberg, E. W. "Interpreting the Book of Job." *Classical Evangelical Essays in Old Testament Interpretation*. Ed. E. W. Hengstenberg. Grand Rapids: Baker Book House, 1972.

Holy Bible. Revised Standard Version. New York: Nelson, 1952.

Hone, Ralph, ed. *The Voice Out of the Whirlwind: The Book of Job*. Materials for Analysis Series. San Francisco: Chandler, 1960.

Kallen, Horace Meyer. *The Book of Job as a Greek Tragedy*. Intro. George Foote Moore. New York: Hill, 1959.

Kissane, Edward J. *The Book of Job*. Dublin: Brown, 1939.

Lambert, W. G. *Babylonian Wisdom Literature*. Oxford: Clarendon, 1960.

Levin, Saul. *Guide to the Bible*. Two parts. Binghamton, N.Y.: privately printed, 1987.

Mitchell, Stephen. "The Book of Job." *Tikkun* 1.1 (May 1986): 56–64.

———. *The Book of Job: Translated and with an Introduction*. San Francisco: North Point, 1987.

———. *Into the Whirlwind: A Translation of the Book of Job*. New York: Doubleday, 1979.

Mitchell, Stephen, Steven M. Joseph, and Gerson H. Brodie. Discussion of Mitchell 1986. *Tikkun* 1.2 (1986): 3–5, 125.

Pope, Marvin H. *Job: Introduction, Translation, and Notes*. 3d ed. Anchor Bible 15. New York: Doubleday, 1973.

Pritchard, James Bennett, ed. *Ancient Near Eastern Texts Relating to the Old Testament*. 2d ed., corrected and enlarged. Princeton University Press, 1955.

Reichert, V. E., ed. *Job*. London: Soncino, 1946.

Renan, Ernest. *The Book of Job*. Trans. A. F. G. and W. M. T. London: 1889.

Sanders, Paul S. *Twentieth Century Interpretations of the Book of Job*. Englewood Cliffs, N.J.: Prentice, 1968.

Sasson, Jack M., comp. and ed. *Oriental Wisdom: Six Essays on the Sapiential Traditions of Eastern Civilizations*. *Journal of the American Oriental Society* 101.1 (1981).

The Septuagint Version of the Old Testament. 3 vols. London: Bagster, 1884.

Scherer, Paul. "Exposition [of the Book of Job]." *The Interpreter's Bible*. Ed. George Arthur Buttrick et al. 12 vols. New York: Abingdon, 1954. 3:905–1198.

Snaith, Norman Henry. *The Book of Job: Its Origin and Purpose*. London: SCM, 1968.

Soler, Jean. "Dietary Prohibitions of the Hebrews." Trans. E. Forster. *New York Review of Books* 26 (June 14, 1979): 24–30.

Terrien, Samuel. "Introduction and Exegesis [for the Book of Job]." *The Interpreter's Bible*. Ed. George Arthur Buttrick et al. 12 vols. New York: Abingdon, 1954. 3:877–1198.

———. "Job." *The Encyclopedia of Religion*. Ed. Mircea Eliade. 16 vols. New York: Macmillan, 1987.

———. *Job, Poet of Existence*. Indianapolis: Bobbs, 1957.

Weiss, Meir. *The Story of Job's Beginning: Job 1–2: A Literary Analysis*. Jerusalem: Magnes Press, Hebrew University, 1983.

Philosophical, Theological, Psychological, or Literary

Austin, John Langshaw. *How to Do Things with Words*. Cambridge: Harvard University Press, 1962.

Bergson, Henri. *The Two Sources of Morality and Religion*. Trans. R. Ashley Audra and Cloudesley Brereton, with the assistance of W. Horsfall Carter. New York: Holt, 1935.

Berkovitz, Eliezer. *Faith After the Holocaust*. New York: NTAV, 1973.

———. "The Hiding God of History." *The Catastrophe of European Jewry: Antecedents, History, Reflections*. Ed. Yisrael Gutman and Livia Rothkirchen, 684–704. Jerusalem: Yad Vashem, 1976.

Bidney, Martin. "Thinking about God and Mozart: The Salieris of Puškin and Peter Shaffer." *Slavic and East European Journal* 30 (1986): 183–95.

Buber, Martin. *I and Thou*. With postscript by the author added. Trans. Ronald Gregor Smith. 2d ed. New York: Scribner, 1958.

Butler, Joseph. *Five Sermons*. Library of Liberal Arts. Indianapolis: Bobbs, 1950.

Camus, Albert. *The Rebel: An Essay on Man in Revolt*. New York: Knopf, 1961.

Conrad, Joseph. *Nostromo: A Tale of the Seaboard*. Garden City, N.Y.: Doubleday, 1931.

Cutter, Charles, and Micha Falk Oppenheim. *Jewish Reference Sources: A Selective, Annotated Bibliographic Guide*. New York: Garland, 1982.

Douglas, Mary. *Purity and Danger*. New York: Praeger, 1966.

Eckardt, A. Roy, and Alice L. Eckardt. *Long Night's Journey into Day: Life and Faith after the Holocaust*. Foreward by Robert McAfee Brown. Detroit: Wayne State University Press, 1982.

Edinger, Edward F. *Ego and Archetype*. New York: Penguin, 1973.

Ehrenfeld, David, and Joan C. Ehrenfeld. "Judaism and Nature." *Environmental Ethics* 7 (1985): 93-96.

Fackenheim, Emil. *Encounters between Judaism and Modern Philosophy*. New York: Basic, 1973.

———. *God's Presence in History: Jewish Affirmations and Philosophical Reflections*. New York: New York University Press, 1970.

———. *Quest for Past and Future: Essays in Jewish Theology*. Bloomington: Indiana University Press, 1968.

Freud, Sigmund. *The Future of an Illusion*. Trans. and ed. James Strachey. New York: Norton, 1961.

Friedlander, Albert H., ed. *Out of the Whirlwind: A Reader of Holocaust Literature*. Garden City, N.Y.: Doubleday, 1968.

Friedman, Maurice S. *Abraham Joshua Heschel and Elie Wiesel: You Are My Witnesses*. New York: Farrar, 1987.

Frost, Robert. *The Poetry of Robert Frost*. Ed. Edward Connery Lathem. New York: Holt, 1969.

Gardner, Jo Ann. "Jews and Nature." *Midstream: A Monthly Jewish Review*, May 1987, 43–45.

Greenberg, Uri Zvi. "To God in Europe." Trans. Robert Friend. *Anthology of Modern Hebrew Poetry*. Selected by S. Y. Penueli and A. Ukhmani, 2:264–78. 2 vols. Jerusalem: Israel University Press, 1966.

Hare, R. M. *Freedom and Reason*. 1963. New York: Galaxy–Oxford University Press, 1965.

Hartshorne, Charles. *Omnipotence and Other Theological Mistakes*. Albany: State University of New York Press, 1984.

Hick, John. *Evil and the God of Love*. Rev. ed. New York: Harper, 1977.

Hobbes, Thomas. *Leviathan*. Intro. Herbert W. Schneider. Library of Liberal Arts. New York: Macmillan, 1958.

Hunt, Leigh. "Abou Ben Adhem." *The Poetical Works of Leigh Hunt*. Ed. H. S. Milford. London: Oxford University Press, 1923.

Jung, C[arl] G[ustav]. *Answer to Job*. Trans. R. F. C. Hull. London: Routledge, 1958.

Kaufmann, Walter. *Nietzsche: Psychologist, Philosopher, Antichrist*. 4th ed. Princeton: Princeton University Press, 1974.

Kierkegaard, Søren. *Edifying Discourses*. Trans. David F. Swenson and Lillian Marvin Swenson. 2 vols. Minneapolis: Augsburg, 1962.

Kleist, Heinrich von. *Three Stories* [including *Michael Kohlhaas*]. Ed. H. B. Garland. Manchester: Manchester University Press, 1953.

Langer, Ellen J. "The Illusion of Control." *Journal of Personality and Social Psychology* 32 (1975): 311–28.

———. "The Illusion of Control." *Judgment under Uncertainty: Heuristics and Biases*. Ed. Daniel Kahneman, Paul Slovic, and Amos Tversky, 231–38. Cambridge University Press, 1982.

Lelyveld, Arthur J. *Atheism Is Dead: A Jewish Response to Radical Theology*. Lanham, Md.: University Press of America, 1985.

Lerner, Melvin J. *The Belief in a Just World: A Fundamental Delusion*. Perspectives in Social Psychology Series. New York: Plenum, 1980.

Levin, Nora. *The Holocaust: The Destruction of European Jewry, 1933–1945*. New York: Crowell, 1968.

———. "Life Over Death." *Congress Bi-Weekly* 40.8 (1973): 22–23.

Maclean, Norman. *A River Runs Through It, And Other Stories*. Chicago: University of Chicago Press, 1976.

Magnus, Bernd. *Nietzsche's Existential Imperative*. Bloomington: Indiana University Press, 1978.

Maimonides, Moses. *Code [Mishneh Torah]*, Laws of Idolatry, chap. 2, paras. 7 and 8. Trans. Samuel Morell. Unpublished typescript, 1989.

Melville, Herman. *Moby-Dick: or, The Whale*. Ed. Luther S. Mansfield and Howard P. Vincent. New York: Hendricks, 1952.

Miller, Perry, ed. *Margaret Fuller: American Romantic.* Garden City, N.Y.: Anchor-Doubleday, 1963.

Moore, Marianne. *Collected Poems.* New York: Macmillan, 1952.

Nietzsche, Friedrich. *Thus Spoke Zarathustra. The Portable Nietzsche.* Trans. and ed. Walter Kaufmann, 103–439. New York: Viking, 1973.

———. *Werke: Kritische Gesamtaugabe.* Ed. Giorgio Colli and Mazzino Montinari. ca. 30 vols. Berlin: De Gruyter, 1967–.

Otto, Rudolf. *The Idea of the Holy.* Trans. John W. Harvey. 2d ed. 1950. New York: Galaxy–Oxford University Press, 1958.

Penelhum, Terence. *Butler.* Arguments of the Philosophers. London: Routledge, 1985.

Plato. *Plato's Republic.* Indianapolis: Hackett, 1974.

Rawls, John. *A Theory of Justice.* Cambridge: Belknap–Harvard University Press, 1971.

Rubenstein, Richard L. *After Auschwitz: Radical Theology and Contemporary Judaism.* Indianapolis: Bobbs, 1966.

Rubenstein, Richard L., and John K. Roth. *Approaches to Auschwitz.* Atlanta: John Knox, 1987.

Schwarzschild, Steven. "The Unnatural Jew." *Environmental Ethics* 6 (1984): 347–62.

Searle, John R. *Speech Acts: An Essay in the Philosophy of Language.* London: Cambridge University Press, 1969.

Troster, Lawrence. "The Definition of Evil in Post-Holocaust Theology." *Conservative Judaism* 39.1 (1986): 81–98.

Wiesel, Elie[zer]. *The Gates of the Forest.* New York: Holt, 1966.

———. *Legends of Our Time.* New York: Holt, 1968.

———. *Night.* New York: Hill, 1960.

———. *The Town Beyond the Wall.* New York: Atheneum, 1964.

———. *The Trial of God (as It Was Held on February 15, 1649, in Shamgorod): A Play in Three Acts.* Trans. Marion Wiesel. 1979. New York: Schocken, 1986.

Wilcox, John T. *Truth and Value in Nietzsche: A Study of His Metaethics and Epistemology.* Ann Arbor: University of Michigan Press, 1974. Reprint Washington, D.C.: University Press of America, 1982.

———. "Zarathustra's Yes (and the Yes in *The Birth of Tragedy*)." *The Great Year of Zarathustra (1881–1981).* Ed. and intro. David Goicoechea, 20–32. Lanham, Md.: University Press of America, 1983.

Wilcox, Patricia. "Death Valley Suite." *Denver Quarterly,* 23.3/4 (Winter/Spring 1989): 60–76.

———. *An Exile from Silence: Poems to God.* Ithaca, N.Y.: Alembic, 1981.

Index